ALL ABOUT BONDS

FROM THE INSIDE OUT

ESMÉ FAERBER

McGraw-Hill
New York   San Francisco   Washington, D.C.   Auckland   Bogotá
Caracas   Lisbon   London   Madrid   Mexico City   Milan
Montreal   New Delhi   San Juan   Singapore
Sydney   Tokyo   Toronto

McGraw-Hill

A Division of The McGraw·Hill Companies

ISBN 1-55738-437-1

Printed in the United States of America

BB

  6 7 8 9 0

TAQ/BJS

Table of Contents

Chapter 6

Chapter 7

Chapter 8

Chapter 11

Fixed Income Mutual Funds   *165*

How Do Mutual Funds Work?
The Different Types of Bond Funds
How Does Performance Affect the Choice of Mutual Fund?
What Is the Significance of the Prospectus?
What Are the Tax Consequences of Buying and Selling
   Shares in Mutual Funds?
What Are the Risks of Mutual Funds?
How to Buy and Sell Mutual Funds
What Are the Advantages of Mutual Funds?
What Are the Disadvantages of Municipal Bond Funds?
Caveats
Should You Invest in Bond Mutual Funds or in Individual
   Bonds?
References

Chapter 12

Closed-End Funds   *193*

What Are Unit Investment Trusts?
What Are the Risks of Closed-End Bond Funds and Unit
   Investment Trusts?
How to Buy and Sell Closed-End Funds and Unit
   Investment Trusts
What Are the Advantages of Closed-End Funds and Unit
   Investment Trusts?
What Are the Disadvantages of Closed-End Funds and Unit
   Investment Trusts?
Caveats
Are Closed-End Funds and Unit Investment Trusts Suitable
   for Me?
References

Preface

All About Bonds is a practical guide written for bond investors and potential bond investors. The purpose of this book is to introduce and explain the information needed to purchase individual bonds and bond mutual funds, as lucidly and simply as possible. While the book covers the basics of investing in the different types of bonds, there are many sophisticated concepts which are included. These concepts may be difficult for beginning investors, but then the nature of determining the choices of different investments is not an easy matter.

The first chapter explains what bonds are, the characteristics and terminology of bonds, the advantages of investing in bonds, how to buy and sell bonds, and how the bond markets function.

The second chapter introduces the different types of bonds, their risks, rates of return, liquidity and valuation.

The third chapter includes an overview of the economic influences which have a bearing on the valuation of bonds. Understanding the relationship between the economy and the bond markets is of great significance for bond investors. The second part of the chapter includes tables on how to read the different bond quotations listed in the newspapers. Beginning investors should read these first three chapters in their entirety.

Chapters four through ten discuss the different individual bond securities, namely, short-term instruments (money market mutual funds, Treasury bills, commercial paper, bankers' acceptances), corporate bonds, treasury securities, government agency bonds, municipal bonds, corporate convertible bonds and zero-coupon bonds. These may be read in any order.

Chapters eleven and twelve include information on fixed income mutual funds and closed end funds. Each of these bond investments is analyzed as to how they work, their risks, how to buy and sell them, their advantages, disadvantages, their caveats and whether this type of investment is suitable for you.

Chapter thirteen discusses the management of a bond portfolio.

Investing money is not easy, and the aim of this book is to make the task a little less difficult. Investors should choose only those investments that they feel comfortable with.

Esmé Faerber

Acknowledgments

A special note of thanks to my husband, Eric, and our children, Jennifer and Michael, for their continued support.

Chapter 1

Why Invest in Bonds?

Key Concepts

◆ Advantages of investing in bonds

◆ Terminology of bonds

◆ Nuances of buying and selling bonds

◆ Description of the bond markets

Investors are faced with two choices with regard to their disposable income: they can spend it or save it. If they choose to save it, they are faced with a vast array of investment choices. Despite the great number of investment alternatives, many investors choose the same few alternatives.

After buying a house, the average investor's savings goes into bank savings accounts. Only the more adventurous investors add stocks. The stock markets are volatile, and investing in stocks makes many investors feel uncomfortable.

Investing the bulk of savings in low yielding bank accounts translates into lower rates of return, greater income taxes, and also the loss of capital appreciation (price growth). Bank savings accounts tend to pay interest at the low end of the yield scale and do not provide the tax advantages or capital appreciation opportunities of some other investment vehicles.

This book is about fixed income investments which, despite their advantages over savings accounts, have been ignored by many investors.

For example, bank money market deposit accounts are currently paying 3.41 percent, and six-month certificates of deposit are paying 3.47 percent. Good quality municipal bonds with a 10-year maturity are yielding 5.8 percent before federal income taxes (an after tax yield of 8.056 percent for the 28 percent income bracket) and 30-year U.S. Treasury Bonds are yielding 7.84 percent.

Investing in bonds used to be boring, but in the 1980s the bond markets became more volatile and thus provided investors with large

1

capital appreciation as well as regular fixed income payments. In the early 1990s, more investors have realized the benefits of bonds and have been investing more money in the bond markets.

Stock Market versus Bond Market

Stocks have historically produced higher rates of return than other investments, but they are also more volatile. Dr. Roger Ibottson (1985) found that rates of return earned by different securities over the 60-year period from 1926-1986 were the greatest for common stocks of small companies, averaging 18.2 percent per year. This was followed by 11.7 percent for common stocks of both large and small companies. Next were corporate bonds with a 4.4 percent return, then long-term government bonds with 3.7 percent and then U.S. Treasury bills with the lowest rate of return (3.3 percent).

The astute reader at this stage will ask the question "why invest in bonds?" when you can get higher rates of return from investing in common stocks.

Common stock prices are historically more volatile. Investing in common stocks needs a longer time horizon so that the variability of the returns can be averaged out. Gregory, a money manager in San Francisco, estimates that the risk of losing money on an investment in a basket of common stocks resembling the S&P index diminishes over time: 30 percent over a one-year period versus 15 percent over a three-year period, and 3-4 percent over a 10-year period (Gottschalk and Donnelly 1989).

Investors in common stocks are not guaranteed dividends. Dividends on common stock are declared at the discretion of the company's board of directors. If the board decides to use the money for alternate purposes or earnings go down, dividends may be reduced or may not be declared. Thus, investors who cannot tolerate the risk of reduced or terminated current income should not buy common stock.

Bonds have a maturity date, at which time the bond is redeemed at the par value (usually the original issue price). U.S. Treasury bond interest and redemption payments are backed by the U.S. Treasury and are considered risk-free. A corporate bondholder has a priority claim to payment over an equity, or common stockholder.

Bond investments tend to offer less variability in returns than stocks (7.6 percent risk for corporate bonds versus 21.2 percent risk for common stocks in the Ibottson study (1985)). In addition to less volatility than stocks, bonds offer the following:

◆ the potential for higher returns than those earned on savings accounts;

◆ the ability to reduce federal, state and local income taxes by investing in municipal and government bonds;

◆ the potential for capital gains by investing in bonds of companies that are on the road to financial recovery and through interest rate declines.

Investment Plan

Before making investment decisions, investors should assess their financial situation and then devise an investment plan.

The first step in an investment plan is to keep enough funds in liquid investments such as money market mutual funds, savings accounts and Treasury bills to meet emergencies. The amount to keep in liquid investments will vary according to individual circumstances. An examination of your personal assets will determine how much to keep. A conservative rule of thumb is to keep three to six months worth of expenses in liquid investments.

Included in your monthly expenses should be premiums on life, health and disability insurance. It is especially important for families that the breadwinner have adequate life and disability insurance. Health insurance is important for all members of the family. Similarly, auto and home insurance premiums should be included in your monthly expenses.

An investment program should include only amounts in excess of all living expenses and contingent emergency expenses.

The second step in an investment plan is to consider your medium- and long-term objectives. Listing your objectives is a good place to start because they will determine the purpose of your investments.

For example, the following objectives have a time frame:

◆ Buy a car in one year;

◆ Redo the kitchen in two years;

◆ Fund a college education in 10 years;

◆ Accumulate savings for retirement in 30 years.

The types of investments can then be geared to the maturities of the objectives. The first two objectives will encompass liquid or short-term investments such as Treasury bills and money market mutual funds. Investment options to fund a college education in 10 years are greater and could include a mixture of common stocks and bonds. With a 30-year investment horizon, the mix of investments could be weighted more heavily towards stocks than bonds. Consult a financial planner or one of the many books on financial planning to help you devise your individual investment plan. My book *Managing Your Investments, Savings, and Credit* (1992) would be helpful.

What Are Bonds?

Before describing the characteristics of bonds, we need to answer the question, "What are bonds?"

Bonds bear certain similarities to savings accounts. When an investor deposits money in a savings account, that investor is in effect lending the bank money. The bank will pay the investor interest on the deposit. Similarly, the investor who buys bonds lends the issuer of the bonds money in return for interest payments. When the bonds mature (come due) the investor will receive the principal amount of the bonds back, as the investor would had he withdrawn the amount from the savings account. A bond is an IOU.

The major difference between savings accounts and bonds is that investors can sell their bonds to others before they mature. Savings accounts cannot be sold to other investors. Thus, bonds are negotiable IOUs, unlike savings accounts.

Bond Terminology

In examining bonds, we need to understand the basic terminology that is used.

Par Value

The par value is also known as the face value of the bond, which is the amount that is returned to the investor when the bond matures. For example, if a bond is bought at issuance for $1,000, the investor bought it at its par value. At the maturity date, the investor will get back the $1,000. The par value of bonds is usually $1,000, although there are some exceptions.

Discount

Bonds do not necessarily trade at their par values. They may trade at a discount which is less than $1,000. For example, Kodak bonds are currently trading on the New York Bond Exchange at $997.50 per bond.

Premium

Bonds may trade at a premium which is more than par value. Bell of Pennsylvania's 9.625 percent bonds are currently trading at $1,052.50 per bond.

Coupon Interest Rate

The coupon rate is the interest rate that the issuer of the bond promises to pay the bondholder. If the coupon rate is five percent, the issuer of these bonds will pay $50 (5% x $1,000) in interest on each bond per year.

Many bonds pay interest semi-annually. In the example above (a five percent coupon rate paid semi-annually) the bondholder would receive $25 every six months. Some bonds have an adjustable, or floating, interest rate; in this case the coupon payment will fluctuate based on an underlying index.

Maturity

The maturity of a bond is the length of time until the bond comes due and the bondholder receives the par value of the bond.

Market Rates of Interest

Market rates of interest affect bond prices. For example, suppose you bought a bond with a coupon rate of five percent when market rates of interest were five percent, and you paid $1,000 per bond. A year later market rates of interest have risen to six percent. What would an investor pay for this bond yielding five percent when that investor can get six percent on other investments in the market?

Obviously, the investor will not pay $1,000 as the return would be less than six percent. The investor would expect to get at least six percent, which means that the bond will sell at a discount (less than $1,000) in order to be competitive.

Conversely, if market rates of interest fall below the coupon rate, investors will be willing to pay a premium (above $1,000) for the bond. Thus, bond prices are vulnerable to market rates of interest as well as other factors which will be discussed in Chapter 2.

Call Provision

Many bonds have a call provision which means that the issuer of the bonds can call or redeem the bonds at a specified price before their scheduled maturity.

Issuers exercise the call provision when market rates of interest fall well below the coupon rates of the bonds.

Bid Price

Bonds are quoted on a bid and ask price. The bid price is the highest price buyers will pay for the bonds.

Ask Price

The ask price is the lowest price offered by sellers of the issue.

Spread

The spread is the difference between the bid and the ask price of the bond, part of which is a commission that goes to the broker/dealer. A large spread indicates that the bonds are inactively traded.

The Bond Markets

There are many different types of fixed income securities, each with varying maturities. The short term securities such as Treasury bills, commercial paper and bankers' acceptances are traded in the money market. Large institutional borrowers (such as the U.S. government, corporations and financial institutions) raise money by selling their short-term securities in the *money market*. Buyers of these securities can sell them before maturity in an active secondary market which exists for some of these securities. The secondary market is where the already issued securities trade. Dealers will buy and sell these securities from their own inventories.

The issues with longer maturities are traded in the *bond markets,* which are differentiated by the types of issues: the U.S. Treasury bond market; the municipal bond market; the corporate bond market; the government agency market; the Eurobond market; etc. These markets are not located in a central place like the New York Stock Exchange, but instead are made up of dealers in the different financial centers. These dealers sell bonds from their own accounts to institutional buyers and broker/dealers. They also buy for their own accounts. Markets which are made up of dealers are referred to as over-the-counter markets. However, the New York and American Stock Exchanges do list a small number of corporate bonds.

Individual investors are not able to compete with the institutions which trade in large blocks (in the millions of dollars). Individual investors typically trade in small quantities, usually called odd lots, and thus face greater dealer/broker mark-ups. Individuals are also at a disadvantage in their access to specific bond issues. Brokerage firms may not have inventories of a particular issue; and hence, the broker may try to convince the investor to buy a similar but different bond issue.

How to Buy and Sell Bonds

There are many more complexities involved in buying and selling bonds than there are for other investments. Certainly, investors can buy and sell bonds through their brokerage firms as they do with common stocks; and for certain bonds, such as U.S. Treasury bonds investors can bypass their brokers and deal directly with the Federal Reserve Bank. However, there are significant differences in the buying and selling of bonds, which if appreciated can reduce the transaction costs and increase the investor's overall return.

Investors can find the prices of listed common stocks on the New York and American Stock Exchanges, and over-the-counter markets in the daily newspapers. This is not so for all bonds. Only a small percentage of the listed corporate bond issues and only the major government agency issues are quoted in the daily *Wall Street Journal.* Price quotes of municipal bonds are quoted in a costly publication titled "The Blue List of Current Municipal Offerings." Thus, individual investors do not readily have access to the majority of daily bond price quotes like they have for common stocks.

Prices of bonds vary from broker to broker and dealer to dealer. This price variance is due to many factors such as availability of the bonds, size of the order, the mark-up on the bonds and the commission costs.

By understanding the process behind the buying and selling of the different types of bonds, investors will be able to reduce the amount of commissions that they are charged.

Suppose an investor wants to buy a particular corporate bond. If that investor's brokerage firm does not have inventories of that bond, that brokerage firm will have to buy those bonds from a dealer. Hence, the price quoted to that investor for those bonds may be higher than that quoted by another brokerage firm that has existing inventories of that bond.

Individual investors should shop around at different brokerage firms to get the best price. It can never hurt to negotiate with the brokers for a better price. When comparing prices, investors should compare the bid/ask prices because the difference or spread between the bid and ask price represents the commission. Needless to say this spread varies from broker to broker (and dealer to dealer). The spread also varies for the different types of bonds. For example, spreads on government agency bonds and municipal bonds are wider than those for U.S. Treasury bonds. This is because the former two bonds are not as actively traded. Similarly, spreads are wider for thinly or inactively traded issues of all types.

Dealers make their money from buying and selling bonds; therefore, they would not want to buy an inactively traded issue at a price where they would lose money when they resell. Consequently, they will quote a wider spread. Investors should be cautious in buying bonds with large spreads (four percent or more, Thau 1992), because this is an indication that they may have difficulty selling the bond. In general, large spreads may also indicate that the credit worthiness of the bond issuer may be low. There are many other reasons which could be attributed towards a wide spread which will be discussed in later chapters.

The importance of the discussion so far is to highlight some of the reasons why bond prices vary, so that investors know to shop around at different brokerage firms to get the best price when they buy and sell their bonds. Even if the differences in price appear to be small per bond, when multiplied by the total number of bonds bought and sold, it can amount to quite a substantial savings. Keep these savings in your pocket rather than in your broker's.

With this brief discussion of the advantages of bonds, the nuances of buying and selling, and the mechanics of the bond markets, the investor will want to evaluate bonds with regard to their liquidity, risk, and return. Chapter 2 discusses these characteristics and the evaluation process.

References

Faerber, Esmé. *Managing Your Investments, Savings and Credit.* Chicago: Probus Publishing Co., 1992.

Gottschalk, Earl C. Jr., and Barbara Donnelly. "Despite Market Swings, Stocks Make Sense." *Wall Street Journal,* October 1989, page C1.

Ibbotson, Roger G. & Associates. "Stocks, Bonds, Bills and Inflation." *Yearbook.* Chicago: Ibbotson Associates, 1985.

Thau, Annette. *The Bond Book.* Chicago: Probus Publishing Co., 1992.

Chapter 2

Evaluating Bond Characteristics

Key Concepts

◆ Short-term debt securities

◆ Long-term debt securities

◆ Risks

◆ Rate of return

◆ Liquidity

◆ Valuation of bonds

◆ Why bonds fluctuate in price

The main advantages of investing in bonds, as pointed out in Chapter 1, are that investors can count on a steady stream of interest income, and if bonds are held to maturity, investors will receive the face value of the bonds back.

However, with the wide fluctuations in market rates of interest in the past decade, bond markets have become more volatile. Investors should become more cautious as to the types of bonds to chose and as to the timing of when to buy and sell bonds. There are many different types of bonds to choose from, each with their own characteristics. For example, bonds vary in their safety, marketability, return, liquidity, tax treatment, maturity as well as the frequency that interest is paid.

Investors can improve their returns and lessen their risks of loss by examining the characteristics of bonds before investing. A good starting point is to match bond maturities to financial needs, which can limit the loss of principal. Maturities of bonds range from less than a year to 30 years. For example, an investor who has funds to invest for six months would not want to invest in 30-year U.S. Treasury bonds because, if interest rates rise during that period, the investor will lose a portion of his investment. However, if interest rates go down during that period, the investor will be able to sell the bonds at a profit. By matching bond maturities to financial needs, investors can limit their losses due to market interest rate fluctuations.

Short-Term Debt Securities

Generally, the longer the maturity of the investment, the higher the yield for the investor. This higher yield is due to the uncertainty of interest rates, inflation, and the credit risk of the issuer in the future. Thus, by investing in shorter maturity issues, investors will generally receive lower yields but the risk of loss of principal will be limited.

There are many different short-term IOUs which are negotiable and actively traded in the money market. The money market is a collection of markets consisting of brokers and dealers who trade in billions of dollars of short-term securities such as Treasury bills, bankers' acceptances, negotiable certificates of deposit, and commercial paper. There is a market for newly issued securities and an active secondary market where issues that have already been issued trade.

The primary money market instruments are as follows:

Treasury Bills are sold by the U.S. Treasury to finance some of the Federal government's expenditures. Their maturities are for 13, 26 or 52 weeks.

Bankers' Acceptances are promissory notes which are used mainly to finance international trade transactions. Their maturities are nine months or less.

Commercial Paper is issued by the most creditworthy companies as a source of short-term credit and is in essence an unsecured promissory note. Maturities are 270 days or less.

Negotiable Certificates of Deposit are deposits of $100,000 or more deposited in commercial banks at a specific rate of interest. These can be bought and sold in the open market.

These short-term securities are relatively safe from default and are also fairly liquid due to the active secondary markets. These short-term debt instruments will be discussed in greater detail in Chapter 4.

By tailoring your investment options to your financial needs you can build stability into your financial program. Short-term money would be matched with short-term securities and longer term funds would be invested in longer term maturities.

Long-Term Debt Securities

There are medium-term notes and bonds with maturities of one to 10 years, and long-term bonds maturing 10 to 30 years after issuance. These are referred to as capital market securities. However, there isn't always a clear distinction between short-term and long-term debt instruments, because there are municipal bond issues with maturities of less than a year and U.S. Treasury bonds and notes that are about to mature which could be considered money market securities.

Long-term debt securities which make regular interest payments are U.S. Treasury notes and bonds, *U.S. agency* issues, municipal bond issues and corporate issues. Zero-coupon bonds and convertible bonds are hybrid debt securities which have different characteristics but are also considered to be capital market securities.

The U.S. Treasury issues two types of long-term securities: *Treasury notes* which have maturities of less than 10 years and *Treasury bonds* which have maturities in excess of 10 years.

U.S. governmental agencies sell long-term debt issues to finance various activities. Although they are not backed by the full credit of the U.S. government, these U.S. agency issues are considered to be of good investment quality. There are many different agencies selling obligations with varying maturities, liquidity, and marketability.

Municipal bonds are issues sold by states, counties and cities. The main advantage of municipal bonds is their special tax treatment. The interest received from municipal bonds is exempt from federal income tax and exempt from state and/or local tax if issued in that state and county.

Corporate bonds are debt obligations of corporations and vary considerably in their features and their risk.

Among the hybrids, *zero-coupon bonds* pay no periodic interest but are issued at a deep discount and are redeemed at face value ($1,000) at maturity. *Convertible bonds* are debt securities which can be exchanged for the common stock of the issuing company at the option of the bondholder.

Each of these long term securities differ in risk, return, taxability, liquidity and marketability. Investors should analyze the characteristics of the different types of bonds before investing.

The advantages of investing in long-term maturities are the higher yields, and the potential to ride out the price fluctuations.

Risks

All bond instruments carry risk, but the degree of risk varies with the type of debt and the issuer. There is always the risk that if you try to sell a bond before maturity, you could lose money on it if market rates of interest have risen. This does not mean that you should resort to stashing your money under the mattress, because this too involves a risk of loss. There are different types of risk and you should be aware of how these affect your bond investments.

Interest rate risk refers to the changes in market rates of interest which have a direct effect on bond investments. The price of fixed income securities changes inversely to the changes in interest rates. During periods of rising interest rates, investors holding fixed income securities will find that the market prices of their bonds will fall, because new investors in these bonds will want a competitive yield. Similarly in periods of declining interest rates, prices of fixed income securities will rise. The longer the time to maturity the greater the interest rate risk.

Interest rate risk can be lessened by reducing the maturities and also by staggering bond investments with different maturities. Interest rate risk is minimized if investors hold onto their bonds until maturity.

Another risk involving bonds depends on the *creditworthiness* of the issuer of the debt. Creditworthiness is the ability of the issuer to make the scheduled interest payments and to repay the principal when the bonds mature. Credit risk varies with bond issuers. U.S. Treasury issues carry virtually no risk of default. We would all be in a sorry state of affairs if the U.S. Treasury defaulted on its interest and principal repayments.

U.S. agency debt has slightly increased risks of default. Bonds issued by state and local governments depend on the financial health of the particular issuer and their ability to raise revenue. For corporate issuers, credit risks are linked to their balance sheets, income statements and their earnings capacities.

There are independent ratings services that evaluate the credit risks of municipal and corporate bonds. See Table 2–1 for a list of credit ratings ranging from the best credit quality for the issuers with the strongest financial status to the lowest ratings for issuers in default.

Moody's and Standard & Poor's (S&P) are two of the best known ratings agencies, and their ratings are similar though not identical.

Table 2–1 Bond Ratings

Moody's	Standard & Poor's	Interpretation of Rating
Aaa	AAA	Highest quality obligations
Aa	AA	High quality obligations
A	A	Bonds that have a strong capacity to repay principal and interest but may be impaired in the future.
Baa Ba	BBB BB B	Medium grade quality. Interest and principal is neither highly protected nor poorly secured. Lower ratings in this category have some speculative characteristics.
B Caa Ca	CCC CC C	Speculative bonds with great uncertainty.
C	DDD DD D	In default

Ratings of AAA, AA, A and BBB from S&P are considered to be investment grade quality. Bonds with ratings below BBB are considered to be junk bonds and are speculative. These junk bonds have lower ratings which means that the issuers have a greater likelihood of default on their interest and principal repayments. Before buying a bond issue, investors should ask their brokers for the ratings on that issue.

Individual investors should stick to issues with ratings of BBB and above to insure against sleepless nights. However, these ratings provide only a relative guide for investors, because the financial status of the issuer could deteriorate over time and result in the issue being downgraded to a lower rating. A downgrading usually causes a decline in the market price of the bond. The opposite occurs when a bond issue is upgraded. The same issuer with many different bond issues outstanding could have different ratings for each issue. For example, in August 1992, Standard & Poor's downgraded Progressive Corporation's senior debt from A+ to BBB and its subordinated debt from A to BBB.

Investors need not be duly alarmed if their bonds are down-graded from AAA to A for example, because this still indicates good quality. However, if the issue is downgraded below BBB, an investor should review whether to continue owning that bond.

Credit risks can be minimized by buying bonds with investment grade ratings (A and above by S&P) which have a reduced likelihood of default, and by diversifying investments. In other words, instead of investing all your money in the bonds of one issuer, buy bonds of different issuers.

Bonds with a call provision have *call risk*. Many corporate and municipal bond issues are callable by their issuers. This means that the issuers can repurchase their bonds at a specified (call) price before maturity. This is beneficial to the issuer and detrimental to the investor because when interest rates drop to less than the coupon rate of the bond, the issuer can call the bonds. The issuer can then reissue bonds at a lower coupon rate.

Call risk poses a potential loss of principal when the bonds are purchased at a premium and the call price is less than the premium price. Call risk can be anticipated by estimating the level to which the interest rates must fall before the issuer would find it worthwhile to call the issue. As will be explained in a later chapter, the call provision of a bond makes the duration of the bond uncertain.

To minimize call risks, examine the call provisions of the bond and choose bonds which are unlikely to be called. This is particularly important if you are contemplating the purchase of bonds that are trading above their par values (at a premium).

Purchasing power risk affects bonds. Bond coupon or interest payments are generally fixed amounts, thus the value of the payments are affected by inflation. When the rate of inflation rises, bond prices tend to fall because the purchasing power of the coupon payments is reduced. Thus, to say the least, bonds are not a good hedge against inflation. Bond prices react favorably to low rates of inflation. When the monthly announcement of the Consumer Price Index or Producer Price Index (measures of inflation in the economy) is less than antici-pated, bond prices rise.

To combat purchasing power risk, invest in bonds whose rates of return exceed that of anticipated inflation. If you anticipate inflation in the future, invest in floating rate bonds whose coupon rate adjusts up and down with market interest rates.

All coupon bonds are subject to *reinvestment rate risk*. Interest payments received may be reinvested at a lower interest rate than the coupon rate of the bond, particularly if market rates of interest decline or have declined. Zero-coupon bonds which make no periodic interest payments have no reinvestment risk.

If you decide to escape it all by investing in foreign bonds, these are subject to *foreign currency risks*. A rise in the dollar against a foreign currency can decimate any returns and result in a loss in principal when the bond matures.

It is evident that risk cannot be avoided even with the most conservative investments such as savings accounts and Treasury bills, or even stashing money under the mattress entails risks. However, through diversification, which is investing in different types of bonds rather than investing completely in one bond issue, certain levels of risk can be minimized. By understanding and recognizing the different levels of risk for each type of bond, the total risk can be better managed in the construction of a bond portfolio.

There is a direct correlation between risk and return. The greater the risk in an investment, the greater the return to entice investors. However, in most cases investing in bonds with the greatest rate of return and therefore the greatest risk can lead to financial ruin.

Rate of Return

Investors invest in bonds to earn interest income and/or capital appreciation (when the face value of the bond at maturity or the sale price is greater than the purchase price). The simple definition of total return includes both income and capital gains/losses.

Why is calculating a rate of return so important?

There are a number of reasons. First, it is a measure of the growth or decline of your wealth; and second, it is a yardstick with which to evaluate the performance of your bond investments against your objectives.

The total rate of return can be calculated as follows:

$$\text{Rate of Return} = \frac{(\text{Ending Value} - \text{Beginning Value}) + \text{Income}}{\text{Gross Purchase Price}}$$

Spreads and commissions should be included in the calculations. For example, if the gross purchase price of a bond bought at the beginning of the year is $850 and the bond is sold for $950 at the end of the year with a commission of $25, and interest of $50 was received, the rate of return is:

$$\text{Rate of Return} = \frac{(925 - 850) + 50}{850}$$

$$= 14.71\%$$

This is not the most accurate rate of return as it ignores the time value of money. A more comprehensive measure of the rate of return of a bond is the yield to maturity, which takes into account the time value of money. The time value of money is a concept that recognizes that a dollar today is worth more in the future because of its earnings potential. A dollar invested at five percent for one year would equal $1.05 at the end of the year. Similarly, a dollar to be received at the end of one year would be worth less than a dollar at the beginning of the year.

This average rate of return of 14.71 percent discussed above does not take into account the earnings capacity of the interest received. In other words, the $50 of interest received would be reinvested which would increase the rate of return above 14.71 percent.

Yield to Maturity

The yield to maturity is the discount rate calculated by mathematically equaling the cash flows of the interest payments and principal payments with the price of the bond. This is also referred to as the internal rate of return of the bond.

The yield to maturity can be solved easily with the use of a financial calculator, which has built-in financial tables. For example, a bond that was purchased for $770.36 and pays a coupon of 5% ($50 annually) with a maturity of 10 years, has a yield to maturity of 8.5 percent:

The process on the financial calculator would be

1. The purchase price of $770.36 is entered into the PV (present value) button;
2. The coupon payment of $50 is entered into the PMT (payment) button;
3. The maturity value ($1,000 par value) is entered into the FV (future value) button;
4. The time to maturity is entered into the n (number of payment periods per year multiplied by the number of years) button;
5. Press the i (interest/yield to maturity) button and the calculator will solve the yield to maturity for you.

If you don't have a financial calculator, you can use the following formula which will approximate the yield to maturity (YTM):

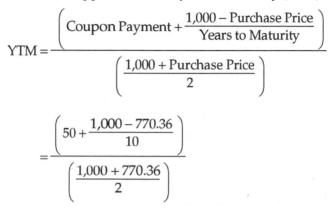

$$YTM = \frac{\left(\text{Coupon Payment} + \dfrac{1{,}000 - \text{Purchase Price}}{\text{Years to Maturity}}\right)}{\left(\dfrac{1{,}000 + \text{Purchase Price}}{2}\right)}$$

$$= \frac{\left(50 + \dfrac{1{,}000 - 770.36}{10}\right)}{\left(\dfrac{1{,}000 + 770.36}{2}\right)}$$

$$= 8.24\%$$

Using the approximation formula, the yield of 8.24 percent understates the true yield to maturity calculated with a financial calculator.

The yield to maturity can also be calculated with pencil, paper, and financial tables. You would solve the following equation for r (which is the yield to maturity):

$$\text{Purchase Price of Bond} = \sum \frac{\text{Coupon}}{(1+r)^n} + \frac{1{,}000}{(1+r)^n}$$

where $\sum$ is the summation

n is the number of years to maturity

For the above:

$$770.36 = \sum \frac{50}{(1+r)^{10}} + \frac{1{,}000}{(1+r)^{10}}$$

Solving this equation can be a tedious task as you would have to use a trial and error approach to determine the value of r. Choose a value for r and plug it into the calculation. If this value does not equate the right side of the equation to the left hand side, choose another value until you find the right value. (This is not the calculation recommended for investors who get squeamish at the thought of adding three figures together.)

The yield to maturity incorporates the compounding effects of the interest payments, but it also hinges on two assumptions:

1. that the investor holds the bond to maturity; and
2. the investor reinvests the interest payments received at the same yield to maturity rate.

If the bond is not held to maturity, then the internal rate of return of the bond can be calculated by substituting the sale price of the bond for the maturity value.

Similarly, when the bond has a call feature, investors can calculate the *yield to call* by substituting the call price for the maturity price in the equations.

The yield to maturity rate assumes that the investor will reinvest the interest received at the same yield to maturity. If this does not occur, the investor's actual rate of return will differ from the quoted yield to maturity rate. For example, if the interest received is spent and not reinvested, the interest does not earn interest; the investor will earn much less than the stated yield to maturity. Similarly, if the stated yield to maturity is eight percent and the investor reinvests the interest at lesser (or greater) rates, then the 8 percent will not be achieved.

In reality, it is difficult to match the yield to maturity rate for the interest received, because interest rates are constantly changing. The interest received is usually reinvested at different rates from the stated yield to maturity rate.

Some readers may throw in the towel at this stage, because the yield to maturity can't even convey a dependable rate of return for a bond.

The yield to maturity is useful, however, in comparing and evaluating different bonds of varying quality with different coupons and prices (Thau 1992, 49). For example, by comparing the yield to maturity of an AAA rated bond with a BBB rated bond, the investor can easily see how much the increment in yield would be in choosing the lower rated bond. The investor can also see the yield differential between bonds with different maturities.

The yield to maturity does not indicate the price volatility of different coupon bonds with different maturities. When comparing different bonds with different maturities, investors will want to know which of the bond's price will fall more when interest rates rise. This can be answered by calculating the bond's duration.

Duration

Duration is defined as the average time that it takes for a bondholder to receive the total interest and principal. It is the point in time in the life of the bond where the bond's return remains the same or unchanged despite the movement of market rates of interest. For example, the duration on a $1,000 face value bond with a coupon of six percent maturing in three years with a market price of $973.44 and current market rates of interest of seven percent can be calculated using the following formula (Mayo, 1991):

$$\text{Duration} = \left(\frac{1+y}{y} \right) - \left(\frac{(1+y) + n\,(c-y)}{c[(1+y)^n - 1] + y} \right)$$

where c = coupon rate

$\quad y$ = yield to maturity

$\quad n$ = number of years to maturity

Substituting the figures in the example:

$$\text{Duration} = \left(\frac{1 + .07}{.07} \right) - \left(\frac{(1 + .07) + 3\,(.06 - .07)}{.06[(1 + .07)^3 - 1] + .07} \right)$$

$$= 2.83 \text{ years}$$

The duration is 2.83 years which means that the bondholder will collect on the average the coupon and principal payments in 2.83 years. What this means is that different bonds with the same duration will have similar price fluctuations to changes in market rates of interest. Bonds that have higher durations will experience greater price volatility as market rates of interest change.

Duration can be used as a management tool to reduce the interest rate risk and for matching the duration of bonds with the timing of investor's needs for the funds.

Current Yield

Another useful measure is the current yield. This is the coupon divided by the purchase price of the bond. For example, if a bond is purchased at par, $1,000, and the coupon is five percent (interest will be $50 per year), then the current yield is five percent (same as the coupon rate). However, on the secondary market most bonds trade above or below par. For a bond purchased at $1100 with a five percent coupon, the current yield is 4.54% (50/1100). Bonds trading at a discount to their par value have current yields which are higher than their coupon rates. For investors who are concerned with high income the current yield would be a useful measure.

What Rate of Return Should I Expect?

Overall, the rate of return of a bond will depend on the type of bond, the levels of risk, and the time period to maturity. For instance, as pointed out earlier, U.S. agency bonds have slightly increased risks of default over U.S. Treasury bonds of the same maturity. Similarly, a junk bond with a S&P rating of CCC will have to pay a considerably higher yield than a bond with an A rating to entice investors.

The question that is always asked by investors is: What rate of return should I expect?

Although there is no obvious answer, you need to take the following factors into account:

1. The spectrum of rates for the different types of fixed income securities;
2. The levels of risk that will give you the comfort of being able to sleep well at night; and
3. The maturities that match your financial needs and objectives.

Market rates of interest have been falling over the past decade which means that bond investors currently may not be able to match the double digit returns of the 1980s. Table 2–1 lists the yields of the different types of maturities at the time of this writing.

By increasing the level of risk and extending the maturities of bonds, investors can increase their rates of return. However, basing investments on the greatest yield may be disastrous. Going for higher

Table 2–1

Treasuries

30-year U.S. Treasury Bonds	7.5%
7-year U.S. Treasury Notes	6.15%
5-year U.S. Treasury Notes	5.6%
2-year U.S. Treasury Notes	4.25%

Agency Issues

10+ year U.S. Agencies	7.84%
1-10-year U.S. Agencies	5.84%

Municipal Issues
New Tax Exempt Issues

30-year Revenue Bonds (A rating)	6.1%
20-year Government Obligation (AA)	5.85%
10-year Government Obligation (AA)	5.25%

Corporate Bonds

10+ year AAA-AA rated	8.13%
10+ year A-BBB	8.53%
1-10-year AAA-AA	6.62%
1-10-year A-BBB	7.04%

Money Market Securities

3-month Treasury Bill	3.19%
3-month CD	2.96%
Dealer Commercial Paper (90 days)	3.37%

yields and ignoring risks does not guarantee high returns over a period of time. For example, investing in lower quality corporate bond issues which go into default translates into a loss of principal and negative returns. Investors must decide whether the additional returns warrant the additional risks. This is known as the risk-return trade-off: choose the level of risk that you feel comfortable with.

On the other hand, by playing it too safe and investing in securities with minimal risks, you will be assured of low, minimal returns. To get higher returns, you have to accept greater risks.

As pointed out earlier, by extending the maturities on your investments without regard for your financial needs can result in a loss in principal due to interest rate risk. The other extreme is just as bad: investors invest every cent of their savings in short-term bank accounts and money market funds. This approach ensures the safety of principal but produces low yields. Currently short-term and long-term yields are spread widely (up to three percent in Table 2–1). Many investors are not taking advantage of the opportunity this spread presents. For example, instead of investing everything in money market instruments currently yielding around three percent, some money can be invested in two-year U.S. Treasuries which increases the yield to 4.25 percent. Increasing the rate of return by 1.25 percent by investing in Treasury notes which still falls within acceptable risk levels enhances the overall value for the investor. Consider the future values of the two investments if $1,000 is invested in each:

Over a 10-year period, by investing in Treasury notes with an additional yield of 1.25 percent, an investor can increase his investment by $172.29 ($1,516.21–1,343.92).

		End of Yr 1	End of Yr 5	End Yr 10
Money Market Funds	3.00%	$1,030.00	$1,159.27	$1,343.92
Treasury Notes	4.25%	$1,042.50	$1,231.35	$1,516.21

The optimal approach is to ladder your investments in terms of yields and maturities. Cash and funds needed currently for living expenses and contingencies (medical expenses and emergencies) could be invested in money market funds and bank accounts where there is little risk. Savings to fund longer term objectives can be invested in higher yield, longer maturity investments such as U.S. Treasury notes and bonds, U.S. agency bonds, municipal and corporate bonds with compatible levels of risk.

There are two important factors which affect the rates of return earned on investments and these are inflation and taxes. If an investment earns four percent per year and inflation is three percent for the same period, the real rate of return is only one percent. If inflation rises to four percent or above, investors holding fixed income securities yielding four percent will not be jumping for joy at the prospect of earning zero or negative returns. This is why market prices of long-term bonds decline so rapidly when the inflation rate rises, because bondholders receive fixed amounts of interest. Market prices of existing bonds on the secondary markets will go down in price in order to make their rates of return more competitive (to include the rate of inflation) which will entice investors to buy them.

If you anticipate inflation, you should choose investments that will yield rates of return which will cover the rate of inflation. In times of rising inflation, investors tend to avoid long-term fixed income securities and invest in short-term investments (money market accounts and Treasury bills) where rates of return can increase with the rates of inflation.

Taxes and Returns

Taxes also diminish investors' rate of return. Interest income is taxed at ordinary rates at the federal level. At the time of this writing, capital gains are also taxed at ordinary income tax rates, although the capital gains provisions still remain in the Internal Revenue Code. This implies that if ordinary tax rates go up, capital gains may then be taxed at special lower rates as was the case before the changes to the Tax Code.

As taxes (federal, state and possibly local) are levied on income and capital gains, the after-tax rates of return of different bonds should be compared. The after-tax rate of return is calculated as follows:

$$\text{After Tax Return} = (1 - \text{tax rate})\ (\text{Rate before Taxes})$$

For example, an investor in the 31 percent marginal tax bracket who invests in a corporate bond yielding 10 percent has an after-tax return of 6.9 percent:

$$\text{After Tax Return} = (1 - .31)\ (.10)$$

$$= 6.9\%$$

This can be compared to the rate of return of a municipal bond which is tax free at the federal level. In many cases, taxes affect the choice of investments, and effective tax planning may reduce the level of taxes paid.

Rates of return are diminished by inflation, taxes, and commissions (spreads), and investors should consider these factors to ensure that their investments yield positive returns after these have been deducted.

Liquidity

Liquidity is defined as the ability to convert an investment into cash without losing a significant amount of the funds invested. Funds which are to be used in a short period of time should be invested in assets which are high in liquidity (savings accounts, certificates of deposit, Treasury bills, money market funds). A Treasury bill can be sold very quickly with a slight concession in selling price, whereas a 20-year to maturity junk bond may not only take time to sell, but may also sell at a significant price concession. This is especially true for bonds that are thinly traded, i.e., where relatively few of these bonds are traded and the trades take place only with large spreads between the bid and the ask prices. Thus, thinly traded bonds are not *marketable*, which means they can't be sold quickly.

All bonds have different characteristics and varying levels of risk, return, tax status, marketability and liquidity. To make the appropriate choices of bonds for your portfolio, you must understand these characteristics, which also determine the value of the bond.

Valuation of Bonds

As noted earlier in the chapter, bond prices fluctuate up and down due to the relationship between their coupon and market rates of interest, their creditworthiness and the length of time to maturity. After bonds are issued, they rarely trade at their par values ($1,000) in the secondary markets because interest rates are always changing. Certain bonds will sell at premiums and others will sell at discounts.

There is a mathematical formula for determining the price of a bond, but bear in mind that this is conceptual. The market price of a bond depends on the stream of the bond's coupon payments and the principal repayment in the future. Using the time value of money, this stream of future payments is discounted at market rates of interest to its present value in today's dollars. It is the same formula as used in the financial calculator for yield to maturity, except you solve for PV (present value) and input i (yield to maturity) that reflets market rates of interest and a risk premium.

For example, a bond which pays coupon interest of $100 per year and will mature in three years time with market rates of interest projected at an average of six percent per year will have a price of

$1,107.30 according to the calculation. Thus, the price of the bond is linked to the coupon yield, market rates of interest, discount rate, and the length of time to maturity.

If we compare the price of a U.S. Treasury note with the same coupon rate and maturity as that of a corporate bond, we will find that their prices will differ. The Treasury note will trade at a higher price than that of the corporate bond because there is a greater risk of default with the corporate bond and thus the price will be calculated with a higher discount rate (or yield to maturity). Thus, investors will require a greater yield on the corporate bond for assuming greater risks of default. This confirms why a AAA rated corporate bond will trade at a higher price than a BBB rated corporate bond if the coupon and maturity are the same. The difference in yield between the AAA and BBB rated bonds is referred to as the excess yield which issuers must pay for the extra grade of credit risk.

Bond prices fluctuate depending on investors assessment of their risks. The greater the risk the greater the yield (and the lower the market price).

Why Bonds Fluctuate in Price

To sum up, bond prices fluctuate in price due to the following:

1. Changes in risk assessment by the market—the lesser the quality the lower the price and the greater the quality the higher the price;
2. The length of time to maturity—the longer the maturity, the more volatile the fluctuations in price; and
3. The coupon rate relative to market rates of interest—when market rates of interest rise and exceed the coupon rate of a bond, the price of the bond will decline in order to relate the current yield to the market rate of interest. When interest rates fall the price of the bond will rise.

References

Mayo, Herbert B. *Investments,* 3rd Edition. New York: Dryden Press, 1991.

Thau, Annette. *The Bond Book.* Chicago: Probus Publishing Co., 1992.

Chapter 3

How to Read the Financial Pages

Key Concepts

◆ The relationships between the economy and the financial markets

◆ Monetary policy and the markets

◆ Fiscal policy and the markets

◆ The dollar and the markets

◆ Bond markets and how to read bond quotations

For many people, the financial pages of the newspaper do not read like a story book. There is a wealth of confusing interrelationships between the effects of economic events and bond prices, in addition to the use of many terms such as CPI, M-1, M-2, and Barron's Confidence Index, which sound more like the code words to the entrance of some secret society!

To better understand the relationship between bond prices and the influence of the economic environment, the first part of this chapter will include a brief overview of some of the key terms which are used to measure the economy and their effects on the bond markets. The latter part of this chapter will focus on bond indices and the different bond price quotations in the newspapers.

The tremendous interest rate swings during the decade of the 1980s changed the nature of bond investing from passive buy and hold strategies to those of the more glamorous, exciting investments which produce large capital gains (and unfortunately, capital losses also) and shorter holding periods.

The previous chapter detailed the different characteristics of bonds and pointed out that the value of a bond is determined by the

---

Portions of this chapter have been previously published by Esmé Faerber in *Managing Your Investments, Savings, and Credit,* published by Probus Publishing Co., 1992.

interest payments and the investor's required rate of return, both of which are related to the economy. If interest rates and levels of risk are influenced by the state of the economy, it then becomes important to understand the relationship between the bond markets and the economy. An understanding of the economic indicators can help you make timely decisions in the credit (bond) markets.

What Is the State of the Economy?

No longer can investors make money by leaving their funds in money market accounts and CDs when interest rates are low. With a sluggish economy, rising unemployment, rising health care costs, increased tuition for higher education, and low interest rates, investors will need to take on more risks in their investment strategies. This means placing a greater emphasis on longer term securities which offer higher yields. Investors must then contend with the gyrations of bond prices in the credit markets which react to different economic and political events.

Investors are better equipped to plan their investment strategies if they are able to understand and forecast the state of the economy. This section outlines the effects of the most common economic indicators which can then be used to identify trends in the economy.

Gross National Product (GNP) is a measure in dollar value of the economy's total production of goods and services. Comparing the current GNP with previous periods indicates the economy's rate of growth (or lack of it). An increasing GNP indicates that the economy is expanding.

Inflation distorts the accuracy of this growth, and so there is a measure of the real growth of an economy's output, referred to as "real" GNP. Real GNP is adjusted for price level changes and measures each period's goods and services using prices which prevailed in a selected base year. A comparison of real GNP figures with those of prior periods provides a more accurate measurement of the rate of growth of an economy.

A more narrowly focused measure of a nation's output is *industrial production,* which measures the manufacturing output.

The *unemployment rate* is the percentage of the labor force that is out of work, and it is another indicator of the economy's strength. Currently, the U.S. has a tight job market with increasing layoffs in various sectors of the economy.

Governments become concerned when the unemployment rate rises above a certain level (currently about seven percent) and they will stimulate the economy (through fiscal and monetary policies) to reduce the unemployment rate. These actions may also stimulate inflation.

In the early 1980s, the U.S. experienced both high rates of unemployment and inflation. The government dealt with the inflation first by pursuing restrictive economic policies. This sent the economy into a recession and the unemployment rate increased further. In 1992, the U.S. experienced low inflation but high unemployment. The government's approach was to stimulate the economy by lowering interest rates (through the Federal Reserve Bank).

Inflation is defined as the rate at which the prices for goods and services rise in an economy. Inflation often prevails in a growing economy where the demand for goods and services outstrips production, which then leads to rising prices. In other words, too much money chasing too few goods and services.

The economic goal of most governments is full employment (nearly full employment, approximately five percent unemployment is acceptable) which also tends to be inflationary. The unemployment versus inflation trade-off is an ongoing dilemma for policy makers.

The *Consumer Price Index* (CPI) is one measure of inflation which is calculated monthly by the Bureau of Labor Statistics. The Bureau monitors the changes in prices of items (such as food, clothing housing, transportation, medical care, entertainment) in the CPI. It is a gauge of the level of inflation and is more meaningful when it is compared relative to the CPI of previous periods.

Some economists believe that the CPI fuels inflation similar to a cat chasing its tail. Social Security payments and many cost of living increases in employment contracts are tied to increases in the CPI. The CPI may, in fact, exacerbate the level of inflation.

When the level of inflation is high (relative to previous periods) governments will pursue restrictive economic policies to try and reduce the level of inflation.

The *Producer Price Index* (PPI) is announced monthly and monitors the costs of raw materials used to produce products. It is a better predictor of inflation than the CPI, because when prices of raw materials increase there is a time lag before consumers experience these price increases.

Inflation has a detrimental effect on both the bond markets and the economy. When the level of inflation increases, real GNP falls (in 1980 in the U.S.) and, similarly, when inflation declines, real GNP increases (in 1983 in the U.S.). This inverse relationship may not always hold out as evidenced by the economy in 1992. Despite lower levels of inflation, real GNP showed insignificant growth, which translated into the economy taking a long time to move out of the recession.

Housing starts are released monthly and show the strength in housing production. An increase in housing starts relative to previous months indicates optimism about the economy as more people are buying homes. Thus, strength in housing starts shows consumer confidence in the economy.

These are some of the pieces to the overall economic picture. By examining these indicators and statistics, investors are better able to fine tune their opinions and forecasts of the economy. The author is not suggesting that, with a brief overview of some economic terms, you are now an expert who can dispense with all the economists' forecasts. On the contrary, it is difficult to predict economic behavior; economists are notorious for differing in their forecasts of economic growth, inflation, unemployment. This highlights the complexities of the economy, but this does not mean that the investor should throw in the towel and discount the economy. Instead, by using a consensus of economic forecasts, investors are better prepared in deciding how to invest their funds.

Generally, the credit markets tend to react to the economy in the following way:

◆ an expanding, growing economy may have a negative effect on the bond markets, because expansion may be perceived to be inflationary.

◆ a sluggish economy is good news for the bond markets due to the fact that interest rates and inflation would tend to be low.

Bond markets tend to thrive on bad news about the economy. This is evidenced by some of the headlines in the financial pages of the newspapers: "Bond prices rise on the anticipated announcement of higher unemployment figures, lower increase in the monthly CPI statistic and housing starts."

Inflation fears plague bond markets. Increasing levels of inflation can have a devastating effect on bond prices by accelerating a sell-off in the bond markets.

Monetary Policy and the Financial Markets

Monetary policy can have a substantial impact on the economy and thus, the financial markets. The Federal Reserve Bank (the Fed) controls the nation's supply of money, and by regulating the supply of credit and money, the Federal Reserve Bank can affect the country's economic growth, inflation, unemployment, and production.

How the Federal Reserve
Changes the Supply of Money

The principal tools used by the Federal Reserve Bank to change the supply of money are: open market operations; reserve requirements; discount rate.

Open Market Operations The Federal Reserve will buy and sell securities in the open market to change the money supply and the reserves of commercial banks. When the Fed buys government securities, it is expanding the nation's supply of money. The Fed will pay for the securities by check, which will increase the reserves in banks, and thus, banks will be able to increase their loans and deposits.

When the Fed wants to contract the nation's money supply, it will sell government securities from its portfolio to the open market. This has the effect of siphoning off money from the nation's money supply; commercial banks' reserves are reduced, therefore reducing banks' ability to lend money.

Reserve Requirements The Federal Reserve Bank requires banks to maintain reserves with the Fed. The percentage of banks' deposits held as reserves is determined by the Fed and is called the reserve requirement. The Fed can increase the money supply by reducing the reserve requirement: banks will need to keep less reserves and can therefore increase their lending. The reverse is true when the Fed increases the reserve requirements.

Not only will the money supply increase or decrease due to changes in the reserve requirements, but there will also be a multiplier effect on the money supply. This can be illustrated by using a simple example:

Suppose I deposit $100 in Bank X and the reserve requirement is 10 percent. Bank X now has $100 on deposit of which $10 is kept on reserve and $90 is lent to Corporation A. Corporation A deposits this

Figure 3–1 The Multiplier Process

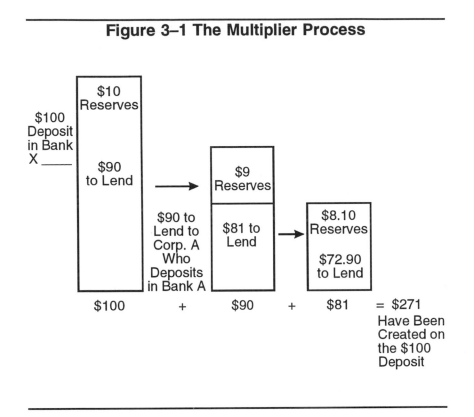

$90 check in its Bank A. Bank A will keep $9 on reserve and lends the remaining $81. This process is repeated, which shows how the original $100 is increased through the banking system to expand the money supply. Figure 3-1 illustrates the multiplier process graphically.

Thus, the Fed can stimulate the multiplier effect by lowering reserve requirements which correspondingly increases the banks' capacities to lend.

Discount Rate The discount rate is the Fed's third tool. The discount rate is the rate of interest that the Fed charges banks when they borrow from the Fed. When the discount rate is too high, banks are discouraged from borrowing reserves from the Fed. When the discount rate is low or lowered, banks are encouraged to borrow. Thus, by changing the discount rate, the Fed can expand or contract the money supply.

Defining the Money Supply

Before looking at the relationship between the money supply and the financial markets, we need to define the different measures of the money supply. This can be likened to measuring our own money supply, although a bit finite by comparison!

How much cash do we have? We have the cash in our pockets, wallets, under the mattress, and in our checking accounts. However, savings accounts, money market funds, and some investments can easily be converted into cash. Similarly, the narrowest measure of the nation's money supply is referred to as M-1, a broader definition M-2, and the broadest category as M-3.

M-1 consists of the nation's cash, coins, traveler's checks, checking accounts (NOW accounts which are interest-bearing checking accounts are included), and demand deposits.

M-2 includes M-1, but also adds savings and time deposit accounts (e.g., CDs, money market deposit accounts, of less than $100,000).

M-3 includes M-1 and M-2 as well as time deposits and financial instruments of large financial institutions.

Which is the best measure of the economy's money supply? That is hard to answer, because economists continue to argue this point. The Federal Reserves' preferred measure is M-2, which is America's broad money supply. Some economists argue that the slow growth of M-2 in the U.S. (1.7 percent from January–August 1992) stunted the economic recovery and that the Fed's policy of broad monetary growth was too tight. Others complain that the nation's narrow money supply, M-1, was too lax, as evidenced by a 12.3 percent jump (*Economist* 1992, page 95).

Interest rate changes explain this discrepancy. Short-term interest rates have fallen, therefore investors moved their savings out of low yielding bank deposits (included in M-2) into higher yielding bonds, as long-term rates remained relatively high. Thus, economists argue that portfolio shifts make the definitions of the money supply unreliable as indicators of the economy. For example, you can see at once that M-1 could increase when people transfer money from their savings accounts to checking accounts without affecting M-2. There will be discrepancies between the classifications of the money supply from week to week, but the investor should be more concerned with the overall changes over a period of time so that a trend can be established. By monitoring the Fed's open market transactions, changes in the reserve requirements and the discount rate, along with the rate of growth or decline in the money supply, investors are better able to make their investment decisions.

However, evidence suggests that changes in the money supply have an influence on nominal economic activity, but the influence on real economic growth is still hotly contested.

Impact on the Financial Markets

When the Fed pursues a restrictive monetary policy, it may sell securities on the open market to siphon money from the money supply, and/or raise the reserve requirements which reduce banks' capacity to lend money, and/or raise the discount rate to discourage banks from borrowing money.

These changes in monetary conditions will have an effect on corporate earnings. When the money supply is decreased, interest rates will go up, making it more costly for companies and individuals to borrow money. This will cause them to delay their purchases and leads to reduced sales. With lowered sales and higher credit costs, companies will have decreased earnings which translate to lower stock prices.

When interest rates are rising, investors will earn more by investing in fixed income securities and money market instruments. Therefore, many investors will take their money out of the stock markets and invest in liquid short-term securities and longer-term debt securities, which puts more downward pressure on stock prices. Higher interest rates also translate into higher borrowing costs for margin investors. These investors will move their money to debt instruments to justify their higher interest costs.

Monetary policy has a direct effect on interest rates, and interest rates and the stock market are strongly correlated. Rising interest rates tend to depress stock market prices, and falling interest rates have the opposite effect. Stock market investors move into bonds when interest rates go up and out of bonds when interest rates go down.

The open market operations of the Fed have a direct impact on interest rates and the bond markets. When the Fed buys Treasury securities on the open market, it competes with other buyers, thus driving up prices and causing a decrease in Treasury yields. This creates a rate discrepancy between the yields on government debt and corporate debt. As a result, investors will purchase corporate debt, causing prices to increase and yields to decrease. The reverse is true when the Fed sells government securities on the open market.

This suggests that if investors anticipate changes in monetary policy they can make the appropriate changes to their investment strategies.

Fiscal Policy and the Markets

The goals of both monetary and fiscal policy are the same: the pursuit of full employment, economic growth, and price stability. The government can use its fiscal policy to stimulate or restrain the economy. The tools of fiscal policy are taxation, government expenditures, and the government's debt management. Changes in fiscal policy can affect the financial markets.

The federal government uses *taxation* to raise revenue and also to reduce the amount of money in the economy. Taxation policies can stimulate or depress the economy and the stock markets. When taxes are increased, consumers have less money to invest and spend on goods and services, and corporations have reduced earnings which will lead to lower dividends.

Tax cuts, however, have the opposite effect. Individuals will have more money to spend and invest, and corporations will experience the benefits of greater consumer spending along with lower corporate taxes which generally leads to higher sales and higher earnings.

Government Spending. A tax cut has a similar effect to an increase in government spending. A tax cut has a favorable effect on savings and investments whereas government spending has a greater effect on the goods and services produced in the economy. Government spending can also be used, therefore, as a tool to stimulate or restrain the economy.

Debt Management. When the government's revenues are less than its expenditures, it runs a deficit. Deficit spending can have a significant effect on the financial markets in general and the stock market in particular. The government can finance its deficit by: borrowing in the financial markets, or increasing the money supply.

Borrowing in the Financial Markets. By borrowing in the financial markets, the government will drive up yields on the bond markets which will have a depressing effect on the stock market. By selling securities on the market, prices of government securities will go down which increases their yields. To counter the rate differential (between corporate and government securities) investors will invest in government securities rather than in corporate securities, which will reduce the prices of corporate bonds which leads to increased yields (on corporate bonds). Thus, borrowing in the market by the government has the effect of depressing bond prices and increasing interest rates. The opposite is true of the government buying securities in the market: bond prices are pushed up and interest rates are lowered.

When a government is faced with financing an increasing deficit, it will have to pay high rates of interest to attract buyers to invest in all its securities. This leads to higher interest rates in the economy. As we saw, this has a depressing effect on stock prices and tends to drive up yields.

Increasing the Money Supply. If the government increases the money supply, inflation may raise its "ugly head," and inflation has a negative effect on the economy and the bond markets in particular.

In summary, when a government is unable to reduce the growth of its deficit spending, there will be an effect on the bond and stock markets. Investors will constantly be looking for policies or budgets that can effectively change the direction of growth of the deficit.

Increased government spending can be inflationary and can bring an immediate response from bondholders. Due to computerized global trading, bondholders can unload millions of dollars of U.S. Treasuries within hours and can send bond prices plummeting and long-term yields soaring.

Fiscal policies affect the security markets and by anticipating changes in the policies, you can formulate your investment strategies.

The Dollar and the Financial Markets

Great attention is paid to the relative value of the dollar, the trade deficit, and whether the Japanese and Europeans will continue to fund the budget deficit through the Treasury auctions. The financial markets react to these financial events. In fact, by now you have come to realize that the financial markets react on a daily basis to almost all economic, political, and financial announcements. In some cases the markets will anticipate the news. For example, the bond market may go up or down in anticipation of the announcement of the balance of trade figures for the quarter.

International Trade and the Dollar

There is a relationship between the markets, international trade, and the relative value of the currency. Readers of the financial press will come across an assortment of terms such as balance of payments, trade deficit (not the same as a budget deficit), current account surplus, foreign portfolio investment and wonder how these can guide (or misguide) economic policy makers. Great care should be used in interpreting balance of payments figures because of the complexities and ramifications involved.

Balance of Payments is an accounting of all the transactions that take place between the residents of a country and the rest of the world. The balance of payments will show whether a country is a net importer or exporter of goods and services, whether foreigners are net investors in that country or whether that country is a net exporter of capital, and the changes in the country's reserves.

Balance of Trade shows whether a country imports or exports more merchandise. The balance of trade is, therefore, the difference between a country's exports and its imports of merchandise. A balance of trade surplus indicates that the country exports more goods than it imports, and a deficit indicates the opposite (imports more goods than it exports).

A balance of trade deficit is not necessarily a bad financial omen, and should not be judged in isolation from the rest of the country's balance of payment figures. For example, Switzerland has had balance of trade deficits, but it also has surpluses in its balance of services account. Thus, as long as a country can finance its balance of trade deficit through its other current accounts and capital accounts, it is economically acceptable.

Current Account is the first major section of the balance of payments, and includes all the country's imports and exports of merchandise (balance of trade), services (balance of services), and transfers (includes foreign aid). A country with a current account surplus will be able to contribute to its capital and reserve accounts. A country with a current account deficit will have to finance it from capital inflows from abroad or run down its reserves.

Capital Account indicates whether the country is a net importer or exporter of capital. In other words, has the rest of the world invested more in this country or has this country invested more in the rest of the world? Thus, a country with a current account deficit will need to finance this deficit with imported capital or it will be forced to run down its reserves.

Reserve Account includes liquid assets such as gold, foreign currencies, special drawing rights (SDRs), and the country's reserve position at the International Monetary Fund. All of these can be converted into foreign currencies to settle the country's international claims.

International trade, investments and the country's actual or relative reserves affects the value of its currency. When Americans buy goods from abroad they pay in U.S. dollars which are exchanged at the going rate into the foreign currency. Since 1973, most of the currencies of the industrialized nations have been allowed to float against each other. Thus, the value of one currency is measured against the value of other currencies, through the forces of supply and demand. When there is great demand for a currency, it will appreciate in value relative to other currencies, and when demand is low, the currency will lose value. Prices of currencies are determined on the foreign exchange market which is composed of international banks and foreign exchange traders.

Inflation and interest rates are important economic factors which influence a currency's value.

Inflation. High inflation in a country will cause the currency in that country to depreciate. For example, if inflation rises in the U.S., the price of goods that originally cost $100 will increase in price to $105. Thus, American consumers may prefer to buy imported goods for the equivalent of $100. This will increase demand for foreign currencies and put downward pressure on the dollar. The theory of purchasing power parity addresses this issue by stating: if the prices of goods go up in one country relative to another, then in order to keep parity in prices of goods between the two countries, the currency must depreciate.

Inflation will also have a detrimental effect on foreign investments, as foreigners will not invest in financial assets which will lose value. Therefore, higher inflation will put upward pressure on interest rates to attract foreign investors.

Rising interest rates will have a downward pressure on the bond markets, as investors may sell their long-term bonds and invest in shorter-term securities whose yields will increase as interest rates go up.

Interest Rates. When interest rates are higher in one country relative to another, foreigners will then invest in that country's T-bills, CDs, and other higher yielding investments. This will mean a greater demand for that country's currency, and thus, theoretically an appreciation in value of that currency. The opposite holds true for low interest rates and lower rates of inflation.

The relationships between interest rates, inflation, and the value of the currency all add an important dimension to international investments.

This discussion points to the overall relationship between economic activity and the financial markets. An expanding economy is generally accompanied by a nervous bond market due to fears of inflation, and a declining economy is generally associated with a rising bond market (in anticipation of lower interest rates). Thus, by forecasting the direction of the economy, investors can anticipate the direction of the bond market.

Bond Markets and How to Read Bond Prices

Bonds are issued by corporations, the federal government, agencies of the federal government, municipal governments, and foreign corporations and governments.

Exchanges

A large number of corporate bonds are listed on the New York Bond Exchange and the American Bond Exchange. Bonds are also traded over-the-counter among bond dealers.

There is an active secondary market for Treasury bills, notes, and bonds. The secondary market is where buyers can buy securities when the Treasury is not selling them and where sellers can sell their securities before they mature. Security dealers make up this market. The Federal Reserve Bank will buy and sell Treasury securities as part of its open market operations.

There is also a secondary market for government agency bonds such as FNMAs (Federal National Mortgage Association), GNMAs (Government National Mortgage Association); municipal bonds such as state and local government issues, highway authorities; and foreign bonds.

Indices

Bond market indices differ from equity market indices in two respects. Bond market indices are not followed as extensively as stock market indices; and secondly, bond market indices focus on rates of return or bond prices, whereas equity indices focus on price movements only. There are several indices for assessing the behavior of the bond markets.

Dow Jones Bond Average consists of 10 utility bonds and 10 industrial bonds. The focus is on the closing prices of these bonds and the average shows the percent of face value that these bonds would sell at.

Shearson Lehman Hutton Indices are more extensive than the Dow Jones Bond Average. The *Corporate Bond Index* includes all the publicly issued debt of industrial, finance, and utility companies whose issues are non-convertible and have a fixed rate. Only bonds with maturities of at least one year or more and a minimum outstanding principal balance of $25 million are included.

The *Government Bond Index* includes all the publicly issued debt of the federal government and its agencies whose issues are non-convertible and have fixed rates. Only issues with a maturity of one year or more and with a principal balance of $25 million are included.

The *Treasury Bond Index* includes debt issues of the U.S. Treasury.

The *Mortgage Backed Securities Index* includes all the fixed rate debt issues which are backed by the mortgages of the GNMA, FNMA, and the Federal Home Loan Corporation.

The *Yankee Bond Index* includes U.S. dollar bonds registered with the Securities and Exchange Commission which are issued or backed by non U.S. governments.

The *Government Corporate Bond Index* combines the Government Bond Index and the Corporate Bond Index. This is the most representative of all the bond market indices.

Barron's Confidence Index is the ratio of Barron's average yield of 10 high grade corporate bonds to the yield on the more speculative Dow Jones average of 40 bonds. This index shows the yield spread between high grade bonds and more speculative bonds.

Users of the index believe that during periods of optimism, investors will invest more in speculative bonds (to get the higher rate of return) which will push their prices up and thus lower their yields. This causes the confidence index to increase.

The opposite happens when investors are pessimistic: they will invest in high quality bonds which will increase the yield differential between the low quality and high quality debt and the confidence index will decline.

Other notable bond indices include the *Salomon Brothers Indices, Bond Buyer Municipal Index* and the *Merrill Lynch Corporate Index.*

Although bond market indices are not as widely known or used as are the stock market indicators, the bond indices are becoming more important. More investors have been investing in bonds and fixed income mutual funds during the 1980s and these indices are excellent yardsticks for investors to evaluate the performance of their fixed income investments.

How to Read Bond Quotations

Corporate Bonds

The daily quotations of listed bonds on the New York and American Exchanges can be found in the financial newspapers. For example, a typical listing of a corporate bond from the financial pages would appear as follows:

Bonds	Mat	Cur Yld	Vol	Close	Net Chg
ATT 4¾	98	5.1	6	92½	–⅜

Reading from left to right:

◆ After the name of the bond, AT&T, is the coupon yield of 4 3/4 percent (i.e., each bondholder will receive $47.50 in interest every year until maturity). If an "s" follows the coupon rate, it means that the issue pays interest semi-annually.

◆ The 98 is the maturity date for this bond—it matures in 1998.

◆ The current yield is 5.1 percent. Determine this by dividing the interest received $47.50 (which is the coupon rate) by the market price at the close of the day which is $925 (47.50/925 = 5.1%).

◆ The volume indicates the number of bonds traded which was six (or $6,000 in terms of face value of the bonds) for that day.

◆ Close indicates the closing price of $925. Bonds are quoted in 100's (the last digit is dropped—a $1,000 face value bond is quoted as $100). Bonds under 100 are selling at a discount and over 100 are selling at a premium.

◆ The net change column shows the change from the previous day's close. In this case AT&T was down by 3/8 of a point.

Corporate Convertible Bonds

These are listed on the same exchanges and read the same way as corporate bonds. A **cv** in the current yield column would signify that it is a convertible bond.

Zero-Coupon Bonds

These are quoted in the same tables as corporate bonds. A **zr** following the name of the bond would signify that it is a zero-coupon bond. There would be no coupon rate as zero-coupon bonds pay no periodic interest.

Municipal Bonds

The financial newspapers list some municipal bonds, but the most complete listing is found in the *Blue List* which a daily brochure published by Standard & Poor's. It is appropriately printed on (you guessed) blue paper and with blue ink.

Tax-Exempt bonds are listed as follows:

Issue	Coupon	Mat	Price	Chg	Bid Yld
NJ Hwy Auth Ser 9	6.25	01-01-14	96½	+⅝	6.55

◆ The issue is the New Jersey Highway Authority Series 9.

◆ The coupon rate is the percentage of par value that is paid in interest. These bonds pay 6.25 percent of par ($1,000) which is $62.50 in interest per bond per year.

◆ The maturity date is the date that the bonds will be retired (paid back) which is on January 1, 2014.

◆ The next column is the dollar price of the bonds which is $96.50 ($965.00 per bond).

◆ The change indicates the difference from the previous day's price. In this case the bonds increased 5/8th of a percentage point from the previous day's price.

◆ The last column is the bid yield. If investors bought these bonds and paid $965.00 per bond and held them until Jan. 1, 2014, their return would be 6.55%.

Treasury Bonds and Notes

There is a separate table listing Treasury bonds and notes in the financial newspapers. The issues are listed in order of maturity. The following is an example of a Treasury note:

Rate	Maturity Mo/Yr	Bid	Asked	Chg	Ask Yld
5⅛	May 94n	101:11	101:13	+2	4.19

◆ The rate in the first column signifies the percentage of par value that is paid as interest. This note pays interest of $51.25 per year.

◆ The maturity date is when the note matures which is May 1994. An n after the date signifies that it is a Treasury note (rather than a Treasury bond).

◆ Treasury bonds and notes are quoted on a bid and asked basis. The bid price is the highest price buyers of this issue will pay: they are willing to pay 101 11/32 or $1,013.44 per note.

◆ The asked price is the lowest price offered by sellers: sellers are asking 101 13/32 or $1,014.06 per note.

◆ The change shows the change in 32nds of a point between the bid price as quoted here and the bid price as quoted the previous day. This issue increased by 2/32 of a point from the previous day's bid price.

◆ The ask yield is the return investors would get if they paid the asked price for the note and held it until maturity. The return is 4.19%.

Government Agency Bonds

These are listed and read the same way as Treasury notes and bonds.

Treasury Bills

Treasury bills are quoted separately in a section marked Treasury bills in most financial newspapers. They are listed in order of their maturity. The following is an example of a Treasury bill quote:

Maturity	Days to Mat.	Bid	Asked	Chg	Ask Yld
Jan 14 '93	70	2.95	2.93	. . .	3.00

◆ Treasury bills are short-term securities so all the listed T-bills will mature within one year, in this case on January 14, 1993.

◆ There are 70 days from this date until the maturity of this issue.

◆ Treasury bills are sold at a discount which is less than the par or face amount of $1,000 and then redeemed at par at maturity. This difference is attributed to interest. The bid discount of 2.95 percent was the highest discount (price) that a dealer was willing to pay on that day, and the asked discount of 2.93 percent was the lowest discount that a dealer was willing to sell on that day.

The dealer's selling price can be calculated as follows:

$$= \text{Par value} - \text{Par value (ask discount)} \left(\frac{\text{days to maturity}}{360} \right)$$

$$= \$100 - 100\,(0.0293) \left(\frac{70}{360} \right)$$

$$= \$99.430 \text{ or } \$994.30 \text{ per T–bill}$$

The dealer's purchase price

$$= 100 - 100\,(\,0.0295\,) \left(\frac{70}{360} \right)$$

$$= \$99.4263 \text{ or } \$994.26 \text{ per T–bill}$$

◆ The ask yield is 3.00 percent which is the return an investor would get on this issue if bought at the asked discount.

The aim of this chapter has been to explain some of the financial and economic jargon found in the financial sections of the newspapers, to enable you to better understand the financial markets and follow your investments in the newspapers. It is not meant to be a comprehensive guide to the understanding of economics and finance.

References

Antilla, Susan. "Comparing Stocks with Boring Bonds." *New York Times,* September 20, 1992.

Faerber, Esmé. *Managing Your Investments, Savings and Credit.* Chicago: Probus Publishing Co., 1992.

"Monetary Smoke Signals." *Economist,* October 10, 1992, page 95.

Chapter 4

Short-Term Fixed Income Securities

Key Concepts

◆ Money market mutual funds

◆ Treasury bills

◆ Commercial paper

◆ Bankers' acceptances

Short-term, liquid, safe investments are used by investors for emergency and short-term funds. Examples of these types of investments are certificates of deposit, money market mutual funds, Treasury bills, commercial paper, and bankers' acceptances. These investments are also used as temporary, short-term cash substitutes. In other words, idle cash can be invested in these to earn a return. The characteristics of these short-term investments are: low risk of default and high liquidity and marketability.

Money Market Mutual Funds

Money market funds compete directly with bank deposit accounts, and over the years money market funds have grown considerably at the expense of bank accounts.

Money market funds are offered by investment companies who also offer mutual funds. These funds provide an alternative to investing in individual stocks and bonds. Investment companies managing money market funds pool investors' money and issue shares to the investors. They then invest the money in high yielding short-term securities such as Treasury bills, commercial paper, bankers' acceptances, CDs, Eurodollars, repurchase agreements, and government agency obligations.

Some of the material in this chapter has been previously published by Esmé Faerber in *Managing Your Investments, Savings and Credit,* published by Probus Publishing Co., 1992.

There are three types of money market funds:

◆ *General purpose funds* which invest in a wide range of money market securities such as Treasury bills, commercial paper, bankers' acceptances, certificates of deposit, repurchase agreements, and short-term off-shore securities;

◆ *U.S. government funds* which invest in short-term Treasury securities and U.S. agency obligations; and

◆ *Tax-exempt money market funds* which invest in short-term municipal securities. The income from these securities are exempt from federal income taxes.

How Safe Are Money Market Funds?

Money market mutual funds do not carry the FDIC insurance carried by bank money market deposit accounts. The safest money market funds invest in U.S. Treasury securities only, as these are backed by the full faith and credit of the U.S. government. However, all money market funds are relatively safe because: (i) their investments are in securities issued by governments and its agencies, and large corporations; and (ii) the maturities of these securities are short-term which lowers the risk. Large institutions are unlikely to default on securities issued for a short period of time, and the prices of short-term securities will not fluctuate widely.

If you are still concerned about the risks of default, limit your investments to high quality funds and U.S. government funds.

Before investing, read the prospectus which will list the types of securities that the fund invests in. The risk of default has been zero to very low for Treasury bills, certificates of deposit, bankers' acceptances, and commercial paper. Although the risks of default on commercial paper are low, a few companies have defaulted, which affected money market funds holding those issues. However, the investment companies running the funds absorbed the losses instead of the investors in the fund.

This does not mean that there are no high-risk short-term securities. High-yielding, high-risk short-term securities do exist and some aggressive money market funds will invest in these to raise yields. Read the prospectus which will outline the investment restrictions for that fund. If the stated objectives are to invest in low-risk securities, the Securities and Exchange Commission (SEC) will monitor and regulate the investment company's adherence to the stated objectives.

Fraud is another concern of investors. What if someone in the fund steals or embezzles their savings from their accounts? This, of course, could happen with all investments, but there are certain safeguards with money market funds, such as:

◆ the investment company does not physically handle the funds. Instead there is a custodial bank which makes the deposits into and transfers from the investors' accounts in the funds; and

◆ the custodial bank has insurance as well as being bonded in the event of theft or loss due to embezzlement or fraud.

Thus, money market funds have the same safeguards against fraud as other short-term investments, such as in savings accounts, and investors' fears should be allayed.

How to Invest in Money Market Funds

Money market funds sell shares which generally do not fluctuate in value as stock and bond mutual funds do. Money market funds typically have a constant share price of $1 (due to the short maturities of their investments) and this constant price is maintained by the investment company.

To invest in a money market fund, call the fund (most have 800 telephone numbers) or write to them for a prospectus and application form. The prospectus is required to be sent by the SEC, and it includes information about the fund, such as:

◆ the minimum dollar investment necessary to open an account,

◆ how the investor can withdraw funds from the account,

◆ the investment objectives and policies as well as the investment restrictions,

◆ who manages the fund, the fees charged by the management company, and an outline of the operating expenses and other charges,

◆ the fund's financial statements.

Read the prospectus before filling out the application form. The completed form can be sent back with a check to open the account. Investors will then receive monthly statements showing the number of shares in their accounts, their deposits, withdrawals and dividend income. Most funds have a minimum amount (usually $100) for additional investments.

Investors can withdraw money on demand from their money market funds in various ways which vary from fund to fund, including:

◆ through check writing (if check writing is available for that fund);

◆ wire transfers from the fund to a bank account;

◆ check written by fund and mailed to account-holder in response to a written request;

◆ transfer money to other funds within the same investment company's family of funds;

◆ the investor may request a systematic withdrawal plan (SWP) and the fund will send a periodic check to the investor, a third party, or bank.

How to Select a Money Market Fund

There are hundreds of money market funds to choose from and you may want to read the prospectus for the following criteria before choosing:

◆ If there is a selling commission or load charge, eliminate that fund. Most, if not all, money market funds today are no load (NL) funds which means that all of your investment is being invested in the fund.

◆ Know your own objectives to determine which type of money market fund you want to invest in. If you want a high quality fund, make sure that the fund that you choose invests in top grade securities. If you are looking for federally tax-exempt income, choose funds that invest in short-term, tax-exempt municipal bonds.

◆ Examine the return of the fund. The yield or return depends on the earnings of the fund, and the fees and operating charges deducted by that fund. Generally, the safer the fund, the lower the yield. U.S. government securities (T-bills) will have a lower yield than commercial paper and repurchase agreements, but the U.S. government will not default on its obligations.

Picking a fund which earns a higher yield may not give a higher overall return due to the operating expenses which may be considerably higher than other money market funds. Unfortunately, investors are at a disadvantage in comparing yields because of two factors: (i) some funds use the cost basis while others use the market value approach to calculate yields, which makes a comparison of yields misleading. Investors can find a list of the seven-day yields in the Thursday *New York Times* and *Wall Street Journal;* and (ii) there is variability in the funds' management fees and operating expenses.

Thus, choosing a fund on yields alone could be misleading. However, a newsletter published by the Donaghue organization, *Donaghue's Money Letter,* lists the yields of the money market funds so that they are comparable.

◆ Compare the features that the funds offer such as check writing, and whether the fund provides free check writing privileges; the number of funds within that investment family; if there are limitations on the number and amount of transfers within the family of funds; the minimum dollar amount to open a fund (typically varies from $500 to $2,000).

A comparison of these features will guide you in your choice of a money market fund.

Advantages of Money Market Funds

The advantages of money market funds are:

◆ They offer high liquidity, relative safety of principal, and competitive money market rates of return.

◆ They can be used as a parking place for funds between financial transactions or investments.

◆ They earn daily income on money that can be used for paying bills.

◆ It is easy to open a money market account, and the small minimum investment amount required to open a fund makes this type of account accessible to small investors.

Disadvantages

◆ Interest income on regular money market funds is fully taxed (federal, state and local levels).

◆ Sometimes investors can earn greater yields by investing directly in money market instruments than indirectly through money market funds.

Caveats

◆ Choose a money market fund from an investment company which has a wide range of different funds allowing you greater flexibility in your transfers to other types of investment funds.

◆ Avoid funds which have sales charges, redemption fees, and high management and expense ratios.

◆ Avoid keeping too much money in money market funds, as over the long-term real rates of return from money market funds are unlikely to exceed the rate of inflation.

Summary

Money market funds are a convenient place to invest short-term money due to their high liquidity, relative safety and high money market yields. There have been a few times historically when money market funds have outperformed all other investments. In the late 1970s and early 1980s, interest rates rose rapidly, investors took their money out of stocks and long term bonds and purchased money market securities to take advantage of the rising yields. However, mostly there is a normal term structure of interest rates (short-term rates are lower than long-term rates), and investors should not keep their long-term funds invested in money market funds.

Treasury Bills

Treasury bills are slightly more awkward to purchase than money market funds, but many investors prefer to invest directly in Treasury bills than indirectly through money market funds.

What Are Treasury Bills?

Treasury bills (T-bills) are short-term, safe haven investments, which are issued by the U.S. Treasury and are fully backed by the U.S. government. The risk of default is extremely low. In fact, if the U.S. government defaulted on any of its obligations, all investments in the U.S. would be suspect. Treasury bills are considered to be the safest of all fixed income investments.

Treasury bills are negotiable, non-interest bearing securities which mature in three months, six months or one year. They are available in minimum denominations of $10,000 and multiples of $5,000 above that.

They are issued at a discount from their face value. The amount of the discount depends on the prices bid in the Treasury bill auctions. At maturity, the bills are redeemed at full face value. The difference in the amount between the discount value and the face value is treated as interest income.

As there is no stated rate of interest, the yield on Treasury bills can be determined as follows:

$$\text{Yield} = \left(\frac{\text{Face value} - \text{Price paid}}{\text{Price paid}} \right) \times \left(\frac{365}{\text{Days to maturity}} \right)$$

A six-month Treasury bill purchased for $9,600 and redeemed at face value has an annual yield of 8.33 percent:

$$\text{Yield} = \left(\frac{\$10,000 - 9,600}{9,600} \right) \times \left(\frac{365}{182.5} \right)$$

$$= 8.33\%$$

However, to make matters more complex, bids submitted to the Federal Reserve Banks are not quoted on an annual basis, as above, but on a bank discount basis which is computed as follows:

$$\text{Yield} = \left(\frac{\text{Face value} - \text{Price paid}}{100^*} \right) \times \left(\frac{360^{**}}{\text{Days to maturity}} \right)$$

* yield is quoted for each $100 of face value
** note the use of 360 as opposed to 365 days

Using the same example as above, the discount is $4 for the T-bill selling at $96 per $100 face value with a maturity of six months. The bank discount yield is:

$$= \left(\frac{100 - 96}{100} \right) \times \left(\frac{360}{180} \right)$$

$$= 8\%$$

Thus, the bank discount yield is always less than the annual yield.

How to Buy and Sell Treasury Bills

New issues of Treasury bills can be bought either directly from any of the Federal Reserve Banks or indirectly through banks and brokerage firms. The easiest way to buy T-bills is through banks and brokerage firms.

Buying T-bills at Banks and Brokers

T-bills can be bought and sold through banks and brokerage firms who charge fees for their services ranging from $20 to $60 per T-bill. Smaller banks who are not dealers in government securities will generally charge higher fees (these banks will have to purchase the T-bills from their correspondent banks who are dealers). Similarly, small brokerage firms that are not dealers in T-bills will charge higher commissions (to cover their purchases of these securities from dealers).

Dealers make a market (known as the secondary market) in these securities by buying, at the bid price, and then selling, at the ask price, which is a higher price.

The payment of fees or commissions will reduce your yields due to the increased amount that you have to pay for the buying or selling of T-bills.

For a little extra effort, you can buy T-bills directly from Federal Reserve Banks and eliminate the fees and commissions charged by banks/brokers.

Direct Purchase

You can buy directly from the Treasury by opening an account and then submitting a tender form. See Figures 4–1, 4–2, 4–3 for a list of the offices of the Federal Reserve Banks where you can obtain the forms; a copy of a new account request form; and a copy of a tender form for a 13-week Treasury bill, respectively. Along with the new account registration form and tender form, there is a booklet "Buying Treasury Securities at the Federal Reserve Banks" which can be obtained at no charge from the Federal Reserve Banks.

The first step is to fill out the new account request form (Figure 4–2) to establish an account with the Department of the Treasury. Besides your name, address, social security or employer identification number, you will need to fill in your bank/savings & loan association information, so that payments by the Treasury can be made by direct deposit to your account. The routing number on the form is the identify-

Figure 4–1 List of Federal Reserve Banks and Treasury Servicing Offices

For In-Person Visits:	For Written Correspondence:	For In-Person Visits:	For Written Correspondence:
FRB Atlanta 104 Marietta Street, N.W Atlanta Georgia 404-521-8657 404-521-8653	104 Marietta Street, N.W. Atlanta, Georgia 30303	**FRB Denver** 1020 16th Street Denver, Colorado 303-572-2475 (Recording) 303-572-2470 or 2473	P.O. Box 5228 Terminal Annex Denver, CO 80217
FRB Baltimore 502 South Sharp Street Baltimore, Maryland 301-576-3300	P.O. Box 1378 Baltimore, MD 21230	**FRB Detroit** 160 West Fort Street Detroit, Michigan 313-964-6153 (Recording)	P.O. Box 1059 Detroit, MI 48231
FRB Birmingham 1801 Fifth Avenue, North Birmingham, Alabama 205-252-3141 Ext. 215 (Recording) 205-252-3141 Ext. 264	P.O. Box 10447 Birmingham, AL 35283	**FRB Houston** 1701 San Jacinto Street Houston, Texas 713-659-4433	P.O. Box 2578 Houston, TX 77001
FRB Boston 600 Atlantic Avenue Boston, Massachusetts 617-973-3805 (Recording) 617-973-3810	P.O. Box 2076 Boston, MA 02106	**FRB Jacksonville** 800 West Water Street Jacksonville, Florida 904-632-1179	P.O. Box 2499 Jacksonville,FL 32231-2499
FRB Buffalo 160 Delaware Avenue Buffalo, New York 716-849-5046 (Recording) 716-849-5030	P.O. Box 961 Buffalo, NY 14240-0961	**FRB Kansas City** 925 Grand Avenue Kansas City, Missouri 816-881-2767 (Recording) 816-881-2409	P.O. Box 440 Kansas City,MO 64198
FRB Charlotte 401 South Tryon Street Charlotte, North Carolina 704-336-7100	P.O. Box 30248 Charlotte, NC 28230	**FRB Little Rock** 325 West Capitol Avenue Little Rock, Arkansas 501-372-5451 Ext. 273	P.O. Box 1261 Little Rock, AR 72203
FRB Chicago 230 S. LaSalle Street Chicago, Illinois 312-786-1110 (Recording) 312-322-5369	P.O. Box 834 Chicago, IL 60690	**FRB Los Angeles** 950 South Grand Avenue Los Angeles, California 213-624-7398	P.O. Box 2077 Terminal Annex Los Angeles, CA 90051
FRB Cincinnati 150 East Fourth Street Cincinnati, Ohio 513-721-4787 Ext. 334	P.O. Box 999 Cincinnati, OH 45201	**FRB Louisville** 410 South Fifth Street Louisville, Kentucky 502-568-9232 (Recording) 502-568-9236 or 9238	P.O. Box 32710 Louisville, KY 40232
FRB Cleveland 1455 East Sixth Street Cleveland, Ohio 216-579-2490	P.O. Box 6387 Cleveland, OH 44101	**FRB Memphis** 200 North Main Street Memphis, Tennessee 901-523-7171 Ext. 225 or 641	P.O. Box 407 Memphis, TN 38101
FRB Dallas 400 South Akard Street Dallas, Texas 214-651-6362	Securities Dept. Station K 400 South Akard Street Dallas, TX 75222	**FRB Miami** 9100 N.W. Thirty-Sixth St. Miami, Florida 305-593-9923 (Recording) 305-591-2065	P.O. Box 520847 Miami, FL 33152

Figure 4–1 List of Federal Reserve Banks and Treasury Servicing Offices (continued)

For In-Person Visits:	For Written Correspondence:	For In-Person Visits:	For Written Correspondence:
FRB Minneapolis 250 Marquette Avenue Minneapolis, Minnesota 612-340-2051 (Recording) 612-340-2075	250 Marquette Avenue Minneapolis, MN 55480	**FRB Portland** 915 S.W. Stark Street Portland, Oregon 503-221-5931 (Recording) 503-221-5932	P.O. Box 3436 Portland, OR 97208-3436
FRB Nashville 301 Eighth Avenue, North Nashville, Tennessee 615-251-7236 (Recording) 615-251-7100	301 Eighth Ave., N. Nashville, TN 37203-4407	**FRB Richmond** 701 East Byrd Street Richmond, Virginia 804-697-8355 804-697-8372	P.O. Box 27622 Richmond, VA 23261
FRB Charlotte 530 East Trade Street Charlotte, North Carolina 704-358-2424 (Recording) 704-358-2100	P.O. Box 30248 Charlotte, NC 28230	**FRB Salt Lake City** 120 South State Street Salt Lake City, Utah 801-322-7844 801-322-7900	P.O. Box 30780 Salt Lake City, UT 84130
FRB Chicago 230 South LaSalle Street Chicago, Illinois 312-786-1110 (Recording) 312-322-5369	P.O. Box 834 Chicago, IL 60690	**FRB San Antonio** 126 East Nueva Street San Antonio, Texas 512-978-1330 (Recording) 512-978-1303 or 1305	P.O. Box 1471 San Antonio, TX 78295
FRB New Orleans 525 St. Charles Avenue New Orleans, Louisiana 504-593-3290 (Recording) 504-593-3200	P.O. Box 61630 New Orleans, LA 70161	**FRB San Francisco** 101 Market Street San Francisco, California 415-974-3491 (Recording) 415-974-2330	P.O. Box 7702 San Francisco, CA 94120
FRB New York 33 Liberty Street New York, New York 212-720-5823 (Recording) 212-720-6619	Federal Reserve P.O. Station 70161 10045	**FRB Seattle** 1015 Second Avenue Seattle, Washington 206-343-3615 206-343-3605	Securities Services Dept. P.O. Box 3567 Terminal Annex Seattle, WA 98124
FRB Oklahoma City 226 Dean A McGee Ave. Oklahoma City, Oklahoma 405-270-8660 405-270-8652	P.O. Box 25129 Oklahoma City, OK 73125	**FRB St. Louis** 411 Locust Street St. Louis, Missouri 314-444-8602 (Recording) 314-444-8665	P.O. Box 14915 St. Louis, MO 63178
FRB Omaha 2201 Farnam Street Omaha, Nebraska 402-221-5638 (Recording)	2201 Farnam Street Omaha, NE 68102	**United States Treasury** Washington, DC Bureau of the Public Dept. Sec. Transactions Branch 1300 C Street, S.W. Washington, DC 202-874-4000	**Mail Inquiries to:** Bureau of the Public Dept. Div. of Customer Services Washington, DC 20239-0001
FRB Philadelphia Ten Independence Mall Philadelphia, Pennsylvania 215-574-6580 (Recording) 215-574-6680	P.O. Box 90 Philadelphia, PA 19105	**Device for Hearing Impaired** 202-874-4026	**Mail Tenders to:** Bureau of the Public Dept. Department N Washington, DC 20239-1500
FRB Pittsburgh 717 Grant Street Pittsburgh, Pennsylvania 412-261-7988 (Recording) 412-261-7863	P.O. Box 867 Pittsburgh, PA 19105		

Figure 4–2 New Account Request Form to Open an Account

PD F 5182
(May 1990)

TREASURY DIRECT®

OMB NO. 1535-0069
Expires 9-30-92

NEW ACCOUNT REQUEST

INVESTOR INFORMATION

ACCOUNT NAME

FOR DEPARTMENT USE

DOCUMENT AUTHORITY

APPROVED BY

DATE APPROVED

ADDRESS

CITY   STATE   ZIP CODE

EXT REG ☐
FOREIGN ☐
BACKUP ☐
REVIEW ☐

TAXPAYER IDENTIFICATION NUMBER

1ST NAMED OWNER   —   —   **OR**   —

SOCIAL SECURITY NUMBER   EMPLOYER IDENTIFICATION NUMBER

CLASS ☐

TELEPHONE NUMBERS

(   )   —   (   )   —

WORK   HOME

DIRECT DEPOSIT INFORMATION

ROUTING NUMBER

FINANCIAL INSTITUTION NAME

ACCOUNT NUMBER

ACCOUNT NAME

ACCOUNT TYPE
(Check One)

☐ CHECKING
☐ SAVINGS

AUTHORIZATION

I submit this request pursuant to the provisions of Department of the Treasury Circulars, Public Debt Series Nos. 1-86 and 2-86.

Under penalties of perjury, I certify that the number shown on this form is my correct taxpayer identification number and that I am not subject to backup withholding because (1) I have not been notified that I am subject to backup withholding as a result of a failure to report all interest or dividends, or (2) the Internal Revenue Service has notified me that I am no longer subject to backup withholding. I further certify that all other information provided on this form is true, correct and complete.

SIGNATURE   DATE

Figure 4–3 13-Week Tender Form
for Treasury Bills

FORM PD F 5176-1
(February 1990)

OMB No. 1535-0089
Expires: 09-30-92

TREASURY DIRECT ®

TENDER FOR 13-WEEK TREASURY BILL

TENDER INFORMATION

AMOUNT OF TENDER: $ _____

FOR DEPARTMENT USE

BID TYPE (Check One) ☐ NONCOMPETITIVE   ☐ COMPETITIVE AT ▓▓ . ▓▓ %

ACCOUNT NUMBER   ▓▓▓▓ – ▓▓▓ – ▓▓▓▓▓

INVESTOR INFORMATION

ACCOUNT NAME

ADDRESS

CITY   STATE   ZIP CODE

TAXPAYER IDENTIFICATION NUMBER

1ST NAMED OWNER   ▓▓▓ – ▓▓ – ▓▓▓▓   OR   ▓▓ – ▓▓▓▓▓▓▓

SOCIAL SECURITY NUMBER   EMPLOYER IDENTIFICATION NUMBER

TELEPHONE NUMBERS

WORK (▓▓▓) ▓▓▓ – ▓▓▓▓   HOME (▓▓▓) ▓▓▓ – ▓▓▓▓

PAYMENT ATTACHED

TOTAL PAYMENT: $ _____

NUMBERS

CASH (01): $ _____   CHECKS (02/03): $ _____

SECURITIES (05): $ _____ $ _____

OTHER (06): $ _____ $ _____

DIRECT DEPOSIT INFORMATION

ROUTING NUMBER

FINANCIAL INSTITUTION NAME

ACCOUNT NUMBER

ACCOUNT TYPE (Check One)   ☐ CHECKING   ☐ SAVINGS

ACCOUNT NAME

AUTOMATIC REINVESTMENT

1   2   3   4   5   6   7   8   Circle the number of sequential 13-week reinvestments you want to schedule at this time

AUTHORIZATION

For the notice required under the Privacy and Paperwork Reduction Acts, see the accompanying instructions.

I submit this tender pursuant to the provisions of Department of the Treasury Circulars, Public Debt Series Nos. 1-86 and 2-86 and the public announcement issued by the Department of the Treasury.

Under penalties of perjury, I certify that the number shown on this form is my correct taxpayer identification number and that I am not subject to backup withholding because (1) I have not been notified that I am subject to backup withholding as a result of a failure to report all interest or dividends, or (2) the Internal Revenue Service has notified me that I am no longer subject to backup withholding. I further certify that all other information provided on this form is true, correct and complete.

SIGNATURE _____   DATE _____

SEE INSTRUCTIONS FOR PRIVACY ACT AND PAPERWORK REDUCTION ACT NOTICE

★U.S.GPO:1990-268-403/20484

FOR DEPARTMENT USE: TENDER NUMBER, CUSIP, ISSUE DATE, RECEIVED BY, DATE RECEIVED, EXT REG ☐, FOREIGN ☐, BACKUP ☐, REVIEW ☐, CLASS ☐

ing number of your financial institution. It can be found on the bottom line of your check before your account number or on your deposit slip before your account number. It is a nine digit number.

After submitting this form to the Federal Reserve Bank/branch in your geographic area, you will receive a confirmation of the establishment of your account. You are now ready to fill in the tender form to buy Treasury bills directly from the Federal Reserve Bank. See Figure 4–3 for a copy of a 13-week tender form. The 26-week and 52-week tender forms are the same but printed in different colors.

New issues of Treasury bills are auctioned on a weekly basis by the Federal Reserve Bank and investors may submit their bids either on a competitive or non-competitive basis.

Using *competitive bids*, investors will have to submit their bids on a bank discount basis, with two decimals. For example, if an investor wanted to buy $100,000 of six-month Treasury bills and pay $96,000, the competitive bid submitted to the Federal Reserve Bank would be 8.00 percent. The Federal Reserve will then accept those bids which have the lowest discount rates (the highest prices) from all the bids received. Thus, for the accepted bids there is a range of yields, from the lowest to the highest known as the "stopout yield," which the Federal Reserve will pay. Investors who have their bids accepted at the "stopout yield" or close to it will receive greater returns than those received for bids at the lowest yields.

The yields that investors bid depend upon the money market rates that are currently being offered by competing short-term instruments as well as expectations of what current short-term rates for T-bills will be. By studying these rates, an investor has a better chance of submitting a bid that will be accepted. However, with a competitive bid investors face the risk of not having their bids accepted, if their bids are above the "stopout yield."

For the less expert investors who may not want to work out their bids or for those who want to be assured of purchasing T-bills, they can submit *non-competitive bids*. With non-competitive bids, investors will be able to buy T-bills at the average accepted competitive bid in the auction. Generally all non-competitive bids of up to $1 million per investor per auction are accepted which means that investors are assured of their purchases.

Tender forms to submit bids may be sent in mail or in person to the Federal Reserve Banks and branches before the close of the auction. Competitive bids must be received by the time designated in the offering circular. Non-competitive bids that are mailed must be postmarked by no later than midnight the day before the auction and received on or before the issue date of the securities.

Payment must accompany the tender form. Check the type of payment: cash, check, securities or other. The amount of the payment should be no less than the amount of the tender for a non-competitive bid; and for a competitive bid no less than the bid amount. If the payment amount is not correct, the tender will be rejected and returned.

On acceptance of your bid, you will receive a confirmation receipt from the Federal Reserve and a payment, which is the difference between the tender amount you submitted and the discounted price of the T-bills. You can stipulate on the tender form whether you want the Federal Reserve to reinvest the T-bills when they mature. If you do not choose the reinvestment option, the Federal Reserve will credit your account for the face value of the Treasury bills at maturity.

Treasury bills purchased directly through the Federal Reserve system are held in the Treasury direct book-entry system which is designed primarily for investors who would hold their securities to maturity. Should you decide to sell your T-bills before maturity, you would have to fill out a Transfer Request Form (PD 5179) which will transfer your account to the commercial book-entry system, and then your T-bills can be sold. The commercial book-entry system records those treasuries bought through financial institutions and government securities dealers.

The advantages of buying T-bills directly from the Federal Reserve and holding them to maturity is that the investor avoids paying commissions or fees.

The Advantages of Treasury Bills

◆ T-bills provide investors with a flexible range of maturities along with complete safety for the repayment of principal and interest.

◆ T-bills offer excellent liquidity (probably the most liquid of all short-term money market instruments).

◆ Interest income on T-bills is exempt from state and local taxation.

The Disadvantages of Treasury Bills

◆ Need a minimum of $10,000 to invest directly in Treasury bills.

◆ Although Treasury bill yields are benchmarks upon which the yields of other instruments are based, yields on T-bills tend to be less than those on certificates of deposit for similar maturities and money market mutual funds.

◆ Treasury bills are subject to interest rate risk. If market rates of interest go up, the price of existing Treasury bills will go down which may result in capital losses for those Treasury bill owners who are forced to sell before maturity. (If market rates of interest go down, investors who sell before maturity may realize capital gains.)

◆ T-bills do not protect against moderate to high inflation.

Caveats

◆ When buying T-bills through banks and/or brokers, shop around for the lowest fees/commissions.

◆ When submitting competitive bids, there is always the possibility that your bid will not be accepted due to unanticipated fluctuations of money market interest rates on the day of the auction.

◆ Although submitting a non-competitive bid assures the investor of purchase, there is the uncertainty that the investor could receive yields well below current yields due to an unexpected drop in short-term interest rates.

Summary

Treasury bills are very safe, liquid short-term investments which can be used as a parking place for short-term funds.

Commercial Paper

Despite the fact that commercial paper is difficult for individual investors to buy, it is a widely held indirect investment in money market funds. By understanding what commercial paper is all about, investors are better able to assess the risks of their money market funds.

What Is Commercial Paper?

Commercial paper is an unsecured, short-term promissory note (IOU) issued by the largest and most creditworthy financial and non financial corporations. Simply stated, the borrowing corporation promises to pay back the lender an amount of money in a short period of time. The commercial paper is sold at a discount to the amount of money the corporation will pay back at maturity. Commercial paper is generally issued with maturities of less than 270 days (in order to escape registration with the Securities and Exchange Commission (SEC) which is required for maturities in excess of 270 days). Denominations for commercial paper are large ranging from $5,000 to $5,000,000, with most being for $100,000 and over (Kolb and DeMong 1988, 687).

How to Buy Commercial Paper

Commercial paper is sold either through dealers to investors or directly by issuers to investors.

Dealer Paper

Dealers buy commercial paper and then immediately resell the paper in large amounts to institutional investors charging relatively small margins (1/8 of one percent per annum) (Stigum and Fabozzi 1987, page 53). Even if individual investors have large amounts ($150,000) to invest, dealers will not sell commercial paper to individual investors, because the SEC has stated that commercial paper should only be sold to sophisticated investors, and dealers consider all individual investors to be unsophisticated. Thus, individual investors may buy dealer paper through brokers who offer the paper in smaller amounts ($25,000 and over) and charge commissions which can be significant on small purchases (Stigum and Fabozzi 1987, page 58).

Direct Issue

Individual investors may buy commercial paper directly from the issuers in relatively small amounts ($25,000). Individual investors can telephone or write to well known finance companies such as GMAC (General Motors Acceptance Corp.), Chrysler Financial Corp., Sears, etc., to find out their terms, rates and maturities. When investors have decided which paper to buy, they can mail their checks and have the company register the paper in their names, and mail the paper securities to them. Buying directly from the issuer is the cheapest way, as no costs are involved (other than telephone calls and postage). Investors can redeem their paper at maturity for cash by mailing the paper security certificates before they mature to the issuer (or to the bank that handles the collections for the issuer).

The investor also has the option of rolling over the paper when it matures. After a direct purchase from an issuer, a renewal form is routinely sent, and the investor should fill it out and send it back to the issuer before maturity. At maturity the issuer will send the new commercial paper security, and a check for the difference between the maturity value of the old paper and the discounted price of the new commercial paper (Stigum and Fabozzi 1987, page 60).

Commercial paper may also be bought through a bank for which the bank will charge a small fee for their efforts.

Most small investors are indirect holders of commercial paper through their ownership of shares in money market mutual funds (who purchase commercial paper as investments for the funds).

The Advantages of Commercial Paper

◆ Commercial paper offers a higher yield than Treasury bills.

◆ Except for Penn Central's default on their commercial paper in the early 1970s, historically the credit risks of commercial paper have been relatively low. Risk depends on the creditworthiness of the issuing corporation, and the risks of good quality commercial paper are low.

◆ Investors do not need to tie up their funds for long periods due to the short maturities.

The Disadvantages of Commercial Paper

◆ It is difficult for investors to get their money before maturity as there is not a secondary market for commercial paper.

◆ Interest on commercial paper is taxed at the federal, state and local levels whereas interest on Treasury bills is taxed at the federal level only.

◆ Need a minimum of at least $5,000 to $10,000 to be able to buy commercial paper directly.

Caveats

Since the yields on commercial paper have traditionally only been slightly higher than those of Treasury bills, an investor may want to consider the disadvantages of commercial paper (not as liquid and triple taxable) before choosing commercial paper over Treasury bills.

Summary

Commercial paper is a relatively low-risk investment for those investors with larger amounts to invest on a short-term basis. The risks of default are higher than for Treasury bills and they are not as liquid as Treasury bills. However, the yields on commercial paper are higher than those on Treasury bills.

Bankers' Acceptances

Bankers' acceptances are the least understood of all the short-term money market investments, yet they are good investments for individual investors.

What Are Bankers' Acceptances?

Bankers' acceptances are negotiable time drafts commonly issued for import-export transactions. For example, a seller (exporter) sells goods to a buyer (importer) in another country, and would like to get paid when the goods are shipped. On the other hand, the buyer would like to pay for the goods in three months when he receives them. To alleviate the seller's fears, the buyer (importer) applies to the bank for a bankers' acceptance, which is a promise from the buyer to pay the amount in a short period of time—usually between 30 to 180 days. The bank then accepts this promise by obligating itself to pay the seller (exporter).

The bank may either hold the acceptance until it matures, or it may sell the acceptance directly to investors or through dealers to investors. The investor buys the acceptance at a discount and holds it until maturity when it is presented to the bank at face value—(the difference between the amount received and the amount paid to the bank is interest to the investor). Banks generally charge small fees which go towards covering their costs.

The predominant investors in bankers' acceptances are central banks of foreign countries, Federal Reserve Banks and other banks. Due to the large amounts that bankers' acceptances are written for, small investors have not been active participants.

How to Invest in Bankers' Acceptances

As a start, an individual investor may approach his or her bank. If the bank does not offer acceptances, the investor should then try other banks, particularly the larger commercial banks and dealers who deal in bankers' acceptances. The amounts that can be invested in bankers' acceptances vary but typically range from $25,000 to $1,000,000 (Martin et al. 1991, page 558). Bankers will group bankers' acceptances into packages at these higher denominations.

Individual investors may indirectly hold bankers' acceptances through investments in money market mutual funds.

The Advantages of Bankers' Acceptances

◆ Bankers' acceptances are high quality, low risk, safe investments: the risk of default is low as they are bank guaranteed.

◆ Rates of return are generally higher than those of Treasury bills of similar maturities.

◆ If investors do not want to wait until their bankers' acceptances mature, they can sell them in an over the counter market. Investors may have trouble selling one or two low denomination bankers' acceptances.

The Disadvantages of Bankers' Acceptances

◆ Investors have to look for banks or dealers carrying bankers' acceptances. Banks do not advertise that they have bankers' acceptances readily available for investors to invest in.

◆ The amounts to be invested in bankers' acceptances may be high ($25,000 to $1,000,000) for individual investors.

◆ If short-term interest rates are volatile and start to fall, bankers' acceptances, being short term, do not offer the investor the opportunity to "lock into" the higher interest rates for a long period of time.

Caveat

Investors should check that the rates of return on bankers' acceptances offered by the banks that they approach are competitive with prevailing rates on bankers' acceptances (can be found in the *Wall Street Journal, Barron's*).

Summary

For the investor who would like a safe (low default rate), short-term investment, bankers' acceptances are very good. A good time to invest in them is when the spread between long- and short-term interest rates is narrow (in other words, investors do not have to tie up their funds for long periods of time in order to get high yields).

Summary of Short-Term Fixed Income Securities

In this chapter, short-term debt instruments traded in the money market were examined. This is not meant to be an all inclusive discussion because there are other important money market instruments such as negotiable certificates of deposit and repurchase agreements which have been omitted. These money market instruments offer investors the opportunity of having their short-term, liquid funds earn a return rather than allowing the money to sit in non-interest bearing checking accounts and low interest savings accounts. To achieve higher rates of return, investors will need to look to investments with longer maturities, discussed in the forthcoming chapters.

References

Faerber, Esmé. *Managing Your Investments, Savings and Credit.* Chicago: Probus Publishing Co., 1992.

Kolb, Burton A. and Richard F. DeMong. *Principles of Financial Management.* Plano, TX: Business Publications, Inc., 1988.

Martin, John D., J. William Petty, Arthur J. Keown, and David F. Scott, Jr. *Basic Financial Management,* 5th Edition. Englewood Cliffs, N.J.: Prentice Hall, 1991.

Stigum, Marcia and Frank J. Fabozzi. *Dow Jones Guide to Bond and Money Market Investments.* Homewood, IL: Dow Jones-Irwin, 1987.

Chapter 5

Corporate Bonds

Key Concepts

◆ The features of corporate bonds

◆ The types of corporate bonds

◆ The risks of corporate bonds

◆ Junk bonds

◆ How to buy corporate bonds

◆ The advantages of corporate bonds

◆ The disadvantages of corporate bonds

◆ Caveats

In the past, investors have considered corporate bonds to be safe investments that provide a steady stream of income. However, in recent years corporate bonds have become more volatile, and a growing category of corporate junk bonds deviate from the standard of safety referred to at the beginning of this paragraph.

The types of corporate bonds and the bond markets themselves have changed in recent years, and although investors still buy bonds because they offer greater yields than CDs and money market funds, investors need to become more aware of the bond's features and risks in order to protect the safety of their principal.

What Are the Features of Corporate Bonds?

Bonds are debt instruments and all bonds have similar features. A corporate bond is a loan made by a corporation in return for a specified amount of interest and the repayment of the face value of the bond at a specified maturity date. The interest (coupon) rate is generally fixed for the life of the bond (exceptions are variable rate bonds), and the face (par) value of the bond is usually $1,000. The maturity value is the date by which the bond must be paid off. Thus, a corporate bond with a coupon of seven percent and a maturity date of July 1, 1999, would pay interest of $70 per bond every year up to July 1, 1999, when the corporation will pay off the face value of the bond to the bondholder.

If a bond has 20 years to maturity at the date of issuance, it is said to have an *original* maturity of 20 years. After a year, that same bond will have a *current* maturity or term to maturity of 19 years.

Forms of Bonds

Bonds are issued in one of three forms: registered, bearer, or book-entry form. Registered form is similar to owning stock certificates. Bonds are registered in the owner's name, and the interest payments are mailed to the owner. When the bond is sold, the transfer agent will register the bond in the name of the new owner.

In bearer (or coupon) form, possession signifies ownership. The bond does not have a registered owner, and the issuing company does not know where to mail the interest payments. Therefore, attached to the bearer bonds are the coupons for the interest payments. At the due date of the interest payment, the bearer clips the coupon and sends it to the issuer's paying agent who will send a check to the bondholder for the interest. The coupon can also be sent to the bondholder's bank which will collect the interest for the bondholder.

It is easy to sell bearer bonds as they do not need to be registered. However, they do present problems in terms of safekeeping. Bearer bonds are like money and need to be kept in a safe place since possession signifies ownership.

Bonds may also be issued in book-entry form. Instead of a bond certificate, the bondholder receives a confirmation with a computer number which signifies ownership. Bondholders would designate their bank or savings and loan accounts into which interest payments are deposited directly.

Who Should Keep Your Bond Certificates?

Investors often debate whether to take possession of their bond certificates (in bearer or registered form) or whether they should leave them with their brokerage firms.

The advantages of leaving them in the custody of the brokerage firm are:

◆ they are protected against physical loss if that brokerage firm is covered by the SIPC (Securities Insurance Protection Corporation);

◆ in the event that your bonds are called, the brokerage firm is more likely to become aware of the call and redeem the bonds immediately.

The disadvantages of keeping them in the custody of the brokerage firm are:

◆ should you decide to sell your bonds through another broker, you must have your existing brokerage firm transfer them to the new broker's firm. You have five days after the date of sale to deliver the securities before the brokerage firm would assess a late charge;

◆ some brokerage firms are slow in remitting the interest payments. For example, one brokerage firm would receive the interest payments at the beginning of the month and only remit them to their clients at the end of the month. This brokerage firm had the use of clients' money for 30 days; and

◆ when bonds with a sinking fund provision are left in the brokerage firm's name, the brokerage firm will choose which customer's bonds will be redeemed early. This is particularly relevant for the small investor. With a sinking fund provision, you are better off holding your own bonds, which can be called directly, but it is not left to the brokerage firm to chose which client's bonds to redeem. A sinking fund is used by companies to redeem a certain number of bonds each year before maturity. The company will notify bondholders through the mail and in the newspapers of redemptions.

The Types of Corporate Bonds

Corporate bonds can be classified into the following groups (Thau 1992, page 156):

◆ The utilities which consists of bonds issued by the telephone and electric companies. These securities tend to be viewed as safe, conservative investments.

◆ The transportation group which consists of bonds issued by the railroads and the airlines.

◆ The industrials which consist of bonds issued by industrial companies.

◆ The finance companies such as insurance companies and banks.

Within these groups, there are many types of bonds such as mortgage bonds, debenture bonds, variable interest bonds, convertible bonds, and zero-coupon bonds. These bonds are either secured or unsecured. For secured bonds, the issuer pledges an asset as collateral, and in the event of a default, the creditor can seize the asset (after proceeding to court). An example of a secured bond is a mortgage bond which is frequently issued by utility companies. Investors should sleep well at night knowing that their bonds are backed by a power plant, but do investors have the expertise to operate the power plant in the event of a default by the utility company? Although pledging assets increases the safety of the principal of the bonds, in this case investors should hope that the utility company does not default on its interest and principal payments.

The transportation group issues bonds known as equipment trust certificates which are secured by equipment such as airplanes and railroad cars. This equipment may be more marketable than power plants, but investors could still lose some of their principal in the event of a default. For example, when both Braniff Airlines and Freddie Laker's airline declared bankruptcy during the worldwide recession of 1981-1982, the market for used aircraft had declined significantly (Mayo 1991, page 382).

Unsecured bonds or debenture bonds are backed only by the issuer's creditworthiness (ability to pay annual interest and principal at maturity). Some companies issue subordinated debenture bonds, which are riskier in the event of insolvency, as subordinated debenture holders will be last in the line of lenders to be repaid. Seniority becomes important during bankruptcy because secured bonds and senior debt are first in line to be repaid. Riskier issues tend to offer higher coupon rates to entice investors.

Generally, investors should be concerned with the issuer's ability to pay (or creditworthiness) rather than with the security alone. In the event of bankruptcy, pledged property may not be marketable, and it may involve litigation, which can be time consuming.

Corporations also issue convertible bonds which are bonds that may be converted into the issuer's common stock. Zero-coupon bonds are a relatively new type of bond that is issued at a deep discount with interest paid at maturity.

What Are the Risks of Corporate Bonds?

The *risk of default* is more of a concern for investors of corporate bonds as a group than for other types of bonds such as U.S. Treasuries and government agency bonds, where the risks of default are much less. U.S. Treasuries are considered to be free of default risk. This is why corporate bonds offer higher yields than Treasuries and government agency bonds. The greater the risk of default the higher the coupon rate for that issue.

For the risks of default on individual corporate bond issues, most investors rely on the ratings of the issues given by the commercial rating companies such as Standard & Poor's, Moody's, and Fitch. However, as pointed out in an earlier chapter, these ratings are not foolproof and are also subject to change. A company's financial position can deteriorate after being rated. For example, in the early 1980s Washington Public Power Supply System defaulted on some of their bond issues when their ratings by the commercial ratings services were good.

Thus, in addition to the commercial ratings, evaluate the bond issue by yourself by looking at the bond's prospectus or company's financial statements for:

◆ the amount of debt that the company has; and

◆ where you stand in the debt line as to claims in the event of bankruptcy.

There is another risk which has affected bond prices of existing issues and that is called *event risk*. This is the risk that large corporations will issue large amounts of debt to finance the takeovers of other corporations (also known as a leveraged buy out). This causes the existing bond issues of those takeover corporations to plummet in price, because the corporation significantly increases their level of debt, resulting in downgraded ratings.

As a result, investors shunned many corporate bond offerings. To entice investors to buy these new issues, corporate issuers introduced provisions which made takeovers more expensive. These are nicknamed "poison puts" which vary from allowing bondholders to sell their bonds back to the issuer at par in the event of a takeover or in the event that the bond's ratings are downgraded.

Before buying a new corporate issue check with your broker whether there is a "poison put" protection clause.

All bonds, except for floating rate bonds, are subject to *interest rate risk*. Citicorp was the first corporation to introduce floating rate bonds in the 1970s. These were unique at the time in that the coupon rate fluctuated with the rate of Treasury bills, and after a two-year period (after issuance), the bondholders could redeem the bonds at par value. Therefore, floating rate bonds will not fluctuate very much in price due to changes in interest rates, unlike the prices of regular fixed income bonds. As pointed out in a previous chapter, bond prices fluctuate inversely with market rates of interest. The longer the maturity of the bond, the greater the price fluctuation in relation to changes in interest rates.

The impact of interest rate risk can be lessened by:

◆ spreading out the maturities of the different bond issues in your portfolio to even out the impact of changing market rates of interest. (i.e., instead of investing only in bonds with 20 year maturities, ladder the maturities between 2, 5, 10, 15 and 20 years);

◆ diversifying your bond portfolio by buying different types of bonds;

◆ purchasing good quality bonds;

◆ lessening the length of the maturities; and

◆ buying bonds with a put feature which allows bondholders to sell their bonds back to the issuer at face value when interest rates rise.

The downside is that these bonds have lower coupon rates and shorter maturities. However, the optimum strategy, in theory, is to invest in short maturities when market rates of interest are increasing and then when they peak, to buy long term bonds to lock into the high coupon rates. The obvious question is how do you know when market rates of interest are going to peak? Locking in at the peak of market interest rates is not as important as at least trying to follow the strategy.

Many corporate bonds have call features which means that they are subject to *call risk*. This call feature allows the issuer to retire the bonds prior to maturity. When a bond is called, interest no longer accrues, which forces bondholders to retire the bond. The call feature benefits the issuer rather than the bondholder. This is because issuers tend to call their bonds after a period of high interest rates. For example, if a corporation issued 12 percent coupon bonds when interest rates were high, and then rates dropped to eight percent, it would be advantageous for the issuer to refund the old bonds with new bonds at a lower coupon rate.

Early repayment is always disadvantageous for investors as issuers will rarely refund bonds early if market rates of interest are going up. This is especially disadvantageous for investors who had bought bonds when interest rates peaked.

Investors should pay particular attention to a bond issue's call and refunding provisions. There are three types of call provisions:

◆ Noncallable bonds offer investors the most protection, but there are many loopholes. Noncallable implies that the bonds will not be called before maturity. However, there are cases where noncallable bonds have been called such as in the case of a fire or act of God; or when a healthy company stops making its interest payments on the bonds, and the trustees call them in and the debt is paid off early. Noncallable for life bonds would be listed in the dealer's quote sheets as NCL.

◆ Freely callable bonds offer investors no protection as issuers can call them anytime.

◆ Deferred callable bonds offer some protection since the bonds cannot be called until after a period of time (for example, 5, 10 or 15 years after issue). A bond that is noncallable until 1999 would be listed as NC99 on the dealer's quote sheet.

The call provision of the bond will specify the price above the face value that the issuer is willing to pay. This is referred to as the call premium which frequently equals the coupon rate of the bond. It is important to check the call provision of a bond issue before buying. For new issues you may want to go one step further and insist on a final copy of the prospectus from the broker. Often the preliminary prospectus is skimpy on early call details (Antilla 1992).

When buying noncallable or deferred callable bonds, seek written assurances from your broker as to their call status.

Besides the call provision, the refunding provision in the bond indenture may be more important. There are nonrefundable bonds which can indeed be called and refunded. However, the refunding must be with "clean money" which is raised either from internal sources of funds or the selling of stocks or assets. Non refundable bonds cannot be repaid from the proceeds of selling lower coupon rate debt. Currently, May Department Stores has been named in a lawsuit for redeeming more than $160 million of high interest bonds with a simultaneous offering of new bonds at a lower coupon rate. May Department Stores used a technique known as a STAC, which is the simultaneous tender offer and cash call.

A STAC works in the following way: the company with outstanding bonds announces to its bondholders that they can voluntarily turn in their bonds at a premium price. The heavy hand is applied to those bondholders who do not voluntarily turn in their bonds. They are told that their bonds will be called for cash later at a lower price. In other words, the gist of a STAC is: turn in your bonds for a higher price because if you don't, the company has enough cash to call them in.

Thus, call and refunding provisions are important to investors particularly if the bonds are purchased at a premium price, and/or market rates of interest are at or near their peak.

What about Junk Bonds?

Junk bonds are not a special type of bond but are regular high-risk, low-rated bonds. These corporate bonds have ratings of BBB (by Standard & Poor's) and Baa (by Moody's Investor Services, Inc.) or lesser categories, which consist of a range of poor quality debt close to default. Some of these bonds have no ratings.

In order to entice investors, coupon rates of junk bonds are higher than the coupon rates of investment grade bonds. There are two major reasons for these higher coupon yields:

◆ the issuers of junk bonds may be young growth companies with weak balance sheets and/or financially troubled companies where junk bonds are one of the few alternatives left to raise capital; and

◆ many corporations have used junk bonds to finance the takeovers of other corporations.

This latter reason has accounted for the major growth in the junk bond market during the decade of the 1980s. Michael Milken and Drexel Burnham and Lambert opened up the junk bond market and sold these bonds directly to the public. By establishing a network of potential investors, companies had a low cost alternative to raising funds to the traditional sources of borrowing from banks prior to the growth of the junk bond market. However, in the late 1980s with the economic slowdown, the junk bond market was faced with increasing rates of defaults.

This resulted in the collapse of the junk bond market where mutual funds, institutional investors and many small investors bailed out of the junk bond market. The prices of junk bonds plummeted and those investors who were left holding junk bonds found that they had illiquid investments with an erosion of their investment capital. Junk bonds remained in the doldrums during 1990. Then, with the steep declines in bond prices, the junk bond market proved to be an attractive speculation. The junk bond market rallied for about 18 months into 1992.

For those investors who bought and sold junk bonds at the right time, the rewards were large. However, the risks are high and that is why the yields of junk bonds are so attractive. Investors are giving up a degree of safety because junk bonds have greater price swings and have the overhanging specter of default. Junk bonds do default as evidenced by the increase in the junk bond default rate to eight percent in 1990 (Thau 1992, page 165).

Various studies quote different rates of default, and there are studies done by brokerage firms which tout the relative safety of high yield junk bonds.

Regardless of which study you choose to believe you should carefully weigh the following risks against the "promised" higher returns (Faerber 1992, page 151):

◆ if interest rates go down, there is the risk that issuers of the high yielding junk bonds will call them and refinance with lower yielding securities;

◆ there is the risk that junk bond prices could plummet and investors could lose part of their initial investments;

◆ there is the risk that during sell-offs in the junk bond market, investors would find that there are no buyers for their bonds.

Investing in junk bonds is not for unsophisticated investors, but for those who are able to analyze the financial statements of companies in order to differentiate the "quality" high yield bonds from those that are descending along the path to bankruptcy.

Some advice for those who are not deterred by the risks of junk bonds:

◆ Buy only publicly listed bonds as you can follow the price quotes in the newspapers when you buy and sell. The junk bond market has received a reputation which has not enhanced its credibility. As trading is unregulated and investors do not have access to accurate price information, prices quoted by dealers can vary significantly. For example, Equitable Bag Company was quoted by one dealer at a bid and asked price of 80 and 90 respectively, while a second dealer quoted an 85 bid and a 90 asked price on the same bonds (Mitchell 1992). Individual investors are therefore, at a disadvantage if they need to buy or sell quickly.

◆ Diversify your purchases to spread your risks. If you cannot afford to buy many different corporate junk bonds, invest in junk bond mutual funds where diversification can be achieved.

◆ Avoid buying bonds that are part of small issues (less than $75 million) as they can be illiquid.

◆ Limit the amount that you invest in junk bonds to a small percentage of your portfolio. The percentage will vary according to your investment objectives, risks, level of income, stage of the life cycle, and other personal characteristics.

How to Buy Corporate Bonds

Corporate bonds can be bought and sold in the same manner as common stocks. Bonds may be bought through brokerage firms with cash or on margin. The process of purchasing bonds on margin is where the investor uses an amount of borrowed funds from the brokerage firm to purchase the bonds (stocks). The amount that can be borrowed depends on the margin requirement (set by the Federal Reserve) which is the percentage requirement that must be put up by the investor in cash. The rest may be borrowed.

Using borrowed funds to buy bonds could lead to problems if the bonds do not appreciate more than the interest cost on the borrowed funds. On the other hand, if the investment does well, the rate of return is greater for the investor since the investor has invested less money.

When you buy a new issue of bonds, you will pay no commission since it is absorbed by the issuing corporation. Before investing in a new issue, you should examine the company's prospectus to assess the overall risks.

From the balance sheet, you can determine the level of debt and the number of debt issues which are senior to this one. In the event of bankruptcy, the greater the number of senior issues to this one the lower the priority of this bond investor's claims.

From the income statement, you can determine whether the level of earnings will provide adequate coverage of the interest payments on all the debt issues outstanding, including the issue to be financed. If there is a downturn in sales, you would want to see how much of an interest cover the company has before the earnings become insufficient to service its debt.

If the company is currently selling off assets to generate funds and the debt to total assets ratio is high, warning flags should go up about this issue. This process of analyzing the financial statements is particularly important when considering the purchase of lower quality, new corporate issues.

Existing corporate bond issues trade on the over-the-counter market and a number of corporate issues are listed on the New York Stock Exchange and American Exchange. Trading of listed bonds does not take place in the same location as common stocks on these exchanges. Actively listed bonds on the NYSE (New York Stock Exchange) are traded in the Bond Room, where members announce the bid and asked prices. These are either accepted by other members or counter offers are made. Thus, buying and selling is done through these members and not through specialists as in the case of common stocks. Inactively listed bonds are traded through the computer system in the Bond Room. Members respond by entering their orders through the computer terminal.

The advantage of buying listed bonds is that their prices appear in the daily newspapers which gives investors the opportunity to check up on actual trades. Bonds that trade over the counter are unlisted and bond price quotes may vary considerably from dealer to dealer. This is especially true for lower quality, inactively traded bonds where the size of the spread between the bid and asked prices may be quite large. In fact, there is pressure to regulate the unruly trading in the junk bond market by instituting a price quotation system for the most actively traded junk bonds in 1993. This system would have to be approved by the SEC before being implemented.

Until such time, small investors will continue to be disadvantaged by these abusive trading practices. When dealers have to report their prices, many of these inefficiencies will disappear (Mitchell 1992). Thus, when buying unlisted bonds, it is almost imperative that investors shop around for the best quotes from different brokers.

It is always a good idea to ask for both the bid and asked price of the bond that you are interested in buying, because the size of the spread tells you much about that bond issue.

◆ A large spread (four percent or more) indicates that the bond is more than likely illiquid (cannot resell quickly), inactively traded and possibly some other bad news such as a potential downgrading in ratings (Thau 1992, 13).

◆ A small spread indicates the opposite—active trading with little risk of resale.

Higher transaction costs are charged if investors buy or sell a small number of bonds (less than 10 bonds).

For existing bond issues, you will not see a prospectus, but before investing, you should request the latest company information from your broker.

When buying bonds, investors may pay more than the asked price due to the *accrued interest* on that bond. Bonds earn interest daily, but the corporation only pays out the interest once or twice a year. Therefore, if a bond is purchased between the dates that interest is paid, the buyer then owes the seller the accrued interest for the number of days that the seller owned the bond. The amount of accrued interest is added to the purchase price of the bond. The accrued interest will be stated separately on the confirmation statement sent from the brokerage firm when the bonds are bought or sold.

Bonds that are in default and are no longer paying interest are said to trade *flat*. These bonds do not trade with accrued interest. In the bond quotes in the financial pages of the newspapers, an F next to the bonds signifies that it is trading flat.

Bondholders can sell their bonds in the secondary market before maturity or call. For listed bonds, investors can get an idea of the price from the newspapers. Bear in mind that newspapers only list one price for bonds, whereas bonds have a bid and asked price. In case you can never remember which price is which: you buy at the higher price (asked) and you sell at the lower price (bid). The difference or spread is how dealers and brokers make their money from the trade.

As mentioned earlier, bonds may be retired earlier than their maturity dates. Many corporate bonds have *sinking fund* provisions in their indentures which are used to help with the retirement of the bond issues. Instead of the entire bond issue being retired at maturity, a sinking fund allows the corporation to make periodic payments to retire parts of the bond issue before maturity.

With one type of sinking fund, the company will randomly select the bonds to be retired, and then call them for redemption. Once these bonds are called, they no longer earn interest. For bonds with this kind of sinking fund provision, you would not want to leave your bonds in street name (in the custody of the brokerage firm), unless you are a large investor with tremendous clout in that brokerage firm, where you know that they will turn in other investors' bonds first.

In another type of sinking fund, a corporation will make payments to a trustee who will invest this money and then the entire amount accumulated will go towards retiring the bonds at maturity.

Corporations may also repurchase their bonds in the bond market and retire them. This happens more when the bonds are trading at a discount. Investors who sell their corporate bonds may not know that it is the issuing corporation who is buying them back.

Corporations may decide to repurchase their bonds by announcing their intention to bondholders and offering a certain price to buy them back. In this case, bondholders are not required to sell their bonds back to the corporation if they don't want to.

What Are the Advantages of Corporate Bonds?

◆ Corporate bonds, as a group, have greater coupon yields than other types of bonds, namely Treasuries and agency bonds. This varies according to the quality of the corporate bonds. Generally, good quality corporate bonds could pay coupon rates of one to 1 to 1 1/2 percent more than those of Treasuries. The spread on junk bond coupons will be much greater.

◆ Corporate bonds give a higher total return relative to other fixed income securities. Investors can increase their current rates of return by purchasing lower quality bonds, but they face increased risks of default on interest and principal.

◆ Income and principal are relatively safe on high quality corporate bonds.

◆ Investors can get capital gains from purchasing bonds when market interest rates are falling (bond prices and interest rates move in opposite directions). However, capital losses may be incurred if bonds are sold when market interest rates are rising. For investors willing to take higher risks, the junk bond market provides investors with opportunities for larger capital gains and higher returns when nervousness about junk bond defaults drives all the junk bond prices down.

What Are the Disadvantages of Corporate Bonds?

◆ Corporate bond prices are adversely affected by rising inflation and rising interest rates. This affects all fixed income securities and is a basic disadvantage of all bond investments.

◆ Interest from corporate bonds is taxable at all levels (federal, state and local) whereas interest from Treasuries and certain agency bonds are exempt from state and local taxes.

◆ Corporate bonds are exposed to greater credit risk (than Treasuries and government agency bonds) as well as to event risk. The latter risk is nonexistent for both Treasuries and agency bonds. The lower the quality of the corporate bond the greater the credit risk.

◆ Investors who are selling corporate bonds may face illiquidity for several reasons:
— if the ratings of the issuer decline or there is bad news concerning the issuer's financial position. This is especially true in the junk bond market where nervousness can send junk bond prices on a downward spiral;
— if investors only have a small number of bonds to sell;
— when market interest rates are rising existing bond prices will be driven down further.

◆ Corporate bonds with call provisions can be called when investors least want their principal returned to them (after market rates have fallen).

◆ Spreads between bid and asked prices on corporate bonds are greater than those on Treasuries and government agency bonds.

◆ Spreads on unlisted junk bonds can be quite large.

◆ The junk bond market has been plagued by some abusive practices as well as sharp market moves in prices before important corporate news announcements, implying insider trading on advance knowledge.

Caveats

Before buying corporate bonds, check the following:

◆ the credit ratings of the issue;

◆ the seniority of the issue;

◆ the call and refunding provisions. Investors can avoid losses of principal by not buying higher premium priced bonds with higher coupon rates than market rates which could be called at lower premium prices. In other words, check whether the premium price exceeds the call price;

◆ the sinking fund provision;

◆ whether there is "poison put" protection against event risk;

◆ whether the bonds are part of a small issue, less than $75 million— avoid buying bonds of small issues;

◆ whether the bonds are listed or whether they trade over-the-counter.

Compare the coupon yield of the corporate issue to those offered on similar maturity Treasuries and government agency bonds first to see if the spread warrants the additional risks that corporate bonds are exposed to.

Conclusion

The best time to buy corporate bonds is when market rates of interest are high, which means that high yields can be obtained on quality bonds. Bonds should be held when market interest rates are declining which offers investors potential capital gains due to the upward price movement of the bonds.

For investors who cannot tolerate higher risks, avoid junk bonds, which will only guarantee sleepless nights. For risk-averse investors, choose high quality corporate issues.

References

Antilla, Susan. "Nonrefundable Bonds Can Indeed be Refunded," *New York Times,* November 21, 1992.

Faerber, Esmé. *Managing Your Investments, Savings and Credit.* Chicago: Probus Publishing Co., 1992.

Mayo, Herbert B. *Investments.* Orlando, FL: Dryden Press, 1991.

Mitchell, Constance. "Hourly Price Quotes on Some Junk Bonds Planned in Bid to Curb Unruly Trading," *Wall Street Journal,* November 11, 1992, page C1.

Thau, Annette. *The Bond Book.* Chicago: Probus Publishing Co., 1992.

Chapter 6

Treasury Securities

Key Concepts

◆ What Treasury notes and bonds are

◆ The risks of Treasury securities

◆ How to buy and sell Treasury securities

◆ The advantages and disadvantages of Treasuries

◆ What U.S. savings bonds are

◆ How to buy U.S. savings bonds

◆ The advantages and disadvantages of U.S. savings bonds

The U.S. federal government issues a wide variety of debt instruments primarily to fund the ever-increasing budget deficit. This budget deficit is the result of the government spending more than the revenues that it collects from taxes. The government raises money to fund its expenditures by issuing securities in the money and capital markets. There are no limitations on the government's ability to pay its interest obligations, and so the government has few restrictions on its ability to create money. This is a major reason why U.S. Treasury securities are considered to be safe from default. The U.S. Treasury is very unlikely to default on its interest payments and principal repayments due to the fact that the government can not only create money, but it can also print money and tax the public.

The U.S. government is the largest single borrower in the U.S. long-term bond market, and there are many different investors who are snapping up the U.S. Treasury debt offerings. These consist of U.S. individual residents, institutional investors (banks, mutual funds, insurance companies, pension funds), corporations, and foreign buyers. Foreigners have increased their holdings of U.S. Treasury securities to

---

The section on U.S. savings bonds has been previously published by Esmé Faerber in *Managing Your Investments, Savings and Credit,* published by Probus Publishing Co., 1992.

almost $300 billion as of June 30, 1992 (Vogel 1992). These foreign buyers come from both the private and public sectors abroad.

The central banks of the industrialized nations, who acquired U.S. dollars, by buying up dollars to stem the fall in the dollar against other foreign currencies, as well as investors from the private sector abroad have been buying. Of course, the speculation in the credit markets is whether these foreigners will continue to fund the United States deficit through these offerings in the future.

These Treasury offerings consist of U.S. Treasury bills, U.S. Treasury notes and U.S. Treasury bonds. United States savings bonds are also issued by the government to fund the deficit. Treasury bills are non interest-bearing, discount securities with an original maturity of one year or less. These are discussed in Chapter 4. Treasury notes are intermediate securities with maturities ranging from 2 to 10 years and Treasury bonds are long-term bonds that have maturities over 10 years. Both Treasury notes and bonds are marketable securities, whereas U.S. savings bonds are nonmarketable government debt. U.S. savings bonds are small denomination securities with various maturities designed to encourage savings from small investors. Savings bonds will be discussed after Treasury notes and bonds in this chapter.

U.S. Treasury Notes and Bonds

Treasury notes and bonds are coupon securities which differ from Treasury bills. Coupon securities pay interest every six months whereas Treasury bills are discount securities where periodic interest payments are not made. Instead, with Treasury bills the interest is received at maturity, and is the difference between the face value received and the purchase price.

U.S. Treasury Notes

U.S. Treasury notes are issued with original maturities ranging from two to 10 years. New Treasury notes are sold on an auction basis with the following maturities:

2 year issued on the last business day of each month

3 year issued on the 15th of February, May, August, and November

5 year issued on the last business day of each month

7 year issued every three months in January, April, July, and October

10 year issued on the 15th of February, May, August, and November.

As of this writing, the Clinton Administration has proposed eliminating the seven-year Treasury note and increasing the sales of Treasury securities with maturities of three years and less. The five-year and ten-year note maturities can be purchased with a minimum of $1,000, and then in multiples of $1,000 thereafter. The two- and three-year maturities may be purchased with a minimum of $5,000 and then in further multiples of $5,000.

Treasury notes are not callable and interest payments are made semi-annually (beginning six months from the date of issue).

U.S. Treasury Bonds

Treasury bonds have original maturities of more than 10 years. Currently, 30-year Treasury bonds are offered for sale every three months on the 15th of February, May, August and November. However, this schedule for the 30-year Treasury bonds may be drastically curtailed if the Clinton administration's proposals take effect. The Clinton plan is to reduce the sales of 30-year bonds and increase the sales of shorter-term Treasury securities. Currently 30-year Treasury bonds can be bought with a minimum purchase of $1,000 and then in multiples of $1,000 thereafter.

Many outstanding Treasury bond issues are callable, generally within five years of maturity. However, since 1985 the Treasury has not issued any callable bonds.

In the newspapers, callable Treasury bonds can be identified by two dates in the maturity column as shown in the following example:

Rate	Maturity Mo/Yr	Bid	Asked	Chg	Asked Yld
7	May 93-98	100.29	101.05	. . .	3.65

This seven percent coupon Treasury bond matures in May 1998, but may be called beginning in 1993. The yield to maturity is 3.65 percent and is based on the call date and not the maturity date. This is why the yield to maturity (asked yield) is so much less than the coupon rate as well as the fact that the bond is trading at a premium.

There are many outstanding Treasury bonds which are very different from the rest of the Treasuries. They are called *flower bonds* and they have the following coupons and maturities:

Coupon	Maturity
4⅛	May 15,1989-1994
3	February 15, 1995
3½	November 15, 1998

Flower bonds were issued by the Treasury in the 1950s and early 1960s. Many have subsequently matured. Flower bonds are no longer issued. They are used to settle federal estate taxes. For example, if an individual decedent owned $150,000 par (face) value flower bonds, and the decedent's estate owed $150,000 in federal taxes, these bonds would be accepted by the Internal Revenue Service at par values (even though they would be worth less at market value). Due to their low coupon rates, these bonds generally sell at a discount. For instance, the three percent February 15, 1995, bonds had an asked price of $99.10 (99^{10}/32) or $993.125 per bond on January 6, 1993. Thus, if these were used to settle the $150,000 federal estate tax liability in the example above, the Internal Revenue Service would accept 150 of these bonds, even though the market value would only be $148,968.75. However, if flower bonds are sold at a premium at the time of the holder's death, the gain would be taxed at a capital gain.

The Treasury Department does impose some conditions when these bonds are used to settle federal estate liabilities. If you are considering using flower bonds for tax planning purposes, you should discuss your situation first with your tax advisor.

Several brokerage firms in the early 1980s packaged U.S. Treasuries in the form of zero-coupon Treasury packages such as Salomon Brothers' "Certificates of Accrual on Treasury Securities" (CATS) and Merrill Lynch's "Treasury Investment Growth Receipts" (TIGRs). In 1984, the Treasury Department announced its own program of packaging zero-coupon Treasuries known as STRIPS, "Separate Trading of Registered Interest and Principal of Securities." See the chapter on zero-coupon bonds for a detailed description of these securities.

What Are the Risks of Treasuries?

There is no credit risk and no risk of default as Treasuries are direct obligations of the federal government. This is why Treasury securities have lower coupon yields than agency and corporate bonds.

Treasuries are free from both event risk and call risk (if you avoid buying outstanding Treasury bonds which are subject to call).

As with all fixed income securities, Treasuries are subject to interest rate risk. Bond prices react inversely to changes in market rates of interest but prices are also tied to the length of time to maturity. Thus, long-term (30-year) Treasury bond prices will see the greatest volatility due to changes in market rates of interest. The shorter the maturities, the lower the price volatility in relation to changes in interest rates.

How to Buy and Sell Treasury Notes and Bonds

Investors may purchase new issues or outstanding Treasury issues trading on the secondary market.

New Issues

New issues of Treasury notes and bonds may be purchased on auction or through brokerage firms and commercial banks. Buying through banks and brokerage firms would involve paying commissions which would vary depending on the face value of the securities purchased and the markup charged for the purchase. For example, on a purchase of $10,000 in Treasury bonds, the commission would typically be in the range of $50.

To avoid having to pay commissions, investors may purchase new issues being auctioned directly from the Federal Reserve Bank.

Auctions of new issues take place on a regular schedule (listed at the beginning of this section on Treasury notes and bonds). You can also call the Federal Reserve Bank in your area (see the section on Treasury bills in Chapter 4 for the telephone numbers of Federal Reserve Banks in different cities in the U.S.) to put you on their mailing list for new note and bond issues. There is also a 24-hour Reserve Bank information number about forthcoming auctions. The financial newspapers also list the schedule of forthcoming auctions.

When buying directly, you will first need to open an account with the Federal Reserve. By completing a New Account Request Form (see Figure 4-2), you will establish a Treasury Direct account where your Treasury securities will be held in book form. Treasury certificates are no longer issued. After submitting this form to the Federal Reserve Bank/branch in your area, you will receive confirmation of your account with a unique account number pertaining to the information in your account.

You are now ready to fill out a tender form to buy Treasury notes/bonds on auction from the Federal Reserve Bank. See Figure 6–1 for a copy of the five- and 10-year Treasury note tender form. The tender forms for the two-, three-, seven- and 30-year issues are the same just printed on different colored forms.

Besides filling in your personal information on the tender form, you will need to supply information about your bank account so that payments by the Treasury can be made by direct deposit to your account. The routing number is a nine digit number which identifies your financial institution where you bank. The number is on the bottom corner of your check before your account number.

On the form you have a choice of buying Treasuries using a competitive or non-competitive bid.

More sophisticated investors will use the *competitive bid* where they will submit a yield bid for the issue to two decimal places (e.g., 4.06 percent). Investors can get an idea of the probable range of the yield to submit by watching the pre-auction trading of that issue. Dealers will begin trading these securities a few days before the auction on a so called "when issued basis," and the "when issued" yield is often reported in the *Wall Street Journal* and *New York Times* financial section.

Investors submit their sealed, written bids, and the Treasury will accept the bids with the lowest yields until the supply is sold. Thus, within the range of accepted bids, the lowest accepted bidders are penalized with a lesser return than the accepted higher bidders. This is known as the "winner's curse" because the bidders with the lowest accepted yields pay a higher price for the issue, and the higher bidders will receive a greater rate of return than that received by the lowest bidders on the same issue.

Investors who bid too aggressively run the risk of losing out in that auction by not having their bids accepted.

In an attempt to lower their borrowing costs, the Treasury Department is experimenting with a new method of selling the two- and five-year Treasury notes during the period September 1992 through August 1993. This experiment is called the single price or "Dutch" auction and works in the following way:

— Like the regular auction, investors submit their sealed bids.
— The Treasury starts accepting bids from the lowest yield on up to the yield where the supply of notes is used up.

Exhibit 6–1 Tender Form
for Five- and 10-year Treasury Note

FORM PD 5174-3
(January 1986)

OMB No. 1535-0069
Expires 01-31-92

TREASURY DIRECT

TENDER FOR 5-10 YEAR TREASURY NOTE

TENDER INFORMATION	FOR DEPARTMENT USE

AMOUNT OF TENDER: $ _____

TERM _____

BID TYPE (Check One)▪ ☐ NONCOMPETITIVE ☐ COMPETITIVE AT ___ . ___ %

TENDER NUMBER
912627

ACCOUNT NUMBER _____ - _____ - _____

CUSIP

INVESTOR INFORMATION

ISSUE DATE

ACCOUNT NAME

RECEIVED BY

DATE RECEIVED

ADDRESS

EXT REG ☐
FOREIGN ☐
BACKUP ☐
REVIEW ☐

CITY   STATE   ZIP CODE

TAXPAYER IDENTIFICATION NUMBER

1ST NAMED OWNER ___ - ___ - ___   **OR**   ___ - ___

SOCIAL SECURITY NUMBER   EMPLOYER IDENTIFICATION NUMBER

CLASS ☐

TELEPHONE NUMBERS

WORK (___) ___ - ___   HOME (___) ___ - ___

PAYMENT ATTACHED

TOTAL PAYMENT: $ _____

NUMBERS

CASH (01): $ _____   CHECKS (02/03): $ _____

SECURITIES (05): $ _____ $ _____

OTHER (06): $ _____ $ _____

DIRECT DEPOSIT INFORMATION

ROUTING NUMBER

FINANCIAL INSTITUTION NAME

ACCOUNT NUMBER

ACCOUNT TYPE ☐ CHECKING
(Check One)   ☐ SAVINGS

ACCOUNT NAME

AUTHORIZATION

For the notice required under the Privacy and Paperwork Reduction Acts, see the accompanying instructions.

I submit this tender pursuant to the provisions of Department of the Treasury Circulars, Public Debt Series Nos. 1-86 and 2-86 and the public announcement issued by the Department of the Treasury.

Under penalties of perjury, I certify that the number shown on this form is my correct taxpayer identification number and that I am not subject to backup withholding because (1) I have not been notified that I am subject to backup withholding as a result of a failure to report all interest or dividends, or (2) the Internal Revenue Service has notified me that I am no longer subject to backup withholding. I further certify that all other information provided on this form is true, correct and complete.

_____   _____
SIGNATURE   DATE

— The difference in this auction method is that all the winning bidders receive the highest accepted bids for the auction.

For example, if the Treasury announces a $9 billion two-year note sale, and the range of accepted bids is between 4.72 percent and 4.74 percent, all the bidders will receive 4.74 percent. This method eliminates the "winner's curse." Thus, all the accepted bidders pay the same price for the issue.

You might wonder how this method would help the Treasury reduce their borrowing costs when the Treasury ends up paying the highest accepted yields at these "Dutch" auctions. The premise for this type of auction method is that by eliminating the "winner's curse" more bidders would participate and they would offer lower yields (higher prices).

For the four auctions for the two-year and five-year Treasury notes to date (from September 22-23 through December 22-23, 1992) the results have been mixed for the "Dutch" auction. The two-year notes have been more successful than the five-year notes from the Treasury's point of view, in that for the two-year note dealers paid higher prices (lower yields). This has saved some money for the Treasury, but on the five-year notes the Treasury has lost money.

For investors who do not want to run the risks of having their bids rejected, or who may not know what to bid, they can submit *non-competitive bids.* With non-competitive bids, investors will be able to buy Treasury notes and bonds at the average accepted bid in the auction. All non-competitive tenders up to $1,000,000 per bidder will be accepted.

Tender forms to submit bids may be sent in the mail or in person to the Federal Reserve Banks/branches before the close of the auction. Competitive bids must be received by the time designated in the offering circular. Non-competitive bids that are mailed must be postmarked by no later than midnight the day before the auction and received on or before the issue date of the securities.

Payment must accompany the tender form and the amount of the check should be for the face value of the securities. If the auction price is less than the face value, you will receive a check for the difference. If the auction price of the note/bond is higher than the face value you will receive an amount due notice for the difference.

On acceptance of your bid, you will receive a confirmation receipt from the Federal Reserve. Interest on notes and bonds are paid by the Treasury every six months.

About 45 days before maturity of the notes/bonds, a reinvestment option notification will be mailed to all note/bondholders giving them the option of reinvesting in a new issue. If you decline the reinvestment option, the redemption payment will be made directly into your bank account on the maturity date.

Should investors decide to sell their Treasury notes/bonds before maturity, there is an active secondary market composed of dealers. Before selling, you would need to fill out a Transfer Request form (PD 5179) if you bought directly from the Federal Reserve, which will transfer your account from the Treasury Direct book-entry system to the commercial book-entry system. Then you can sell your Treasury notes/bonds. The commercial book-entry system records Treasuries bought through financial institutions and government security dealers. You would need to use a bank/broker to sell Treasuries in the secondary market.

Existing Issues

Investors may buy (and sell) existing issues through banks or brokers. There are many issues with a wide range of maturities trading at discounts or premiums depending on their coupon rates and length of time to maturity. Like corporate bonds, Treasury notes and bonds are quoted in the financial sections of newspapers under the heading "Treasury Issues." Ask your banker/broker for a dealer's quote sheet to see what existing issues are available.

The secondary market for Treasuries is an over-the-counter market where dealers quote bid and asked prices. The spreads on Treasuries are the smallest (rarely larger than 1/8 of a point) of all the fixed income securities due to the liquidity of many of the issues. It is an active market with huge quantities of Treasuries being traded.

What Are the Advantages
of Treasury Notes and Bonds?

◆ Virtually no credit or default risk since they are direct obligations of the federal government.

◆ Wide range of maturities available.

◆ Interest is exempt from state and local taxes.

◆ Extremely liquid and marketable due to the active secondary market.

◆ Transaction costs/fees can be avoided by buying directly from the Federal Reserve Bank/branches.

◆ Markups on trading Treasuries are the lowest of all the fixed income securities.

◆ Some issues (five- and 10-year notes and 30-year bonds) have lower purchase minimums of $1,000, making them affordable for small investors. Treasury notes with two- and three-year maturities have $5,000 minimum purchase amounts.

What Are the Disadvantages of Treasury Notes and Bonds?

◆ Yields on Treasuries are lower than agency and corporate bonds for comparable maturities.

◆ They do not protect against rising inflation. Losses in purchasing power and investment capital would occur if the rate of inflation exceeds the coupon rate.

◆ For the longer maturity Treasury bonds, there is interest rate risk. If interest rates go up after long-term bonds are bought, the market price of these bonds will go down. Investors could lose a significant part of their investment if they are forced to sell during these conditions before maturity.

◆ Interest rates have become quite volatile since 1979 and investors who have locked in to coupons of 7 1/2 percent could find that in the future coupons could rise to 13 percent for equivalent maturities. This happened in 1980.

Caveats

Avoid longer maturities unless you are confident that both inflation and market rates of interest are headed downwards in the future.

Conclusion

Treasury notes and bonds are safe investments. There is a wide range of maturities to choose from. Although yields offered by agency and corporate bonds are greater, they do not match the safety offered by Treasuries. If the yield differential between Treasuries and these other types of fixed income securities is not very wide, Treasuries may be the better investment. However, when the yield differential is significant, you ought to consider their purchase over Treasuries.

Ownership of Treasuries can be staggered due to the wide range of maturities offered. For example, instead of buying 10-year or 30-year Treasuries, investors would apportion amounts to two-, three-, five-, 10- and 30-year issues. This approach provides a steady stream of income and frees up principal on a *piece meal* basis as the shorter term issues mature. The advantages are that the effects of interest rate risk are avoided and yields are averaged over the time period.

U.S. Savings Bonds

U.S. savings bonds are non-marketable securities issued and backed in full by the U.S. government. In the 1960s and 1970s when inflation was high, investing in U.S. savings bonds was a patriotic decision rather than a good investment. Rates of return on savings bonds were low and did not equal the returns of other comparable investments. Thus, in order to compete with other investments, the U. S. Treasury increased the rates of interest on U.S. savings bonds. With market rates of interest currently on the low end of the spectrum, U.S. savings bonds look quite attractive with the guaranteed floor yield of four percent per annum over a five-year period.

In 1980, the Treasury issued EE and HH savings bonds. EE series bonds are issued at a discount: a $50 EE bond cost $25, and similarly, a $200 EE bond costs $100. The interest is paid at maturity or when the bond is cashed in. The new interest rate (after November 1982) is 85 percent of the average rate paid on five-year Treasury securities. The rate changes every six months, but the government guarantees that the rate will not fall below four percent per year if the bonds are held for five years or longer. For EE bonds bought before March 1, 1993, the effective rate, if held for five years, is six percent per annum. This provides a floor on the interest rate and if interest rates go up, investors will be able to receive the higher rates. However, if investors do not hold their bonds for five years, they will receive a lower interest rate than six percent for bonds bought before March 1, 1993, and four percent for bonds bought after March 1, 1993. Interest is credited every six months (twice a year).

Interest earned on EE bonds can be deferred from federal income taxes until the bonds mature or are redeemed. Interest is exempt from state and local taxes. EE bonds can be used for tax planning purposes and have the following tax advantages:

◆ By deferring the interest income annually until the bonds are cashed in, you can lower your federal taxable income in the years that you hold the bonds. You can also postpone the tax on the interest income for a further period by swapping the EE bonds at maturity for HH bonds. However, the interest received semi-annually on the HH bonds are taxable at the federal level each year.

◆ EE bonds can be purchased for children under 14 years of age to avoid the children's income being taxed at their parent's marginal tax rates. At the time of this writing, children under 14 years of age pay no tax on investment income under $600. Investment income between $600 and $1,200 is taxed at the lowest rate, and income over $1,200 is taxed at the parent's marginal tax rates. After 14 years of age, investment income is taxed at the child's marginal rate. By deferring the interest income until the child turns 14 years of age, you can lower the child's tax liability. However, changes are always being made to the Tax Code so check with your accountant whether this treatment is still in effect.

◆ Currently, interest on savings bonds used to finance educational expenses is tax exempt at the federal level for married couples within adjusted gross income limits. This exemption is phased out proportionately over certain levels of adjusted gross incomes. President Bush vetoed the bill that would have eliminated the current limits for a federal tax exemption. Changes are constantly being made to the Tax Code, so check with your accountant as to the changes and adjusted gross income limits.

HH series bonds are only available through an exchange of E, H and EE series savings bonds. (E and H series savings bonds have been replaced by EE and HH respectively). HH bonds differ from EE bonds in the following ways:

◆ HH are issued at par value (or face value) in larger denominations.

◆ Interest is received every six months and is subject to federal tax each year.

◆ Holders receive only the face value at maturity as interest is paid out every six months.

How to Buy U.S. Savings Bonds

EE savings bonds can be bought (and redeemed) directly through the Bureau of Public Debt, or at banks, savings and loan associations, and even through employers as payroll deductions.

Large denomination bonds are handled through any of the Federal Reserve Banks. The denominations of EE bonds range from $50 to $10,000. The maximum investment in EE bonds is $30,000 per person per year.

HH bonds can be acquired through an exchange of E, H, or EE bonds through the Bureau of Public Debt or any of the Federal Reserve Banks or branches. The denominations for HH bonds range from $500 to $10,000.

There are no fees, handling charges or commissions when you buy or sell U.S. savings bonds.

What Are the Advantages of U.S. Savings Bonds?

◆ U.S. savings bonds are safe investments where interest and principal are guaranteed by the U.S. government.

◆ There are no fees, handling charges, or commissions to buy and sell.

◆ EE bonds provide a build up of capital whereas HH bonds provide a steady source of income (every six months).

◆ The interest earned on U.S. savings bonds is exempt from state and local taxes.

◆ Interest earned on EE bonds is deferred from federal income taxes until the bonds are redeemed.

◆ U.S. savings bonds are not subject to interest rate risk.

◆ Investors are assured a minimum rate of return of four percent on their EE bonds held for five years, even if market rates of interest fall below four percent, and if interest rates go up investors can share in the higher yields.

What Are the Disadvantages of U.S. Savings Bonds?

◆ Savings bonds must be held for five years in order to get the floating interest rate. If held for less than five years you receive the lower rates of interest.

◆ They do not protect against rising rates of inflation.

◆ The Treasury does not allow them to be used as collateral and neither can they be transferred as gifts. However, they may be transferred through an estate.

◆ Other securities pay higher rates of interest: EE bonds pay 85 percent of the average five-year Treasury securities.

Caveats

◆ Compare the returns of other "safe" investments such as Treasury bills and Treasury notes where you may be able to increase your rate of return.

◆ As interest on EE bonds is credited semi-annually, always redeem your bonds after the six-month interest has been paid or credited. If you redeem your bonds before the semi-annual interest is credited, you will lose the interest for those months.

◆ Interest is always credited from the first day of month, so when buying U.S. savings bonds, buy them at the end of the month to increase your overall rate of return.

Conclusion

Savings bonds provide a safe, easy way to save money. EE bonds are appealing to conservative investors who would like to build up capital and defer current income. HH bonds will appeal to investors who prefer safe investments which pay current income.

References

Faerber, Esmé. *Managing Your Investments, Savings, and Credit.* Chicago: Probus Publishing Co., 1992.

Vogel, Thomas T. Jr. "Foreigners' U.S. Debt Binge is Seen Easing." *Wall Street Journal,* August 24, 1992, page C1.

Chapter 7
Government Agency Bonds

Key Concepts

◆ Mortgage pass-through securities

◆ Government National Mortgage Securities

◆ How to buy them

◆ Their advantages and disadvantages

◆ Caveats

◆ Federal Home Loan Mortgage Corporation securities

◆ Collateralized mortgage obligations

◆ Their advantages and disadvantages

◆ Caveats

◆ Government agency securities

Government agency bonds appeal to investors who are interested in high quality bonds. Agency bonds are issued by the major federally sponsored agencies such as the Federal Home Loan Mortgage Corporation (FHLMC), Federal National Mortgage Association (FNMA), Federal Home Loan Bank (FHLB) System, Farm Credit Banks, the Student Loan Marketing Association (SLMA), and many others. The first three of these agencies (FHLMC, FNMA, and FHLB) provide funds to the mortgage and housing sectors of the economy. The Farm Credit Banks provide funds for the agricultural sector, and the SLMA provides funds for loans for higher education.

These agencies were created by acts of Congress to form a network of federally sponsored agencies that would provide credit for specific sectors of the economy. These agencies are privately owned financial intermediaries who issue securities in the market to raise funds which are lent through intermediaries to borrowers in these sectors of the economy. Their offerings are exempt from registration with the Securities and Exchange Commission (SEC) since they come under Congressional authority and scrutiny, unlike the issuance of corporate bonds which require registration with the SEC.

The debt of federally sponsored agencies is not backed by the credit of the U.S. government, like Treasury securities. Instead, there is a moral backing that, in the event of a default, the government would cover the obligations of these agencies. This accounts for the excellent credit risks of these agencies' securities. Therefore, the risk of default is slightly greater than those of Treasury issues, and this partly explains why the yields of agency securities are greater than Treasuries of similar maturities. The other major reason for the yield spread is that Treasury issues are more liquid and more marketable.

Besides the five major agencies mentioned, there are many other federally sponsored agencies which offer many issues with slightly higher yields and similar credit risks.

Some of these are the Small Business Administration (SBA) which offers participation certificates; the Department of Housing and Urban Development (HUD) issues U.S. Government Guaranteed Notes; obligations from the Financing Corporation, and secured notes from the Private Export Funding Corporation (Jonson and Silver 1989).

An important sector of the government agency securities market is mortgage backed or pass-through securities. Through the creation of the Government National Mortgage Association (GNMA) by the National Housing Act in 1970, the pass-through securities market has grown to be a very large sector of the agency market. The government succeeded in increasing the investment base in the mortgage market by attracting institutional investors. Since then several government sponsored agencies and private institutions have entered this market. Besides the Government National Mortgage Association, the other major mortgage related agencies are the Federal National Mortgage Association (FNMA), the Federal Home Loan Mortgage Corporation (FHLMC), and the Federal Home Loan Bank System.

Since the securities offered by the different federally sponsored agencies vary considerably, the mortgage related agencies will be discussed first, followed by some of the other major agency offerings.

Mortgage Pass-Through Securities

Mortgage pass-through securities are shares in pools or collections of mortgages. The mortgage holders pool their mortgages and sell shares in the pools to investors. The investor will then receive the interest and principal repayments (less a modest fee normally about one half a percentage point) on a monthly basis—hence, the name pass-through. Mortgage pools vary, with some consisting of several thousand mortgages ranging to others having just a few mortgages. These pools are issued with a minimum of at least $1,000,000.

Pass-through securities can be better understood by examining how mortgages work. For illustrative purposes, assume that this mortgage pool is $1,000,000 and that it consists of a single conventional 30-year mortgage of $1,000,000 at nine percent. The monthly payment that the mortgagor will make to the mortgage holder is $8,046.23. This payment consists of interest and a portion which goes towards the reduction of the principal balance. Table 7-1 shows the amortization schedule for the first 12 months of this mortgage. For the first payment, the amount of interest is $7,500 and the $546.23 goes towards reducing the principal balance from $1,000,000 to $999,453.77. The interest rate is nine percent per year and the interest rate per month is 9%/12 which is .0075. The interest expense is calculated by multiplying the monthly rate by the mortgage balance. Hence, the interest for the first payment is $7,500 (.0075 multiplied by $1,000,000).

These monthly payments are designed to reduce the mortgage balance to zero at the end of the mortgage term (30 years or 360 pay-

Table 7-1 Amortization Schedule
for a 30-year, 9% Mortgage of $1,000,000

Month/Year	Payment	Int. (9.00%)	Principal	Loan Balance
	0.00	0.00	0.00	1000000.00
1/1993	8046.23	7500.00	546.23	999453.77
2/1993	8046.23	7495.90	550.32	998903.45
3/1993	8046.23	7491.78	554.45	998349.00
4/1993	8046.23	7487.62	558.61	997790.39
5/1993	8046.23	7483.43	562.80	997227.59
6/1993	8046.23	7479.21	567.02	996660.57
7/1993	8046.23	7474.95	571.27	996089.30
8/1993	8046.23	7470.67	575.56	995513.75
9/1993	8046.23	7466.35	579.87	994933.87
10/1993	8046.23	7462.00	584.22	994349.65
11/1993	8046.23	7457.62	588.60	993761.05
12/1993	8046.23	7453.21	593.02	993168.03

ments). As you can see from the first 12 payments, the amount of the interest expense declines each month, which means that more of the monthly payment will go towards reducing the outstanding loan (mortgage) balance. In other words, the fixed amount of the payment is the same, but the proportionate amount of interest received declines and the proportionate amount of principal repayments increases.

In this case, the investor in this pass-through security will receive the pass-through interest and principal. The amount that is received will have the servicing fees and any other charges by the servicing institution deducted.

The investor cannot always count on the monthly amount being the same since mortgagors have the option to prepay their mortgages.

This could be the entire amount of the mortgage or a part of it. For example, if the mortgagor prepaid an additional $1,000 a month in the example above, the mortgage pass-through security holder would receive this additional payment which is in essence a return of that holder's principal or investment capital.

For many reasons, mortgagors prepay the entire amount of their mortgages before their maturity dates. This happens when homeowners sell their homes, or refinance their mortgages when interest rates go down; and in the case of the death of the homeowner, fire and other casualties where the property is destroyed, and the insurance proceeds are used to pay off the mortgage.

Thus, in a mortgage pool, if many mortgagors prepay their mortgages, there will be uncertainty as to the amounts of the cash flows to investors and as to the length of time to maturity of the pool.

There is also uncertainty as to the timing of the cash flows. For example, assume that mortgage payments are due by the first day of the month. If the mortgagors are late in sending in their payments and there are delays in the processing of these payments, then the payments to investors will be delayed. The time delay will also vary as to the type of pass-through.

Besides the level payment, conventional mortgage described above, which is the most common for pass-through securities, there are other types of mortgages which are used for pass-through securities.

The *adjustable rate mortgage* (ARM) has a floating rate of interest which varies according to a particular index. For instance, if the adjustable rate mortgage is tied to the rate on short-term Treasury notes, the rate will be adjusted up or down with the movement of the rate on the Treasury note every six months, one year, or whatever period the mortgagee chooses at the outset of the mortgage.

Most ARMs have periodic caps on interest rates. They can only increase or decrease by a certain number of percentage points within a period of time and generally there are also lifetime caps on interest rates—they can only increase or decrease by a certain number of percentage points over the life of the mortgage.

The cash flows of ARMs are even more difficult to predict, which means that the amounts received by investors in the pass-through securities will fluctuate. Similarly, there will also be prepayment risks with ARMs.

Graduated payment mortgages (GPMs) have also been used for pools of pass-through securities. With a GPM, the level monthly payments in the early years of a mortgage (may be five years) are less than the level payments in the later years of the mortgage. The interest rate is fixed (like a conventional mortgage), but the monthly payments in the initial years may not be enough to cover the interest expense each month; hence, negative amortization which means that the shortfall in interest expense gets added back to the mortgage/loan balance. Instead of decreasing the mortgage/loan balance, it increases and so do the monthly payments. Thus, by the end of the mortgage term, the mortgagor will have repaid a greater amount of principal than was originally borrowed at the inception of the mortgage.

All types of mortgages are subject to prepayment risk, which affects the amount of the cash flows for investors in pass-through securities. However, there is a level of comfort for these investors in that historically during times when mortgage rates have fallen to eight percent, there are still many homeowners who hang on to their 13 percent mortgages.

Besides the prepayment risk, mortgage pass-through securities present a challenge for investors in terms of valuation. As mortgages are self amortizing (the principal gets paid back in monthly amounts throughout the mortgage term) they cannot be valued like other fixed income securities such as Treasury bonds where the entire principal is returned at maturity.

The Types of Mortgage Pass-Throughs

There are various types of mortgage pass-through securities, each with their own differences. Despite their differences, investors in all mortgage pass-through securities are concerned with the following criteria:

◆ the safety of the issue,

◆ the liquidity and marketability of the issue,

◆ the overall rate of return of the issue, and

◆ the expected maturity of the issue.

The majority of pass-through securities have been issued by three government agencies, namely the Government National Mortgage Association, the Federal National Mortgage Association, and the Federal Home Loan Mortgage Corporation. There has also been a marked growth in the number of mortgage pass-through securities by private issuers since the mid-1980s.

The main characteristics of each of these major issuers of pass-through securities will be discussed in the remainder of this section.

Government National Mortgage Association (GNMA) Pass-Through Securities

The Government National Mortgage Association also known as Ginnie Mae is a wholly owned agency of the Housing and Urban Development Department (HUD). Hence, the timely interest and principal payments of Ginnie Mae pass-through securities are guaranteed by the full faith and credit of the U.S. government. This means zero credit risk which is very appealing to investors.

The agency does not issue pass-through securities but insures them. These securities are issued by mortgage bankers and thrift institutions who bundle mortgages into pools of at least $1 million. These mortgage bankers apply to the Government National Mortgage Association for backing, and if accepted, they will get a pool number. Part of these pools are sold to investors which consist mainly of banks, pension funds, and insurance companies. The minimum purchase amount is $25,000 which explains why the majority of investors in these pools are institutions.

GNMA will accept only VA (Veterans Administration) and FHA (Federal Housing Administration) mortgages which are assumable mortgages. This feature makes prepayment less variable than on mortgages which are not assumable.

There are a variety of Ginnie Mae pools. The major pools are GNMA I and GNMA II. The former includes fixed rate 20- to 30-year mortgages totaling a minimum face value of $1 million, all with the same interest rates.

GNMA II pools are:

◆ larger than GNMA I pools, and

◆ have mortgages with a variety of interest rates and maturities (Thau, 1992).

There are also GNMA midgets (mortgages with a 15-year term), GNMA GPMs (Graduated Payment Mortgages), GNMA ARMs (Adjustable Rate Mortgages), GNMA mobile homes, GNMA Buydowns and GNMA FHA projects. The different types of mortgages, maturities, interest rates, and pool sizes make the analysis, more difficult for each type of pool. Generally, the larger the pool size the more liquid and the lesser the impact of prepayments. The shorter the term of the mortgages, the shorter the average life and half life of the pool.

The *average life* is defined as the weighted average time that each dollar of principal is outstanding. This is a measure of the investment life of the mortgage backed securities in the pool. The average life depends on the prepayment rate. The greater the prepayments in the pool, the shorter the average life, and the shorter the weighted average life the lower the volatility in price of the GNMA.

The *half life* is defined as the time taken to return half the principal in the pool. The average life and half life are useful measures for comparison purposes because you would use these and not the length of time to maturity to compare GNMAs with other fixed income investments. For example, if you wanted to compare the yield on a GNMA with a five-year half life and a maturity of 12 years with a Treasury note, you would look at Treasury notes with five-year maturities.

GNMA investments are much more complex than the other fixed income investments because there is not only the uncertainty as to the length of time to maturity for that investment, but also as to the amount and timing of the cash flows. GNMA provides statistics as to the prepayment histories for each GNMA pool, but these are not cast in stone and may vary. Hence, these estimated payments are constantly being revised.

The yield on GNMAs are also difficult to accurately determine as the reader might well suspect. If you are not sure what the cash flow will be, you can't determine the precise yield. However, various calculation methods have been developed based on different assumptions of prepayment speed (fast, average and slow). In an offering sheet, you will see a number of yields quoted depending on the FHA estimated experience of prepayment speed. The slowest speed will offer the highest yield. Thus, from a safety point of view, when buying GNMAs, assume that you will earn the lowest of the predicted yields.

When comparing the estimated yields on GNMAs with yields on other fixed income securities you need to keep in mind the following factors:

◆ Reinvestment risk is greater for GNMAs than other fixed income securities because interest and the return of principal payments are made monthly for pass-through securities, as opposed to semi-annually or annually for regular bonds. For example, if there is a significant downturn in market rates of interest, the returned interest and principal will be reinvested at lower rates, and the total return will be lower for the GNMA investment than the quoted yield to maturity assuming reinvestment at the quoted yield.

◆ Exact rates of return cannot be determined due to the uncertainty of reinvestment risk.

◆ If the monthly interest and principal payments are spent instead of reinvested, the total rate of return will be even lower.

◆ The principal repayments should not be included in the cash flow yield as these are a return of the investor's initial investment.

GNMAs and all pass-through securities are sensitive to changes in market rates of interest like all other fixed income securities. When market rates of interest go up, bond prices decline. However, when market rates of interest come down, many homeowners will prepay their mortgages when they refinance them at lower rates. This is a damper on GNMA prices, and so, generally speaking, they will not go up by as much as regular bond prices when market rates come down. Not only will investors receive their principal earlier, but they will also be faced with reinvesting the proceeds in investments with lower yields.

How to Buy GNMAs

GNMAs can be purchased directly from the issuer through dealers or brokers. Minimum purchase amounts are $25,000. However, investors can buy GNMA mutual funds or unit investment trusts by investing as little as $1,000 to $2,500 (the minimum amount specified by the GNMA mutual fund or investment trust). Mutual funds and investment trusts are discussed in detail in later chapters in this book.

Existing GNMA issues may be bought (sold) in the secondary market. GNMAs are both marketable and liquid due to the large volume of issues traded. When buying from a broker/bank you should be aware of the following:

◆ Prices quoted in the newspapers or offering sheets are for large buyers (institutions) and so small investors will be quoted higher spreads (between bid and asked prices).

◆ Yields quoted are based on prepayment assumptions. If only one yield is quoted, ask your broker for the different prepayment assumptions and the corresponding yields. Use the most conservative yield, because even then it may not be realized.

◆ The remaining term of the mortgage pool or length of time to maturity is not as important as the weighted average life, because the former assumes no prepayments. In the secondary market it is assumed that a 30-year GNMA will be repaid on average in 12 years.

◆ Price is important. If the GNMA is trading at a premium, you may be more inclined to suffer a capital loss. If interest rates decline, mortgagors may prepay their mortgages in the pool faster than estimated. Hence, you may not recover the premium paid over the face value, and you will also have to reinvest the money at lower interest rates. Buying at a discount offers the opportunity of capital gains, but the coupon yield for the GNMA is lower than currently offered coupons.

What Are the Advantages of GNMAs?

◆ Large sophisticated investors can use the futures market to hedge their portfolios against adverse swings in interest rates.

◆ GNMAs offer investors cash flows on a monthly basis as opposed to semi-annually or annually for other fixed income investments.

◆ GNMAs have no credit risk as interest and principal payments are guaranteed by the U.S. government.

◆ GNMAs are marketable due to the large size of the GNMA market. They are also liquid in that the bid and asked spreads tend to be similar to those for Treasury securities (about ⅛ of a point), and less than most corporate securities.

◆ Thirty-year GNMAs are not as volatile as 30-year Treasuries, because part of the principal on the GNMA is repaid on a monthly basis.

◆ Yields on GNMAs tend to be higher than those on Treasuries but lower than those offered by corporate bonds.

What Are the Disadvantages of GNMAs?

◆ It is difficult to determine the amount of the monthly cash flows due to the prepayments of mortgages in the pools.

◆ It is difficult to determine the exact yield for GNMAs due to the uncertainties of the cash flows.

◆ Reinvestment risk is greater for GNMAs than Treasuries and corporate bonds, particularly when market rates of interest decline.

◆ Interest is fully taxable at the federal, state, and local levels, whereas Treasuries and certain agency issues are exempt from state and local taxes.

◆ They are subject to interest rate risk. Prices of GNMAs move in the opposite direction to changes in interest rates.

Caveats

◆ To reduce the prepayment risk, investors should avoid buying GNMAs from small mortgage pools. By buying into large mortgage pools, investors can spread out the prepayment risks. For this reason, small investors might consider GNMA mutual funds where diversification can be achieved through the size of the mutual fund's investments in these securities. By investing in one or a few pools, investors with relatively small amounts cannot achieve the diversification that mutual funds can.

◆ With GNMAs, investors receive a return of principal and interest monthly. Investors should not spend their entire monthly checks, but should rather invest a portion of their proceeds to keep their investment capital intact.

◆ When GNMAs are trading at a premium price, their coupon yields are greater than current coupon rates for new GNMAs. Investors should be cautious in buying at a premium because prepayment volatility is greatest for GNMAs whose coupons exceed current mortgage rates by three percent (Hayre and Mohebbi 1989, page 283). A faster rate of prepayments may lead to a capital loss.

Conclusion

GNMAs provide investors with monthly cash flows, and yields have tended to be higher for the past several years than those offered by both Treasuries and top rated corporate issues. There is virtually no credit risk for GNMAs and they are much more liquid than corporate bonds.

However, GNMAs are complex in their make up and provide unpredictable cash flows with yields that are difficult to measure accurately. Invest in GNMAs when yields on them exceed the yields on Treasuries by at least two percent (Thau 1992).

As GNMAs are designed more for institutional investors, individual investors should consider GNMA mutual funds or investment trusts which are discussed in detail in their respective chapters in this book.

Federal Home Loan Mortgage Corporation (FHLMC)

The Federal Home Loan Mortgage Corporation, also known as "Freddie Mac," is the second largest issuer of pass-through securities. Freddie Mac is an agency of the U.S. government and its shares are owned by the 12 Federal Reserve Banks.

The participation certificates offered by Freddie Mac are similar in many ways to GNMAs. The major differences are:

◆ Participation certificate pools contain conventional mortgages (most are single family loans with 30-year terms) which are underwritten and purchased by Freddie Mac. Pools tend to be larger than those of GNMAs.

◆ Freddie Mac guarantees the timely payment of interest and ultimately the repayment of principal (within a year). Being an agency, this is a weaker guarantee than the "full faith and credit" provision by the government for GNMAs. Some participation certificates only guarantee the timely payment of interest.

◆ Participation certificates are not as marketable as GNMAs because less participation certificates are traded in the secondary markets than GNMAs. To improve the marketability of its participation certificates, Freddie Mac will buy them back directly from holders.

◆ Yields on participation certificates are slightly higher than those on GNMAs because of the slight discrepancy in safety and the slightly lesser degree of marketability. This does not mean that participation certificates are not safe or that they are not marketable. Compared with GNMAs, their credit risk is slight (far less than a corporate issue) and they are marketable (and liquid), but because GNMAs have a greater presence in the marketplace, they are not as marketable or liquid.

Besides participation certificates the Federal Home Loan Mortgage Corporation also has a mortgage pass-through called the guaranteed mortgage certificate (GMC). The GMC was designed for institutional investors with minimum amounts of $100,000 (as opposed to $25,000 for GNMAs and participation certificates) and pay semi-annual payments of interest and principal. Freddie Mac guarantees the interest payments and the full payment of principal.

Federal National Mortgage Association (FNMA)

The Federal National Mortgage Association also known as Fannie Mae or FNMA is a quasi-private organization whose common stock is traded on the New York Stock Exchange. Fannie Mae was established by Congress in 1938, but was then rechartered by Congress to become a private corporation in 1968 with a mandate to assist in the development of a secondary market for conventional mortgages.

Some of the features of Fannie Mae pass-throughs are:

◆ FNMA guarantees timely interest and principal payments—a weaker guarantee than that given for GNMA pass-through securities.

◆ FNMA pools tend to be larger than GNMA pools.

◆ FNMAs are not as marketable as GNMAs, and yields on FNMAs tend to be higher than those offered on GNMAs.

In a study comparing the prepayment rates on 30-year FNMA, FHLMC and GNMA fixed rate, mortgage-backed securities, FNMA and Freddie Mac pools prepay at a faster rate than GNMA pools at equivalent interest rates (Scott 1989). To offset the prepayment and cash flow uncertainties, collateralized mortgage obligations were developed.

Collateralized Mortgage Obligations

The first Collateralized Mortgage Obligation (CMO) was issued in 1983. The main innovation of the CMO is that it provides investors with a steady stream of income for predictable terms. A CMO is a debt security based on a pool of mortgages (like GNMAs) where the mortgagors make their interest and principal payments on a monthly basis. However, the return of principal payments are segmented and paid sequentially to a number of different portions of the pool's investors.

CMO pools are divided into three or more tranches (or slices) and investors will buy bonds with varying maturities in these tranches. For example, the classic CMO has four tranches where the first three (Class A, Class B, and Class C) would pay interest at the stated coupon rate to the bondholders of each tranche. The fourth tranche (often referred to as a class Z or a Z bond Class) resembles a zero coupon bond where interest would be accrued.

The cash flows received are used first to pay the interest on the first three classes of bonds and then to retire the bonds in the first tranche. After all the bonds are retired in the first tranche, payments will be used to retire the next shortest maturity bonds in tranche B. This process will continue until class B bonds are paid off, and then C bonds follow. Z bonds receive no payments (interest or principal) until all the other tranches are paid off. The subsequent cash flows are used to pay off the accrued interest, and then the return of principal to retire the Z bonds.

Z bonds are much more complex than the A, B or C bonds in CMOs for a number of reasons. Firstly, the length to maturity cannot be accurately predicted (for Z bonds) whereas regular A, B and C tranches have stated maturities. Secondly, Z bonds are long-term bonds and thus, face greater risks than shorter term securities. Hence,

Z bonds can be quite volatile and you should understand the risks before buying Z tranche bonds in a CMO.

The Advantages of CMOs

◆ For earlier tranches, there is greater certainty as to cash flows (quarterly or semi-annually).

◆ For the earlier tranches there are shorter, predictable maturities. Consequently, there is less exposure to interest rate risk.

◆ The later tranches have less prepayment risk (they cannot receive any principal payments until the earlier tranches have been paid off).

◆ CMO pools are much larger than GNMA pools.

◆ Depending on the backing of the mortgages, CMOs can have very little to no credit risk. Some pools are backed by GNMA, FNMA, or FHLMC which have no credit risk. There are privately backed pools with pool insurance which carry greater credit risks.

◆ Depending on the brokerage firms selling CMOs, minimum amounts for investing can be as low as $10,000.

◆ Yields on Z tranche bonds are higher than those of GNMAs, but the risks are also much greater for Z tranche bonds.

The Disadvantages of CMOs

◆ CMOs are less liquid and may be less marketable than GNMAs, FNMAs and Freddie Macs.

◆ Z tranche bonds can be quite volatile when market rates of interest change.

◆ Yields on the earlier tranches tend to be lower than those on GNMAs.

◆ Z tranche bonds have more complicated tax aspects in that interest is taxed as accrued even though the investor does not receive the actual interest payments in the early years (only when the Z tranche pays out).

Caveats

Before investing in CMOs, investors should:

◆ understand the characteristics of each tranche, the relationship between the tranches as well as the prepayment structure;

◆ understand who has guaranteed or insured the mortgages in the pools;

◆ ascertain from the brokerage firm selling the CMOs whether they make a market in the securities. If not, the CMOs may be difficult to sell.

Conclusion

Many different classes of CMOs have evolved. These have different features and the complexities of each specific class has increased with the evolution of CMOs. Investors should become familiar with the features and characteristics of the CMO before they invest.

CMOs offset some of the problems of the traditional pass-through securities by providing a stream of cash flows for a relatively predictable maturity. Due to the high quality of the bonds (with the underlying collateral of the mortgages) CMOs have less credit risk than corporate bonds, and some CMOs offer slightly higher yields than good quality corporate issues.

Government Agency Securities

Agencies of the government issue traditional securities in addition to mortgage pass-through securities.

Federal Home Loan Bank (FHLB) System

The Federal Home Loan Bank System plays a similar role to the Savings and Loan Associations, as the Federal Reserve Banks do to the commercial banks. The FHLB System consists of 12 regional banks and has a central board in Washington. These 12 banks are owned by the private Savings and Loans that are members of the system. Despite this ownership, the FHLB System is responsible to Congress for regulating the Savings and Loans as well as lending to them.

The FHLB borrows in the open market by issuing consolidated bonds and shorter term discount notes. Consolidated bonds have maturities of one year or more (up to 20 years). Many of the new issues may be purchased in minimum amounts of $10,000 with additional amounts in multiples of $5,000. Interest is paid semi-annually and these bonds are not callable.

The FHLB's consolidated discount notes are short-term securities with maturities ranging from 30 to 360 days, and are sold in minimum denominations of $100,000.

The credit quality of FHLB securities is high because the U.S. government is unlikely to allow one of its agencies to default on its obligations. Interest income on both the consolidated bonds and discount notes is taxable at the federal level, but is exempt at the state and local levels.

Farm Credit Agencies

The Farm Credit Administration oversees the Federal Farm Credit System in which the country is divided into 12 farm credit districts, each with its own Federal Land Bank, a Bank for Cooperatives, and a Federal Intermediate Credit Bank. These banks issue securities through a fiscal agent in New York City to raise funds so that they can lend to agricultural borrowers in their districts.

The Farm Credit Agencies issue three types of securities through its banks:

◆ short-term discount notes which are auctioned daily with maturities ranging from 5 to 270 days in minimum denominations of $50,000;

◆ short-term bonds which are auctioned monthly with maturities of three to nine months in minimum denominations of $50,000;

◆ long-term bonds with maturities of one to ten years in minimum denominations of $1,000.

Interest income from these is taxed at the federal level but exempt at the state and local levels. Credit risk is negligible, due to the de facto backing from the U.S. government. This was evidenced during the middle and late 1980s when Congress passed legislation to aid the Farm Credit system which had experienced financial difficulties.

Conclusion

There are many different government agencies that issue securities which may vary considerably as to their characteristics. However, they do have many common features such as:

◆ new issues of agency securities are sold through a syndicate of dealers. These dealers also buy and sell these securities in the secondary markets;

◆ agencies with large issues have marketable and fairly liquid securities;

◆ agency securities are exempt from registration with the SEC;

◆ some agency issues have tax advantages in that interest income is exempt from state and local taxes;

◆ agency securities have either de facto or de jure backing from the federal government.

Agency securities tend to offer yields which are greater than those of Treasuries for comparable maturities, but lower than most Aa or Aaa rated corporate bonds. The different agency securities, their wide range of offerings and maturities, will appeal to investors who like the slightly higher yields than those offered by Treasuries without sacrificing very much on credit risks.

References

Hayre, Lakhbir S. and Cyrus Mohebbi. "Mortgage Pass-Through Securities," in *Advances and Innovations in the Bond and Mortgage Markets.* Edited by Frank J. Fabozzi. Chicago: Probus Publishing Co., 1989.

Jonson, Judith and Andrew Silver. "NADCO, NASBIC, HUD, PEFCO and FICO: High Quality Investment Opportunities Worth Investigating," in *Advances and Innovations in the Bond and Mortgage Markets.* Edited by Frank J. Fabozzi. Chicago: Probus Publishing Co., 1989.

Scott F. Richard. "Relative Prepayment Rates on Thirty-Year FNMA, FHLMC and GNMA Fixed Rate Mortgage-Backed Securities," in *Ad-*

vances and Innovations in the Bond and Mortgage Markets. Edited by Frank J. Fabozzi. Chicago: Probus Publishing Co., 1989.

Thau, Annette. *The Bond Book.* Chicago: Probus Publishing Co., 1992.

Chapter 8

Municipal Bonds

Key Concepts

◆ What is different about municipal bonds?

◆ Are municipal bonds suitable for you?

◆ The types of municipal bonds

◆ The risks of municipal bonds

◆ How to buy and sell municipal bonds

◆ The advantages and disadvantages of municipal bonds

◆ Caveats

Municipal bonds are debt securities issued by state and local governments, their agencies and those enterprises with a public purpose. The agencies of local governments include authorities for housing, toll roads, transportation facilities, school districts, etc. Some examples of enterprises with a public purpose include hospitals, and universities.

What Is Different about Municipal Bonds?

For investors, the most important feature of municipal bonds is that the interest income is exempt from federal income taxes. Generally, interest income is also exempt from state and local taxes if investors live in the state and county issuing the municipal bonds. Hence, in such a case, the issue would be triple tax exempt. For example, if you live in a high tax state, you may want to buy bonds issued by your state or local government, which can improve your yield by a percentage point or so.

Most of the municipal bonds issued are tax exempt at the federal level, but there are some that are not tax exempt at the federal level. With the Tax Reform Act of 1986, Congress deemed those municipal issues with nonessential purposes to be taxable at the federal level.

However, they are exempt from state and local taxes. Nonessential purposes include those issued to raise funds for sports stadiums, parking facilities, conventions, industrial parks, and pollution control facilities.

Another tax wrinkle from the Tax Reform Act of 1986 involves industrial development bonds issued after 1986. Industrial development bonds are those where 10 percent or more of the proceeds raised by the sale of the bonds are used by private firms. For example, a state may issue industrial development bonds to finance a building which it leases to a private corporation.

Interest income received from industrial development bonds is treated as a preference item and may be subject to the alternative minimum tax (AMT) that some individuals pay. The alternative minimum tax is an additional tax that individuals in high income tax brackets with large deductions may pay. The AMT is designed to ensure that individuals in high income tax brackets who may not be subject to regular federal income taxes (due to large deductions) will be required to pay some federal taxes.

Thus, interest income on industrial development bonds that is exempt from federal income taxes may trigger the alternative minimum tax. This would not concern investors who are not subject to the alternative minimum tax. In fact, industrial development bonds may be attractive to investors as they tend to have slightly higher yields than tax-exempt bonds that are not subject to the alternative minimum tax.

Investors in high tax brackets can circumvent the alternative minimum tax by buying tax-exempt bonds issued before August 7, 1986, in the secondary market. This is the good news. The bad news is that the supply of these bonds is limited due to institutional investors such as mutual funds which have already purchased them. Thus, industrial development bonds may not be that attractive to investors who are subject to the alternative minimum tax.

There is always an exception to the rule, and this is: 501(c) bonds which are not subject to the alternative minimum tax. These are the bonds issued by the private, non-profit hospitals and universities.

Under certain circumstances, interest income on regular municipal bonds may be taxable for some retirees. Interest from municipal bonds currently is added to the retiree's adjusted gross income together with half of their Social Security payments, and if this exceeds a certain dollar amount, then a certain amount becomes taxable. However, the Internal Revenue Tax Code changes with the Congressional flow of ink on a yearly basis, and if in doubt as to the tax status of your municipal bonds, ask your accountant.

Despite the fact that private activity bonds are not tax exempt (at the federal level) and industrial development bonds issued after August 7, 1986, may trigger the alternative minimum tax, the vast majority of municipal bonds issued by state and local governments and their authorities are tax exempt at the federal level. It is this freedom from federal and possibly state and local taxes that makes municipal bonds so appealing to investors in the higher tax brackets.

Are Municipal Bonds Suitable for Me?

Everyone likes to lower their tax bills, but as you can see municipal bonds may not be the right investment for everyone. Buying tax-exempt issues purely to lower tax liability, may mean that some investors in some cases may not be earning as much as they could on an after-tax basis if they had bought taxable bonds. This may be true for investors in low tax brackets where they could earn even more from taxable bonds even after paying the taxes.

In order to compare municipal bonds with taxable bonds you need to convert the tax-exempt yield of a municipal to the equivalent of a taxable bond. See Table 8–1 for some examples of what taxable bonds would have to yield in order to equal the yields of municipal bonds.

The equivalent yield of a taxable bond at the investor's tax bracket is the yield an investor would have to earn on a taxable bond

Table 8–1 Comparison of Taxable Bond Yields to Those of Municipals at Different Tax Brackets

A Municipal Bond with a Yield of:

	5%	5½%	6%	6½%
would be equivalent to a Taxable Bond Yield of:				
Federal Income Tax Bracket				
15%	5.8 %	6.47%	7.06%	7.65%
28%	6.94%	7.64%	8.33%	9.03%
31%	7.24%	7.97%	8.70%	9.42%
36%*	7.81%	8.59%	9.38%	10.16%

* This level of Federal Income Tax is being proposed.

to equal the yield on a municipal bond. For example, an investor in the 15 percent tax bracket purchasing a taxable bond with a yield of 7.65 percent would earn the equivalent from a 6 1/2 percent tax exempt municipal bond. Put another way, the investor in the 15 percent tax bracket would purchase a municipal bond yielding 6 1/2 percent only if taxable bonds of similar maturities were yielding less than 7.65 percent. If this investor could earn more than 7.65 percent on taxable bonds, municipal bonds would not be considered. However, for investors in higher tax brackets, the taxable equivalent yield will be much greater. In the proposed 36 percent tax bracket, the taxable equivalent yield on a 6 1/2 percent municipal bond is 10.16 percent. Thus, as tax brackets (rates) increase, the taxable equivalent yields increase, and municipal bonds become more attractive.

Before buying tax-free municipal bonds you should decide whether the yield at your tax bracket is high enough to warrant the purchase.

Brokerage firms publish tables like the one in Table 8–1 of taxable equivalent yields, but it is a simple calculation to convert municipal bond yields to taxable yield equivalents.

The formula is:

$$\text{Taxable Equivalent Yield} = \frac{\text{Tax Free Yield}}{1 - \text{Tax Rate}}$$

A 6 percent coupon municipal bond bought by an investor in the 28 percent marginal tax bracket will have a before tax return of 8.33 percent:

$$\text{Taxable Equivalent Yield} = \frac{6\%}{1 - .28}$$

$$= 8.33\%$$

Some states have higher rates of taxation than other states and this brings the next question to mind: should you buy an in-state or out-of-state bond?

Most states give favorable tax treatment to in-state municipals by exempting the income from state taxes. This also applies at the local tax level if the issue is a local issue. This exemption from state and local taxes increases the taxable equivalent yield when comparing an in state municipal bond with a taxable bond. To answer the question of whether to buy an in-state or out-of-state bond requires another simple calculation.

Suppose that you are considering an out-of-state municipal bond with a yield of 6 1/2 percent with an in-state bond with a yield of 5 3/4 percent, and the state and local taxes combined are 6 percent.

The after–tax out–of–state yield = (1 – tax rate) × out–of–state yield

$$= (1 - .06) \times .065$$

$$= 6.11\%$$

The after-tax yield on the out-of-state bond is 6.11 percent which is higher than the in-state bond yield, and so, the out-of-state bond would be more attractive in this case. High tax states like New York and California have such a high demand for their in-state issues that their yields are often lower than out-of-state municipal bond issues. Bear in mind for comparison purposes that Treasury issues and certain government agency issues are also exempt from state and local taxes. These, however, are not exempt from federal taxes.

Investors who are subject to the alternative minimum tax should consult their tax advisors or accountants to determine their equivalent yields.

Tax laws change continually and investors should keep abreast of these changes as to the effects on their investments. Municipal bonds are probably the last great tax shelter left in the code. However, they do not benefit all investors. Generally, investors in the higher tax brackets benefit the most from municipal bonds and those in the lower tax brackets may not find them particularly advantageous to own.

Types of Municipal Bonds

State and local governments (and their agencies) issue a variety of debt instruments which are classified either by the length of time to maturity or by the way in which the debt is supported. In the case of the former, the debt would be classified as short-term or long-term, depending on the time to maturity. In the latter type, the debt issue is secured either by the taxing power of the issuer, in which case it is a general obligation bond, or by the revenues generated by the project, called a revenue bond.

General obligation bonds are issued by states, counties, cities, towns, school and special districts. These are usually secured by the taxing power of the issuer. In other words, the interest paid to bond-holders comes from taxes and the ability of the issuer to raise more taxes. Theoretically, issuers may have unlimited taxing authority, but in reality, it may not be that easy to enact their "unlimited" taxing powers. This is evidenced by New York City's default on its general obligation notes in 1978. New York City was later compelled by the courts to pay up on their defaulted issue. Many cities have subsequently seen their bond issues downgraded in ratings. This raises questions as to the so-called ironclad security of general obligation bonds.

The changes in the federal bankruptcy laws of 1979 made it easier for municipal bond issuers to seek protection from bondholders by filing for bankruptcy and this aroused investors' concerns even more. Just because the issue is a general obligation bond backed by the taxing power of the issuer does not mean that there are no credit risks.

There are some obligation bonds which are not secured by the unlimited taxing power of the issuer. There are limits on their taxing sources and these are known as *limited-tax general obligation bonds*. There are also certain obligation bonds which, besides their own characteristics, have certain features of revenue bonds. These are referred to as "double barreled" securities.

Revenue bonds are issued by enterprises such as hospitals, universities, airports, toll roads, public utilities whereby the revenues generated by these enterprises or from their projects are used to pay the interest on the debt.

For example, airport revenue bonds may generate revenues based on traffic usage at the airport or from revenues generated by the use of the airport facilities such as leasing out a terminal building. As to the former case of revenue collection, bondholders should determine whether there is a growing demand for both passenger and airline traffic usage of the airport and as to the latter form of revenue collection, whether the lease payments will be sufficient to service the debt.

Proceeds from highway revenue bonds may be used to build toll roads/bridges or to make improvements to the highway infrastructure. Bondholders will have a claim to tolls collected on the roads and bridges, but what about the improvements to the highways? Improving a highway does not generate revenue. Revenue bonds which are not self supporting will have revenues earmarked to secure the debt. These may be gasoline taxes, license fees, and automobile registration fees.

Thus, the security or safety of the revenue bonds will depend on how essential the services are that the enterprise provides, the flow of revenues, whether these are increasing or decreasing, and whether there are any other claims to the revenues before those of the bond-holders. The relative strength of the issuer of the revenue bonds to generate revenues and the ease with which the issuer can cover the interest payments will determine the rating of the revenue bonds.

Besides general obligation and revenue bonds, state and local governments issue short-term municipal notes which have maturities for periods up to three years. *Anticipation notes* are issued to even out the irregular cash flows of the treasuries of the state and local governments. Among the anticipation notes are tax anticipation notes (TANs) which are issued in anticipation of taxes to be collected; bond anticipation notes (BANs) in anticipation of the proceeds from the sale of long-term bonds; revenue anticipation notes (RANs) which are issued in anticipation of revenues coming in; tax and revenue anticipation notes (TRANs) which are a combination of taxes and revenues coming in.

There are also municipal bonds which have special features. *Zero-coupon municipal bonds* are like regular zero coupon bonds in that they are sold at a deep discount to their face value. Interest is paid at maturity when the investor receives the face value of the bond. The zero-coupon municipal bond offers tax advantages over regular zero-coupon bonds: the interest that accrues is not subject to federal income taxes. For regular zero-coupon bonds, interest accrues each year and is subject to federal income taxes even though the interest is not received until the bond is sold or matures. These bonds are discussed in more detail in Chapter 10.

Put or option tender municipal bonds are those where bondholders have the option of returning the bond to the bond trustee before maturity at face value. Generally, this type of bond is either backed by the revenues of the issuer or by a letter of credit from a bank. The put feature is the opposite of a call feature in the bond provision.

Wall Street bankers, always looking for new types of securities, have dreamed up a new municipal security, a *municipal bond derivative with detachable call option rights*. In November 1992, the Municipal Electric Authority of Georgia sold these securities. The attraction of these to the issuers is that the detachable call option rights can be sold separately from the underlying bond issue (and may also trade separately from the underlying bond), and they have the potential of bringing in additional dollars to the issuers.

These were originally developed by the Paine Webber Group to take out some of the downside effects that call provisions have on municipal bonds. Most tax-exempt securities are issued with call provisions. In periods of falling interest rates, municipal bond issuers are apt to call in their bonds. Thus, municipal bonds tend to appreciate much less than Treasuries and corporate bonds during bond market rallies. This has a direct effect on the performance of municipal bond mutual funds.

Managers of these municipal bond mutual funds can solve this problem by buying the detachable call rights from the issuer. The issuer, therefore, gives up the right to call the bonds in return for an additional sum of money.

The U.S. Treasury is currently questioning whether the detachable call option rights violate the tax laws. This could dampen the potentially lucrative market if the Treasury decides that these securities violate the complex municipal bond tax laws in the Internal Revenue Code. However, if they decide that there is no tax violation these securities will give investors the opportunity to hedge against their bonds being called as well as being able to speculate on the direction of market rates of interest (Mitchell 1993).

For risk averse investors who want a safe investment with some tax advantages, there are *prerefunded municipal bonds*. These are backed by U.S. Treasury bonds. Prerefunded bonds were issued when interest rates were higher and came into existence when municipalities issued new lower coupon bonds. The proceeds of these were used to buy U.S. Treasury securities. The Treasuries are used as security for the first issue of bonds (prerefunded) which will be called at the first call date.

Prerefunded municipals have AAA ratings and generally pay slightly higher premium coupons. The disadvantages are that they generally sell at premium prices and they have relatively short maturities in that they will be called within a few years.

Merrill Lynch & Co. has very recently begun to market a speculative, complex municipal bond to individual investors. It is called an *inverse floater*, or TEEMS, which stands for Tax-Exempt Enhanced Municipal Securities. This security is very new and has been used over the past few years primarily by mutual funds to boost their returns.

Inverse floaters are derivative securities which reflect the changes in price of the underlying bonds sold with them. It seems from the paucity of information available on these inverse floaters that the bond issue which is underwritten is divided into two parts. One part contains bonds which pay holders coupon rates that fluctuate with money market rates and the second part of the issue gets the rest of the interest. The second part contains the inverse floaters. When short-term rates fall, holders of the bonds from the first part will get less interest which leaves more money for the inverse floaters. Similarly, prices of the inverse floaters will increase more than regular municipal bonds when short-term rates of interest fall. Thus, holders of inverse floaters benefit in two ways when interest rates go down: they get more interest and prices of the bonds appreciate more than other bonds.

When short-term rates of interest move up, the price of the inverse floaters will drop more than that of plain vanilla bonds since inverse floaters will get less of the money available for interest payments. When long-term rates increase this will depress the price of the inverse floater even more.

Merrill Lynch offered $15 million of inverse floaters to individual investors in the third week of March 1993 as part of an offering by the Puerto Rico Telephone Authority (Vogel 1993). Along with the offering came a brochure filled with warnings about the risks and complexities of this security. The target market for inverse floaters are affluent clients who are not sensitive to instruments that provide variable income and that are volatile in price.

These securities have performed well for mutual funds during the past few years as market rates of interest have been falling. It is not evident what the downside risk will be when market rates of interest level off and begin to go up. Samuel B. Corliss Jr., a managing director of municipal derivatives at Merrill Lynch is quoted as saying that yields on these inverse floaters will not drop to zero if short-term rates go up rapidly (Vogel 1993). This raises the question who will bear the risks of loss? Another question is who will maintain a market for these securities when interest rates rise? or will investors find that they are stuck with an investment that no one will want to buy when the stakes are down.

Until more is known about this security, individual investors should not be in too much of a hurry to invest in them, bearing in mind that there are no free lunches on Wall Street. New, complex, speculative, derivative securities should be left for institutional investors who can withstand greater variability in prices without their investments being wiped out, and who have more options open to them to deal with the risks involved.

What Are the Risks of Municipal Bonds?

In the past municipal bonds were always perceived to be very safe investments and tended to rank a second to Treasury securities. This changed during the decade of the 1970s when New York City defaulted on some of its obligations. This shattered the perception that there could be no defaults on government obligation bonds since the issuers could always raise revenues by increasing taxes.

A default by a city, town, municipality is very different from a default by a corporation. In the latter case, bondholders will go to court and then the assets will be seized and sold off to pay the creditors. With cities it is very different. In New York's case, bondholders could not easily and practically have sold the New York subway system or parts of it on the market.

So, what is the small investor to do regarding the safety of municipal bond issues? The easiest and also the most glib answer is: avoid issues which are financially shaky.

To follow that advice, ask all those investors who invested in the municipal bonds issued by New York City and Cleveland before their respective defaults, and they would say that they were investing wisely. Both cities had A ratings. In 1973, New York City obligation bonds were upgraded by ratings services to investment grade quality. In 1975, New York City defaulted on these bonds. New York City claimed that they did not default but that they had a "moratorium."

Another major default which shook the municipal bond market was that of the Washington Public Power System (WPPSS, also referred to as WHOOPS). WPPSS sold $2.25 billion of tax exempt bonds to build two nuclear power plants. Construction on the plants was halted midway, and the Power company was unable to raise rates to cover the construction costs resulting in a default on the bonds.

Although the number of defaults on municipal issues have been small, these highly publicized examples have made investors very conscious of the *risk of default*. Following these steps may reduce the risk of default:

◆ **Ratings.** Investors should consider the ratings of the bond offering. Moody's and Standard & Poor's rate these offerings based on a substantial amount of financial information. As municipal bonds do not have to be registered with the Securities and Exchange Commission, there is very little information available about the issuer's financial status for investors. States and municipalities may not publish their annual financial statements. Therefore, limit your purchases to AAA or AA ratings to minimize the risk of default.

◆ **Insurance.** Check whether the issue is insured. Bond insurance can increase the ratings of an issue. When a bond is insured, it is given a AAA rating even if the bond had a lower rating before insurance. A bond issue that has a rating of AAA or AA without insurance is a stronger offering than an insured bond with AAA ratings. Insurance corporations such as Municipal Bond Insurance Association (MBIA), Financial Guaranty Insurance Co. (FGIC) sell insurance whereby they will guarantee the interest payments and the return of principal.

The quality of the insurance company will also affect the ratings of the issue. For example, when Standard & Poor's downgraded the debt of Verex Assurance in 1988, which insured housing authority bonds, their market prices (housing authority bonds) declined. The insurance is only as good as the insurer, and issues with insurance generally have lower yields than uninsured bonds.

◆ **Credit Enhancements.** Instead of insurance, some issuers have letters of credit from banks and insurance companies. These do not guarantee interest payments by the banks/insurance companies. Instead these offer the issuer a line of credit. If the issuer does not have enough cash to cover the interest payments, the bank or insurance company will lend the issuer the money. This is a lower degree of protection than insurance and investors should check the ratings of the bank or insurance company providing the line of credit.

◆ **Official Statement.** Obtain a copy of the official statement or offering circular, which is like the prospectus for corporate securities. In it, review:

   ◆ The legal opinion. If there is any doubt as to the tax exemption avoid the issue.

   ◆ How the issue will be repaid. This ought to be fairly clear.

   ◆ The qualifications, such as "no assurance can be given." If phrases are used that make you nervous, find another issue to invest in.

◆ **Diversification.** Purchase bonds of different issuers which spreads the risks associated with any one particular issuer.

A word of caution, ratings are not cast in stone and they can change over time as evidenced by WPPSS. Standard & Poor's gave WPPSS projects 4 & 5 ratings of A+ in 1980, which by 1984 deteriorated to a D rating. Thus, do not base your decision on ratings alone.

Interest rate risk may be greater than the risk of default if you choose quality tax-exempt issues. This is not unique to municipal bonds but applies to all fixed income securities. Value Line Investments Service estimates that a 20-year municipal bond trading at par will decline 8.6 percent in price for a one percent increase in market rates of interest and will have a 9.9 percent increase in price for a one percentage drop in interest rates (Dunnan 1990). The longer the term to maturity, the greater the price volatility due to fluctuations in interest rates.

Although investors will receive greater yields from long term (30-year) municipals, they should bear in mind the increased volatility and the fact that yield spreads between maturities tend to be wider for municipals than they are for bonds in the taxable bond market.

Investors can lessen interest rate risk and not give up on yield by buying AA rated 15 year municipal bonds instead of AAA rated 30 year municipals. As of this writing, yields on shorter maturities of a notch lower rating will yield the same as a longer maturity higher notch rated municipal bond. Rates change, and this would of course depend on the yield spread at the time of purchase.

The *risk of a municipal bond being called* is a common risk. Most municipal bonds have call or refunding provisions which allow issuers to call the bonds in when interest rates have decreased significantly. This explains the high level of redemptions of municipal bonds currently due to the fall in interest rates. Bondholders receive the face value of the bond (and in some cases more depending on the terms set out in the indenture), but they will have to reinvest their money at a lower rate of return.

Investors should read the call provisions of their bonds before purchase to see if there are any unusual features. Housing revenue bonds, for example, may not stipulate a call date, meaning that they could be called anytime after issue. Be careful if you are paying a premium on these bonds, because if they are called, you may not recoup your premium.

Ask your broker for the yield to call as well as the yield to maturity, because if your bond is called, the yield to call becomes your actual return and not the yield to maturity. If the yield to call is less than the coupon rate, you know that the bond is trading at a premium price.

Remember that there are no free lunches (or if there are, they are very few in number) on Wall Street. The higher the coupon rate of the bond, the more costly it is for the issuer, and hence, the likelihood of that bond issue being called when interest rates fall.

Municipal securities are not as actively traded as government bonds which means that the spreads between the bid and asked prices tend to be relatively wide. This is true even for the most actively traded issues. This makes municipal bonds less liquid than Treasury issues and agency bonds.

The larger issues of general obligation bonds and the well known authorities tend to be marketable, but the smaller, thinly traded issues may not be marketable. In fact, for some small issues there may be no market outside the issuing locality.

Investors should be aware that if they invest in the longer term maturities, they may be exposed to the high costs of selling them due to illiquidity and the lower marketability of municipal issues. The best strategy is to buy and hold municipal bonds through maturity (or call).

How to Buy and Sell Municipal Bonds

Investors may buy municipal bonds at issue or on the secondary market. The financial newspapers, *Barron's, Wall Street Journal,* and *The New York Times* list the forthcoming sales of municipals for the week. *The Bond Buyer,* which is a trade publication for municipal bonds, also gives information on the forthcoming sales, as well as the results of the previous week's sales of municipal bonds.

State and local governments in some cases market their issues by placing them privately in the market, usually directly to institutional buyers. Mostly, they are placed through investment bankers who will offer them for sale to the investment community (the public). The investment banker will form a syndicate of brokerage firms to sell the new issue. If there is an issue that interests you, you can put in your order through your brokerage firm. If your brokerage firm is part of the syndicate, there will be no sales commission on the purchase. The other advantage of buying at issue is that the bonds are priced at a uniform price (the syndicate offering price) until all the orders for the syndicate have been filled. Only then can the bonds trade at market prices.

Buying municipals on the secondary market is slightly more difficult because the financial newspapers only print the prices of a small list of some of the popular revenue bonds. Prices of government obligation bonds are not quoted in the newspapers. To learn what bonds are available in the secondary market you may want to obtain a copy of the "Blue List" which is published daily by Standard & Poor's. It lists the bonds that dealers currently own in their portfolios and wish to sell. The listings of each bond will include information such as:

◆ the number of bonds for sale in each issue;

◆ the name of the issuer;

◆ the coupon rate and maturity date;

◆ the price (this does not include the bid and asked spread); and

◆ the name of the dealer selling the bonds.

The "Blue List" is the best source of information, but it is also very costly for most individual investors to subscribe to. Consequently, you should ask your broker to let you see a copy. Do not be surprised to find that by the time that you see the "Blue List" some of the bond issues may already be sold. Because the bid and asked spreads are not quoted, there may also be some deviation from the price quoted in the "Blue List."

The municipal bond secondary market is supported by many municipal bond dealers throughout the country. Brokers serve as intermediaries between dealers and institutional and individual investors in municipal bond issues. Many brokerage firms will maintain markets in their local and regional issues.

Pricing of municipal bond issues can vary significantly from dealer to dealer so when buying (or selling) you should get several quotes from different brokerage firms. In addition to dealer spreads, commissions may also vary significantly among comparably rated issues. The bottom line is to shop around because paying high commissions and wide spreads will lower your overall return.

Another factor which increases commission costs is whether you buy in round or odd lots. Buying or selling orders of less than $25,000 are considered to be odd lots. Spreads between the bid and asked prices quoted by dealers for these odd lots tend to be wider because dealers find it harder to sell small numbers of municipal bonds. These higher costs will erode investors' returns, so they may want to buy and hold these issues to maturity. Before buying, investors should evaluate the overall risks and returns.

Municipal bonds on the secondary market may trade at a discount or a premium depending on a number of factors such as quality, coupon yield, issuer, length of time to maturity.

When buying municipal bonds at a discount or premium you should be aware of the likelihood of the incurrence of capital gains when sold or called. For example, if you buy 50 municipal bonds with a face value of $50,000 at a discount of $45,000 in 1989, and in 1990 you buy another 50 municipal bonds with a face value of $50,000 at a premium of $55,000 with both issues maturing in 1993, $5,000 will be subject to capital gains in 1993. Puzzled? Well, most people are.

According to the Internal Revenue Tax Code (section 171), for tax-exempt bonds there is no allowable deduction for the amortization of the premium. In other words, the $5,000 gain cannot be offset against the $5,000 loss because the loss is not recognized (which means that the loss cannot be deducted). The premium is amortized down over the life of the bond to maturity or until call. This results in the fact that municipal bondholders could be doubly penalized; they could buy high coupon bonds at a premium, only to find that they could be called at a lower price (than the premium purchase price paid):

◆ one, the loss is not deductible against other capital gains; and

◆ two, the bonds may be called sooner than anticipated, not giving the bondholder the chance to recoup the costs of having paid a premium price for a high coupon security.

This nondeductibility of the amortization is unique to tax-exempt bonds, and investors should be aware that they may be liable for taxes due to gains from buying bonds at a discount and through the process of amortization of a premium. To illustrate the latter process, consider the example where an investor bought a tax-exempt bond at a premium of $1,100 and in five years time sold the bond for $1,100. As a result of having to amortize or write down the premium over time, the adjusted basis of the tax-exempt bond will be less than $1,100. Hence, there will be a taxable gain between the adjusted basis and the selling price.

Municipalities often issue *serial bonds* which are groups of bonds with different maturities within the issue. Bear in mind that with a serial issue investors can choose the maturity they desire when the issue is originally sold in the market.

What Are the Advantages of Municipal Bonds?

◆ Interest on most municipal bond issues is exempt from federal income tax, and may be exempt from state and local taxes if issued in that state and locality. This benefits high income investors in the higher tax brackets.

◆ Provides regular interest payments for income dependent investors.

What Are the Disadvantages of Municipal Bonds?

◆ Municipal bonds are less liquid and less marketable than government securities. Investors may have difficulty in selling some of the smaller, less actively traded issues in the secondary market.

◆ Many high coupon municipals have call provisions. Be aware of the call provision when buying a tax-exempt bond trading at a premium. You could lose part of your investment if the issue is called at a lower price than the purchase price.

◆ When bonds are called, investors are exposed to the reinvestment risk of having to reinvest their money into lower yielding securities.

◆ Default risk is of increasing concern due to a number of defaults in the past and the increasing number of financially troubled cities.

◆ Municipal bond prices fluctuate with the changes in interest rates. The longer the maturity of the issue, the greater the price volatility.

◆ Dealer spreads can be quite wide and vary considerably among dealers.

Caveats

◆ Municipal bonds are not entirely risk free. Buy municipals with the highest quality ratings and stay away from small unrated issues, and speculative revenue bonds.

◆ When buying a new issue, check the offering circular for the legal opinion, and the ratings for the issue.

◆ Be aware of the tax nuances—the possibility of incurring capital gains on the redemption of municipals bought at a discount or premium price.

◆ Interest on IDBs (industrial development bonds) issued after August 7, 1986, is treated as a preference item which may trigger the alternative minimum tax for high income investors.

◆ Interest on private activity bonds for nonessential purposes is not tax exempt from federal income taxes.

Conclusion

The overriding advantage of municipal bonds is their favorable tax status—interest being exempt from federal income taxes. When marginal tax rates are raised, the value of municipal bonds is of greater significance to investors in higher tax brackets. Municipal bonds should be considered by investors who can not only reduce their income taxes, but also receive yields from their municipal bond investments which are comparable to other fixed income bonds on a before-tax basis. The latter point is important because tax advantages can easily be swept away with the stroke of a congressional pen.

Due to the higher transaction costs, as well as the decreased marketability and liquidity of many municipal issues, investors may be better off with a strategy of buying and holding their bonds through to maturity.

Diversification can spread the risks of default. For investors who do not have significant funds to diversify their portfolio (around 15 to 20 different issues), municipal bond funds and unit trusts should be considered. Mutual funds are also excellent investment vehicles for those investors who do not have the time or expertise to pick individual bond issues.

One method of protecting against interest rate risk is "laddering." This is the technique of buying several different municipal bond issues with different maturities over a period of time. Investors will receive their principal back on the shorter maturities which can be reinvested at current market rates of interest. If rates go up, investors will reinvest at higher rates. Of course, if rate go down, the coupons of the reinvested securities will be lower. In essence, investors will average out market rates of interest over the time period.

Most of all choose good quality municipal bond issues. The yield gap between good quality and lesser quality municipal bonds is not large enough (currently) to justify the risks of buying lesser quality issues.

References

Dunnan, Nancy. *Guide to $Your Investments$,* 1990. New York: Harper & Row Publishers, Inc., 1990.

Mitchell, Constance. "Latest Muni Derivative Gets U.S. Scrutiny." *Wall Street Journal,* February 11, 1993, page C1.

Vogel, Thomas T. Jr. "Muni Floaters are Marketed to Individuals." *Wall Street Journal,* March 31, 1993, page C1.

Chapter 9

Convertible Bonds

Key Concepts

◆ Convertible securities

◆ Their features

◆ How they work

◆ The different types of convertibles

◆ Their risks

◆ How to buy and sell convertibles

◆ Their advantages and disadvantages

◆ Caveats

◆ Their suitability for investors

Some years convertible securities out pace all other investments. In 1992 convertible securities measured by Smith Barney's convertible index increased by 25 percent, which was more than six times the increase in the Dow Jones Industrial Average and the Standard & Poor's 500 Index (Bary 1993).

You may think that investors were falling over themselves beating a path to buy convertible securities. Well, you would be wrong. According to mutual fund managers, most investors had either never heard of convertible securities or did not know what they were. Confirming this fact, the convertible fund in the Vanguard Group of mutual funds had the highest return (19 percent) for 1992 and had assets of only $165 million (Bary 1993).

Portions of this chapter have been previously published by Esmé Faerber in *Managing Your Investments, Savings, and Credit,* published by Probus Publishing Co., Chicago, IL 1992.

What Are Convertible Securities?

Convertibles are hybrid securities which come in two primary forms: bonds and preferred stock. These (convertible bonds and preferred stock) can be exchanged for a specified number of common shares of the issuing corporation at the option of the convertible holder. In a few cases, convertible bonds have been exchanged for preferred stock or other bond issues. However, there are some other rare types of hybrid convertibles which include PIKs (payment in kind), hybrid convertibles, LYONs, commodity-backed bonds and stock-indexed bonds. Each of these types of securities has a conversion option or relationship to another type of security or asset. PIKs (payment in kind securities), for example, pay their holders more of the same units of securities that they hold. Each of these types will be discussed in more detail later in the chapter.

Features of Convertible Bonds

Convertible bonds are long-term debt instruments which have many of the features of regular bonds. They are usually issued with a par or face value of $1,000 and have a maturity date (in the event that they are not converted). Interest may be paid by the issuer semi-annually or annually.

Some issues have call provisions which issuers often use to force the holders to convert their bonds. When convertible bondholders convert their bonds, the issuing firm no longer has to repay the bonds.

Why do companies issue convertible bonds when they could raise money by issuing debt or equity? By issuing convertible bonds, companies can tap into the credit markets more easily. Because of the conversion feature, companies can issue convertible bonds with lower coupon rates than they would have to pay on regular bonds. These bonds are usually subordinated to the issuing company's other outstanding debt issues.

Why would investors want to invest in lower quality, lower yielding debt? Again, it is the conversion feature which makes the difference. Investors are willing to accept lower coupon rates and lower quality in return for the possible appreciation, if the stock price of the issuing company rises. In other words, investors are sacrificing current income for possible future capital gains.

The fact that convertibles are subordinated debenture issues does not mean that only weaker financially troubled companies issue them. Many financially weaker companies do issue convertibles because they can raise funds which may not have been available through either ordinary debt or equity issues. However, in many examples, financially strong companies have also issued convertibles in order to lower their interest costs from issuing regular debt. Companies such as Xerox, Westinghouse, Ashland Oil, Compaq Computer, Browning Ferris, and Ford Motor Company have issued convertible securities.

In 1991, Ford Motor Company sold a large convertible issue when the stock price was $25. Ford's stock price has reached a high at the time of this writing of $50 during the 1992-1993 period which is a 100 percent gain on the stock price. The convertible bonds have appreciated by a lesser percentage (70 percent). Due to the conversion feature, convertible bonds appreciate when the stock price goes up, but generally do not appreciate as much as the common stock (as confirmed by the Ford Motor Company issue). When the stock price declines, the coupon rate on the convertible bond acts as a cushion on the downward pressure of the price of the convertible.

How Do Convertibles Work?

Convertible securities have their own terminology and these terms are often confusing to investors. A good starting point to understanding them is to use an example. Suppose a corporation wanting to raise funds decides that it does not want to issue more common stock, because the market price of the stock is low. To raise enough cash it would have to issue many more shares of common stock, which would dilute the earnings for existing shareholders. A straight debt issue would also be too costly because the company would have to match the coupon rate of comparable existing corporate debt issues with similar risks and maturities.

Instead the company decides on a convertible bond which because of the conversion feature investors will accept a lower coupon rate on the issue. The company will need to consider the current market price of its common stock to determine the number of shares that each bondholder will receive on conversion. For instance, if the company's stock is currently trading at $18 per share, the company may decide on a conversion price of $25 to make the bonds more appealing to investors. The *conversion ratio*, which is the number of common shares received for each bond, is 40 (shares per bond 1000/25). This is the face value of the bond divided by the conversion price.

The reader will see immediately that the convertible bond can be valued either in relation to the conversion value of the stock or as a straight bond. In reality, both of these factors are taken into account in the valuation of the convertible security.

Value of Convertible Bond as Stock

The value of the convertible security as stock depends on the market price of the common stock. The value is the number of shares into which the bond is convertible multiplied by the market price of the stock. In the example above, the convertible may be exchanged into 40 shares which is multiplied by $18, the current market price of the stock to give a value of $720.

The relationship between the value of the convertible bond as stock and the price of the common stock is illustrated in Table 9-1.

From Table 9-1, we see that as the market price of the stock (column 2) rises, the value of the convertible increases. The value of the convertible is obtained by multiplying the conversion ratio by the market price of the stock. When the price of the common stock is below the conversion price of $25, the value of the convertible is less than the face amount of the bond ($1,000). When the stock price is above the conversion price of $25, the value of the convertible is greater than the face value of the bond. Thus, the conversion feature allows for the upside potential of capital gains through the appreciation of the stock price. Moreover, there is a floor price below which the price of the convertible will not fall, and that is the straight value of the bond.

Table 9–1

Conversion Ratio*	Market Price of Stock	Value of Convertible as Stock
40	$10	$ 400
40	18	720
40	25	1,000
40	30	1,200
40	35	1,400
40	40	1,600

*The number of shares the convertible is exchanged into.

For example, assume that in the above illustration, the market price of the common stock falls to $10 per share. The conversion value is $400, but the market price will not fall below the value of the bond, due to the value of the coupon interest payments on the bond. Similarly, the market price of the convertible will not be less than the conversion value of the security. This is due in part to the activity of arbitragers who will buy and sell the same security in two different markets to take advantage of price differentials.

For instance, if the market value of the debt is $900 when the stock price is $24, arbitrageurs will exploit this price differential for their own profit. The conversion value is $960 (40 shares x $24 per share), and they will sell short the stock. To sell short is to borrow a security and sell it on the market. They will simultaneously buy the convertible bond for $900 and sell short 40 shares of the stock for $960. The conversion option would be exercised and they would tender the shares that they borrowed. The resulting profit will be $60 per bond before taking into account the commissions for the buying and selling of the securities. Arbitrageurs will bid up the price of the bonds until there is no longer a price differential. In reality, the price of convertible bonds are rarely the same as the conversion value into stock. Mostly, the price of the convertible exceeds that of the conversion value due to the bond's value. In addition to the upside appreciation due to the conversion value, the value of the bond as debt provides a floor price for the convertible bond.

Value of the Convertible Bond as Debt

The value of the convertible as debt will depend on the coupon rate, the risk of default on the interest payments, the length of time to maturity, the call provision and market rates of interest. The investment value of the bond can be determined by discounting both the coupon payment that the convertible pays and the face value of the bond at maturity (assuming it is not converted) at the interest rate paid on similar debt. In other words, the value of the convertible bond is the present value of the cash flows of the coupon payments and the face value of the bond at maturity discounted at an interest rate which includes the risk for that security.

As with regular bonds, the value of the convertible bond as debt will fluctuate with changes in market rates of interest. When interest rates increase, the price of the convertible bond will decline, and conversely when interest rates decline the price of the convertible will go up. This is because the coupon rate on the convertible is fixed.

The value of the convertible as straight debt is important because it sets a floor price. When the stock price is trading below the conversion price, the straight bond value provides the floor value and the convertible will not fall below this value. That is because the convertible option is of no consequence at lower stock prices. When stock prices go up above the conversion price, the minimum price for the convertible bond will be the conversion value as stock. This is where the bond is equity in disguise.

Value of the Convertible Bond as a Hybrid Security

Thus far we have seen that at low stock prices the floor price of the convertible will be no lower than its value as a straight bond, and at sufficiently high stock prices, the price of the convertible will be the same as the conversion value into stock. In between these extremes in stock prices, the convertible security will generally trade at a premium price over its value as equity and over its value as debt.

These relationships are examined in Table 9–2 using the example of a six percent 20-year convertible bond which has a conversion ratio of 40 shares. The market rate of interest used is eight percent.

At low stock prices ($5 and $10 per share) the market price of the convertible bond is the same as its value as straight debt and the

---

Table 9–2 Premiums on Convertible Bonds

Share Price	Conversion Ratio	Value as Stock	Value as Debt	Market Price of Convertible Bond*	Premium over Stock Price	Premium over Bond Price
$ 5	40	$ 200	$ 803.64	$ 803.64	$603.64	$ 0
10	40	400	803.64	803.64	403.64	0
18	40	720	803.64	850.00	130.00	46.36
25	40	1,000	803.64	1,100.00	100.00	296.36
35	40	1,400	803.64	1,420.00	20.00	616.36
40	40	1,600	803.64	1,600.00	0	796.36

* In reality, it is difficult to calculate the market price of the convertible security due to its hybrid nature and the many factors affecting the market price. Therefore, the market prices between the extremes in stock prices in this example are hypothetical and could fluctuate.

premium over the stock price is large. At $25 per share, the conversion price, the market price for the convertible is $1,100 which exceeds both the value of the debt by $296.36 and the value as stock by $100. At a significantly high stock price of $40 for this company, the market price of the convertible is the same as the value as stock and the premium over the value as debt is very high ($796.36).

The example illustrates that as the stock price rises, the premium paid over its value as straight debt increases. This is due to the importance of the conversion feature on the convertible and the fact that the straight debt becomes less important as the stock price increases.

There is also the probability that the bond may be called which would force conversion when the stock price is higher than the conversion price. For example, assume that the convertible bond was bought at $1,420 and the company calls in the bonds when the stock price is trading at $35. Convertible bondholders will not turn in their bonds for $1,000 per bond. Instead, they will convert their bonds into equity receiving $1,400 per bond (40 shares × $35), which results in a loss of $20 per bond for the bondholder. Thus, as the stock price rises, and puts downward pressure on the premium over the stock price, the market price for the convertible converges with the stock value of the convertible.

Most convertible securities trade at a premium over either the stock value or the value as a straight bond. Investors should analyze the fundamentals of the company first before buying. For example, Battle Mountain six percent convertible bonds were trading at a 141% premium over its equity value, whereas another mining company, Couer d'Alene seven percent convertible bonds, were trading at a 31 percent premium over the equity value. In this case, the lower premium over the equity value offers greater appreciation potential than the convertible bond with the higher premium over its equity value.

The Different Types of Convertible Securities

Convertible preferred stock is similar to convertible bonds. The convertible preferred stockholder has the option to convert each share of preferred stock into a fixed number of shares of common stock of the issuing company. Generally, the conversion ratio for convertible preferred securities is small. For example, it may be one share of preferred for one share of common stock.

Convertible preferred stock issues have many similar characteristics to convertible bonds. However, with convertible preferred stock, dividends are paid only if the board of directors of the company declares them. They are not like interest payments on convertible bonds where a default is liable to cause the bondholders to bring action against the company. Although the number of convertible preferred stock issues have increased in the last few years, they are not as popular as convertible bonds.

Another type of combination security is *hybrid convertibles*. These are convertible debentures of one company that are convertible into the common stock of another company. Companies that have accumulated a substantial number of the shares of another company can issue hybrid convertibles as a source of funds. For example, Mesa Petroleum had accumulated shares of General American and it issued hybrid convertibles which were convertible into the shares of General American.

Buying hybrid convertibles means that not only should the debt of the issuing company be attractive to you, but you should also like the equity of the convertible company. The nuance with hybrid convertibles is that it is a taxable exchange because the securities involve those of two companies.

There are many different *zero-coupon convertible bonds*. One of which is Merrill Lynch's LYON or liquid yield option note. Zero coupon bonds are sold at a deep discount from their face value and do not pay yearly cash interest. Instead, the interest accrues and at maturity the bond is redeemed for its face value. However, these also have call provisions which make their valuation more complex.

Zero-coupon convertible bonds tend to be offered by companies that want to conserve their cash. Walt Disney Company issued zero coupon convertibles to raise funds for their European Disneyland in Paris. These securities are convertible into EuroDisney stock traded on the Bourse in Paris, which, unfortunately for its holders, has been declining in value. This points out the disadvantage of this type of security. When the stock price is depressed and there is a call provision, the zero-coupon convertible will trade close to its call price which could be less than what investors paid for the security.

Another similar combination security is the *payment in kind* or PIK. PIKs are in some respects like zero-coupon securities in that interest (or dividends in the case of preferred stock PIKs) is not paid out in cash in the early years. Instead interest (or dividends) is paid in the form of additional securities of the underlying issue. For bonds, interest will be in the form of more bonds and for preferred stock dividends will be additional preferred shares.

PIKs tend to carry higher coupons to entice investors. However, investors need to examine the issuing company's financial status carefully to determine whether the company will be around in future years to be able to make the payoffs in cash. Again we are reminded that there are no free lunches on Wall Street—it is a high yield security in return for high risk.

SIRENs or *step-up income redeemable equity notes* are intermediate convertible bonds with two coupons. The first coupon is below market rates of interest, and then after a few years the coupon increases to a higher rate until maturity. These have a convertible provision where holders can convert their notes into the common stock of the issuer at a price determined by the issuer (conversion price). As with other convertibles, if the price of the common stock goes up, holders stand to profit. If the price of the common stock goes down, holders of SIRENs will have a floor price on their notes but they would earn less than they would on a similar conventional bond.

The clincher is that these are issued with call provisions which allow the issuer to call the bond at the time of the step-up by paying a slight premium over par. Thus, if the stock price has not risen above the conversion price investors would not convert and they would have sacrificed a few years of below market rate yields on their SIRENs.

What Are the Risks of Convertibles?

As with any debt security, investors are concerned about the *risks of default*. This is especially so for convertible bonds, which tend to be subordinated to the issuing firm's other debt securities. Convertible bonds are, therefore, not as safe as the company's senior debt and in the event of bankruptcy, convertible bondholders may only receive a fraction of their invested principal at best.

In addition to default risk, there is *interest rate risk*. Being a fixed income security with coupon rates that tend to be lower than conventional debt issues, an increase in market rates of interest will cause a greater decline in the price of convertible issues than nonconvertible bonds.

Generally, high interest rates tend to depress stock market prices, and the convertible bond is doubly cursed if the issuing company's stock is depressed. Stock prices and stock markets can be both uncertain and volatile which may not help in the appreciation of the convertible.

Convertible bonds mostly have call provisions and so there is always the *risk of call*. Bonds are generally called by corporations when interest rates decline so that the corporations can issue new bonds at lower coupon rates and save money.

How to Buy and Sell Convertible Securities

Convertible bonds may be bought and sold in the same way as corporate bonds. New issues may be bought through the underwriter or participating syndicate broker, in which case the investor will not be charged a commission.

Convertible securities trading on the secondary market may be purchased (sold) through full service brokerage firms, discount brokers and brokerage services offered by banks. Most of the convertible bonds are listed on the over-the-counter markets while the convertible bonds of the larger, better known companies are listed on the New York Bond Exchange. The same applies to convertible preferred stocks-listings on the New York Stock Exchange, American Stock Exchange, and the over-the-counter markets.

Brokerage fees charged for purchasing convertible bonds are similar to those charged for buying regular bonds. Commissions charged per bond could vary depending on several factors such as the number of convertible bonds purchased, the total value of the purchase, the type of broker (full service or discount). It is important to shop around to find the lowest commissions and dealer spreads before buying.

Fees for convertible preferred stock would be similar to buying common stocks. Fees would be higher for purchasing in odd lots (less than 100 shares for the higher priced convertible preferred stocks).

Information on convertible securities can be found in: the weekly *Value Line Convertibles Report* put out by Value Line Investment Survey; the sections on convertible bonds in the Standard & Poor's Bond Guide and Moody's Bond Record; convertible preferred stocks in the Standard & Poor's Stock Guide; as well as research information from brokerage companies. Merrill Lynch publishes *Convertible Securities*, a comprehensive monthly report on existing convertible bonds, convertible preferred stock, and many of the combination convertible securities.

What Are the Advantages
of Convertible Securities?

◆ Experienced investors can use convertible securities to hedge against fluctuations in market prices. Hedging is the buying of one security and simultaneously selling short the related security. For example, buying the convertible and selling short the related stock can result in at worst a small loss or at best profits with fluctuations in the market price of the stock.

◆ Convertible securities offer the upside potential of capital gains through the appreciation of common stock and the downside protection if the market price of the common stock falls below the conversion value, in that the convertible will be valued at no less than as a straight bond/preferred stock.

◆ Interest (dividends) received on convertible bonds (preferred stock) generally exceeds the dividends paid by comparable common stock. Some corporations that have convertible securities may not pay dividends on their common stock and corporations could easily eliminate them if they have a drop in earnings. Failure to pay interest on debt, however, would force the company into bankruptcy.

◆ Convertible securities offer some protection against inflation since the market price of both common stock and convertible bonds rise with inflation. However, if conversion does not take place—when the market price of the common stock does not rise above the conversion value—investors have no protection from inflation as interest/dividends received on convertible securities are fixed.

What Are the Disadvantages
of Convertible Securities?

◆ Yields on convertible securities are often lower than yields on straight bonds.

◆ In the event of liquidation, convertible bonds are subordinated to the other debt of the issuing corporation on their claims to assets. Convertible preferred shareholders would be paid after creditors but before common shareholders. Risk would depend on the overall strength of the issuing company.

◆ Convertible securities, like all fixed income securities, are sensitive to changes in interest rates. The price of convertible securities will fluctuate with changes in market rates of interest.

◆ When market interest rates fall, there is an increased risk that the convertible bonds will be called by the issuing company. The issuing company can then refinance their convertibles with cheaper debt.

◆ Investors may face the risks of dilution of the common stock of the company. This occurs when the value of the common stock decreases due to an increase in the number of common shares outstanding through conversion or new issues of common stock.

◆ In the event of a leveraged buy out of the issuing company, investors may end up with a non-convertible security which has a lower yield than the company's other debt.

Caveats

◆ Do not buy convertible securities unless you are willing to buy that company's common stock. If the convertible security is never converted to common stock, the interest received on the convertible will be less than if you had invested in a regular bond.

◆ Be wary of buying convertibles which are trading at high premiums over both the market values of the common stock and/or the callable price of the convertibles.

◆ Check the provisions of the convertibles before you buy, such as whether there is a sinking fund that will allow the issuing company to redeem a specific number of convertibles each year, the call price, etc.

Are Convertible Securities Suitable for Me?

Convertible securities offer the potential for both appreciation and a steady stream of income, but they may not be the best of both worlds. They certainly allow the investor to hedge their bets in both the debt and the equities markets. However, in certain conditions, they may not be the best investments, and investors would have been better off owning either regular debt or equity.

Generally, convertible securities will do well when interest rates are falling and the stock market is rising. This was the case in 1992 when convertible securities outperformed the stock market indices. However, on an individual basis, much will depend on the fundamentals of the issuing company of the convertible. If investors like the common stock of a particular company but they are not sure if the stock market is going to fall, they could buy the convertible, which will not fall as much in price as the common stock would. The convertible holders would receive regular income even if the stock price does decline.

However, if the stock price of the company goes up, investors will not do as well with convertibles as they would have had they bought the stock instead of the convertible.

The downside of convertibles is that they can be complicated in structure with call provisions which could result in holders losing money if they had bought the convertibles at a premium. Similarly, if convertibles are not converted investors generally would have been better with regular bonds which tend to pay higher coupons.

Convertible securities are suited to investors who have the knowledge of the workings and intricacies of these specialized securities who can hedge their bets in the bond and equity markets.

References

Bary, Andrew. "Trading Points." *Barron's*, February 8, 1993.

Faerber, Esmé. *Managing Your Investments, Savings, and Credit.* Chicago: Probus Publishing Co., 1992.

Chapter 10

Zero-Coupon Bonds

Key Concepts

◆ The relationships influencing the price of zero-coupon bonds

◆ The different types of zero-coupon bonds

◆ The risks of zero-coupon bonds

◆ How to buy and sell zero-coupon bonds

◆ The advantages of zero-coupon bonds

◆ The disadvantages of zero-coupon bonds

◆ Caveats

◆ Conclusion

Zero-coupon bonds are debt securities that are issued at deep discounts from their face values. They pay no periodic interest but are redeemed at face value ($1,000) at maturity. For example, a 10-year zero-coupon bond (with a face value of $1,000) yielding eight percent would cost about $463 at issuance. In other words, the investor of this zero-coupon bond will buy it for $463, receive no interim interest payments and at the end of the tenth year receive $1,000, the face value of the bond. As zero-coupon bonds do not pay interest, they do not have a current yield like regular bonds.

The price of a zero-coupon bond is the present value of the face value of the bond at the maturity date discounted at a particular rate of return. Looked at in another way, the investor's funds grow from $463 to $1,000 in 10 years. The initial price is compounded at a particular rate of interest to equal $1,000 in 10 years.

The rate of return or yield on a zero-coupon bond can be solved either mathematically, or using compound interest tables or a financial calculator.

The yield equation is:

Zero–Coupon Bond Price $(1 + i)^n$ = Face Value at Maturity

where i = yield
       n = periods to maturity

In this example, i is 8%:

$$\$463 \, (1 + i)^{10} = 1{,}000$$

$$(1 + i)^{10} = \frac{1{,}000}{463}$$

$$i = 8\%$$

Knowing what the yield is on the bond is helpful not only for federal tax purposes but also for calculating the price of the bond. Even though the bondholder will receive no interest payments, the bondholder is required to pay federal income taxes on the accrued interest as if it had been paid. For instance, in the example above, the accrued interest for the first year is $37.04:

$$\text{Interest} = \$463 \times .08$$

$$= \$37.04$$

The zero-coupon bondholder will pay taxes on this $37.04 even though it has not been received, thus creating a negative cash flow for this investor. In other words, the bondholder will pay out of pocket cash for the taxes and will not have received the $37.04. Instead, the interest is added to the principal price of the zero-coupon bond so that at the end of the first year, the price of the bond increases to $500.04 ($463 + 37.04).

The accrued interest for year two is $40.00:

$$\text{Interest} = \$500.04 \times .08$$

$$= \$40.00$$

The adjusted price of the bond at the end of the second year is $540.04 ($500.04 + 40.00). Theoretically, the price will rise with the accrued interest until the price reaches $1,000 at maturity. This is illustrated in the graph in Exhibit 10-1. As you will see, there are other factors which affect the price of the zero-coupon bond.

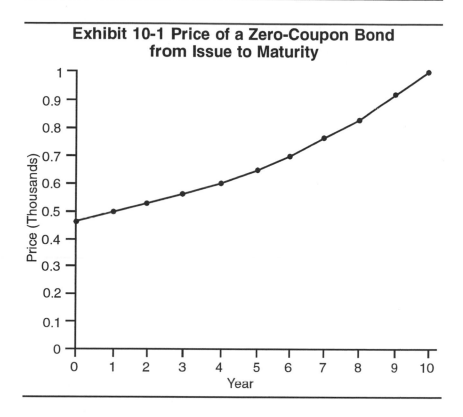

**Exhibit 10-1 Price of a Zero-Coupon Bond
from Issue to Maturity**

Due to the negative cash flows during the life of the bond from paying taxes on accrued (phantom) interest, zero-coupon bonds are better suited in investment accounts which are not subject to taxes. These are pension funds, IRAs (independent retirement accounts), keoughs, and SEP accounts. In these plans, accrued interest is taxed only when the funds are withdrawn. Municipal zero-coupon bonds alleviate the tax problems of zero-coupon bonds.

Zero-coupon bonds have advantages when purchased for minor children because of the low dollar costs of the bonds. However, you need to consider the total income for the child to see if it is worthwhile. Minor children may be exempt from the phantom interest tax payments, if their total passive income is less than a threshold amount ($600 for 1992). Phantom interest is taxed at the child's low marginal tax rate for income between certain amounts ($600 and $1,200 for 1992). For higher incomes the phantom interest on a bond would be taxed at the parent's marginal tax rate, which may make investing in other investments a better alternative. The Internal Revenue Tax Code is constantly changing and investors should keep up with the changes, especially with regard to the effects on the different investment instruments. Thus, in certain instances, zero-coupon bonds are not advantageous because of the negative cash flows and the complexities of calculating the interest for tax purposes.

The Relationships Influencing the Price of Zero-Coupon Bonds

The quality of the bond, the length of time to maturity, the call provision, and the yield will all affect the price of the zero-coupon bond. The *quality* of the zero-coupon bond is important since the return depends on:

◆ the issuer's ability to redeem them at maturity,

◆ or the investor's ability to sell them before maturity at a higher price than their purchase price.

A zero-coupon bondholder has more to lose in the event of a default than a conventional bond, because with the latter, the bondholder would have received some interest payments which could have been reinvested.

The quality of a zero-coupon bond is an assessment of the issuer's ability to pay off the bondholder at maturity. A good quality zero-coupon bond has less risk of default than a speculative, low quality zero-coupon bond. Investors will be willing to pay more for a good quality bond. Thus, there is a positive relationship between *quality* and *price*.

Ratings assigned by the ratings agencies such as Moody's, and Standard & Poor's are a yardstick as to the credit quality, but you should always be aware that these are subject to change.

The quality of a zero-coupon bond is also related to the *yield*. A low quality zero-coupon bond will offer a higher yield than a good quality zero-coupon bond to entice investors. The flip side of the coin is that investors will pay less for a low quality zero-coupon bond than a high quality zero-coupon bond. Price is, therefore, inversely related to yield.

However, the yield is also related to the *length of time to maturity*. The longer the maturity, the lower the price and the higher the yield.

This is because the zero-coupon bondholder will only get the interest payment at maturity (or an accrued amount built into the sale price before maturity).

Besides the length of time to maturity and the quality of the issue, zero-coupon prices are sensitive to the fluctuations in interest rates. The purchase price of a zero-coupon bond determines the yield over the life of the security, because interest is only paid at maturity and interest accrues at that fixed yield. If market rates of interest go up above the fixed yield of the zero-coupon bond, investors will want to sell their zero-coupon bonds and reinvest at higher rates. This has the effect of depressing the price of the zero-coupon bond more than a conventional type bond which pays interest annually or semi-annually. If you recall the concept of duration discussed in Chapter 2, you will see why zero-coupon bonds are more volatile in price than regular fixed interest payment bonds. Zero-coupon bonds will have a higher duration than a conventional bond of similar maturity and yield, because the holder does not receive any interest payments until the zero-coupon bond matures. Similarly, when interest rates fall, zero-coupon bonds will appreciate more than existing conventional bonds due to the fixed yield on the zero-coupon bond.

Market factors also have a bearing on price. An actively traded zero-coupon bond will be priced differently than an inactively traded zero-coupon bond with the same maturity and yield.

The Different Types of Zero-Coupon Bonds

Besides conventional zero-coupon bonds issued by corporations and government entities, there are many different types of zero-coupon bonds. Derivative zero-coupon bonds were constructed by several brokerage houses during the early 1980s, primarily for use in retirement accounts. These are called derivative securities because they are derived from another underlying security.

Stripped Government Securities

In 1982, Salomon Brothers and Merrill Lynch both created *zero-coupon Treasury securities*. To create their respective securities, the brokerage firms bought long term U.S. Treasury bonds and held them in escrow. They then sold zero-coupon bonds representing an ownership interest in the underlying Treasury bonds and their interest payments. These securities were created by stripping the coupon payments on the U.S. Treasury bonds. An important distinction to make with stripped zero-coupon securities is that they are not backed by the faith and credit of the U.S. Treasury. It is true that Treasury bonds are backed by the faith and credit of the U.S. government, but the zero-coupon securities are merely the products of the brokerage houses.

Salomon's product was marketed under the name CATS (Certificates of Accrual on Treasury Securities) and Merrill Lynch's stripped zero-coupon security went under the name TIGRs (Treasury Income Growth Receipts). Other brokerage firms followed with their stripped zero-coupon securities under other feline acronyms.

The major disadvantage to these stripped zero-coupon securities of the brokerage firms is the lack of liquidity. The securities of one brokerage firm are not traded by competing dealers and so to improve liquidity of the stripped zero-coupon bonds, a group of primary dealers in the Treasury bond market decided to issue generic securities. These are called "Treasury Receipts" which are not associated with any of the participating dealers (Fabozzi and Fabozzi 1989).

In 1985, the U.S. Treasury announced its own STRIP (Separate Trading of Registered Interest and Principal) program. Designated Treasury bonds could be stripped to create zero-coupon Treasury bonds. Since these are the direct obligations of the U.S. government, they tend to have slightly lower yields than the brokerage firm's stripped zero-coupon securities. Moreover, the Treasury's STRIP securities offer greater marketability than the generics offered by the brokerage firms.

Salomon Brothers created stripped federal agency zero-coupon bonds in the late 1980s. Salomon purchased $750 million FICO bonds, stripped them of their interest, and sold them as zero-coupon FICO strips. FICO was created by Congress for the purpose of raising money for the financially strapped Federal Savings and Loan Insurance Corporation (FSLIC).

The FICO zeros are not assigned credit ratings by the rating companies but are believed to be relatively safe because of Congress' commitment to FICO and the FSLIC. Hence, yield on FICO zeros are slightly higher than those on Treasury strips. FICO strips may be bought through brokers and trade over the counter in the secondary market.

Mortgage-Backed Zero-Coupon Bonds

Mortgage backed zero-coupon securities were referred to in the chapter on agency bonds in the CMO section. These zeros are backed by Ginnie Mae, Fannie Mae, and Freddie Mac securities as well as the collateral of the real estate on the mortgages. Due to the prepayment risk, investors may find that these zeros may be paid off before their stated maturities.

Municipal Zero-Coupon Bonds

These are issued by state and local governments and are advantageous in that the accrued interest is exempt from federal income taxes and generally from state taxes in the state where issued.

Municipal zero-coupon bonds come in two types: *general obligation zero-coupon bonds* issued by states and *project zero-coupon bonds* issued by highway authorities for highway projects, public power projects for sewer systems, and other municipal projects. General obligation issues are backed by the taxing power of the states issuing them, whereas project securities are backed by the revenues generated from the projects. Hence, project zero-coupon bonds are less secure.

You should check the quality of the issue before buying. There are so many good quality zero-coupon municipal issues that investors need not settle for lower quality issues. This point is especially relevant for long-term issues (over 15 years to maturity) where anything could happen to affect the issuer's ability to repay the bonds. Investors should, therefore, stick to issues with ratings of not less than AA. For better quality zeros investors will sacrifice slightly on yields.

Many municipal zero-coupon issues are callable, and investors should check the call provisions before buying. If there is a choice between a callable and a non-callable issue of similar quality and maturity, avoid the callable issue.

The call price and date listed in the bond's indenture is important. For example, the call price could be above par, at par, less than the par price, or it could also be at a price that is less than the yield to maturity.

The call provision could be extremely disadvantageous, so it is wise to check it out before buying. Some issues have a serial call, which means that some bonds can be called earlier than others in the issue.

Although municipal zero-coupon bonds are exempt form federal income taxes, investors may want to find out how their states tax the accrued interest on the securities. Some states tax the phantom interest as it accrues and others tax the interest at maturity or when the securities are sold. Investors can get the information from their particular State Revenue offices. Before selling a zero-coupon bond, investors should consult with their tax advisors or accountants as to the tax consequences of gains and losses.

Zero-Coupon Convertible Bonds

Zero-coupon convertible bonds were hot products during the late 1980s but have become a dying breed in the early 1990s (Mitchell 1993). These are deeply discounted bonds with conversion provisions. Their yields tend to be lower than those of conventional bonds, and they don't pay out annual interest. Holders are required to accrue interest for federal tax purposes, and like regular zero-coupon bonds they are suitable for tax-deferred accounts such as IRAs and pension plans.

Like convertible bonds, these can be exchanged into a predetermined number of the issuing corporation's common stock. Some zero-coupon convertibles have put options which allow the holders to sell their securities back to the issuer at the original issue price plus accrued interest after a certain date (usually five or 10 years). Everything seemed to be terrific from the investor's standpoint and the brokerage firms led by Merrill Lynch promoted these securities aggressively.

Merrill Lynch called their securities LYONs (liquid yield option notes). However, declining interest rates coupled with the call provisions on many zero-coupon convertible securities have worked to the detriment of investors. Walt Disney's zero-coupon convertible securities scheduled to mature in the year 2005 have been called at a price which is lower than what many investors bought at in the secondary market. The conversion feature has not helped the holders of the Disney convertibles because, the securities were tied to Euro Disney stock, traded on the Paris Exchange, which has been depressed and trading below the conversion price.

Other companies, such as MCI Communications, Inc., Sonat Co., Carnival Cruise Lines, and Berkshire Hathaway Co., have redeemed their LYONs. It is cheaper for these companies to refund the issues and issue new regular bonds due to the sharp decline in interest rates (Mitchell 1993).

The advantage of zero-coupon convertible bonds is the upside potential for appreciation if the common stock rises above the conversion price.

To counter the disadvantage of negative cash flows due to the federal taxation of phantom interest, many municipalities have issued *zero-coupon convertible municipal issues*. These have been sold under different acronyms: FIGS (future income and growth securities), BIGS (bond income and growth securities), PACS (principal appreciation conversion securities) and TEDIS (tax-exempt discount and income securities).

These are much the same as regular zero-coupon convertible securities except for the exemption of accrued interest from federal taxes. However, state taxes may be applicable on the accrued interest and the quality of the issue is, of course, dependent on the financial position of the issuing municipality. These, unfortunately, may also contain call provisions and they fluctuate in price in relation to changes in market rates of interest and other factors.

What Are the Risks of Zero-Coupon Bonds?

The *risk of default* depends on the financial position of the issuer and is of great importance to the zero-coupon bondholder. This is because the interest and principal is made in a single payment at maturity and if the issuer is not able to make this single payment the holder may receive a large zero. With regular bonds, the holder would have received some interest payments. Consequently, the quality of the zero-coupon bond is an assessment of the likelihood of the issuer's ability to be able to pay off the bondholder at maturity. The risk of default can be lessened by choosing high quality zero-coupon bond issues and/or government stripped bonds.

Zero-coupon bonds are also subject to *interest rate risk*. When market rates of interest rise (or fall), zero-coupon bonds, like regular bonds, fall (or rise) in price. However, zero-coupon prices tend to be more volatile than those of regular bonds. This is again due to the fact that the entire amount that the investor receives is a single payment at maturity, whereas for regular fixed interest bearing bonds the price is the discounted cash flows of the interest payments and the principal at maturity. Generally, with fixed interest paying bonds, the lower the coupon rate of the bond the greater the price volatility due to changes in market rates of interest. This then explains the price volatility of zero-coupon bonds, which have no coupon payments. Some zero-coupon bonds will be more volatile in price than other similar yielding zeros as a result of different trading activity, quality differences, call features, and length of time to maturity.

With the decline in interest rates from 1992 to 1993, many outstanding bond issues have been called. Zero-coupon bonds are no exception. They too have call provisions and many have been called. This is the lesson many zero-coupon bondholders have learned the hard way. When interest rates decline, higher yielding zero-coupon bonds appreciate significantly due to the fact that these bonds are locked into an above market rate yield. However, the issuers are not thrilled at paying above market rates, and if their bonds have call provisions they will call them.

Even issuers of zero-coupon bonds without call provisions have tried their luck. Transamerica Finance Corporation issued zero-coupon bonds in 1982 with a yield of 13 percent with maturities from 2007 to the year 2012. Due to the high yield of these zero-coupon bonds in an economic environment with significantly lower interest rates, these bonds have appreciated in price. Because these bonds were not issued with call provisions, the most that the company could do was send out letters to the bondholders to try and entice them to turn in their bonds. However, Transamerica offered such a low price (they were willing to pay 40 percent of the current market price) that most investors did not fall for the trick. This shows the extent that issuers will go to get rid of higher yielding bonds. Thus, if zeros have call provisions, they are subject to call risk, and because Transamerica's bonds were not callable they could not redeem them early. To avoid the risks of call, buy noncallable issues (Bary 1993).

Zero-coupon bonds have no *reinvestment risk* because the yield is determined by the purchase price and then locked in over the life of the bond. With a regular coupon bond, the holder will be faced with the uncertainty of having to reinvest the interest payments at fluctuating market rates of interest. Moreover, the disadvantage is when interest rates rise, zero-coupon bondholders are locked in to their existing lower yields.

How to Buy and Sell Zero-Coupon Bonds

Zero-coupon bonds may be purchased in the primary market at issue (in other words, a new issue to the market). Investors who buy these new issues from the brokerage firms underwriting the issue will avoid paying commissions or fees.

Existing zero-coupon bonds trading in the secondary markets may be bought through securities brokers, dealers, and banks. Brokers charge fees or commissions which can be relatively high for zero-coupon securities, bearing in mind that investors are investing smaller amounts of money (due to the deep discounts) than they would for the same number of regular bonds. These commissions vary considerably from broker to broker and you should not be deceived if your broker announces that his/her firm does not charge a fee or commission. Very often the markups, which include the commissions on zero-coupon bonds, are quite high, as prices on the same zero-coupon bonds can vary considerably at different brokerage firms.

Some brokerage firms may make a market in certain zero-coupon issues. The prices that these are bought and sold at will be determined by the brokerage firm and the conditions on the market. Consequently, the investor may not pay a commission but the size of the markup will determine whether the investor is getting a break.

It is important to shop around at different brokerage firms for the best prices when buying and selling zero-coupon securities. Many brokerage firms have inventories of different zero-coupon issues, and they may be more competitively priced. If the issue is quoted in the newspapers, you have some yardstick in terms of price. Most zero-coupon issues are traded over-the-counter, but there are some issues that are quoted on the New York Bond Exchange.

You should be aware that when buying zero-coupon issues from sponsoring brokerage houses at issue, these brokerage houses are not required or obligated to make a market in these issues.

The high transaction costs on zero-coupon issues make them less liquid than other fixed income securities and, consequently, they are more suited to a buy and hold strategy. By holding zeros to maturity, investors will improve their returns.

Rather than buy individual zero-coupon issues, investors may choose to put their money into mutual funds that specialize in zero-coupon bonds. As with all mutual funds, fees are deducted from the earnings (and/or the net assets) of the funds and can be quite high.

Advantages of Zero-Coupon Bonds

◆ Zero-coupon bonds appreciate more than conventional fixed income securities when interest rates decline. Of course, the opposite is true when market rates of interest go up—prices of zero-coupon bonds will decline more than those of conventional bonds.

◆ Investments in zero-coupon bonds require less of a capital outflow than other fixed income securities, as they are sold at a deep discount. For example, a purchase of 10 regular bonds at face value requires an outlay of $10,000, whereas 10 zero-coupon bonds selling at $180 require capital of $1,800.

◆ Investors need not be concerned with reinvestment risk. With zero-coupon bonds there is no coupon to reinvest at unpredictable market rates of interest.

◆ Zero-coupon bonds have fixed yields when held to maturity and provide predictable payments. Nearly all zero-coupon bonds have a maturity value of $1,000 per bond.

◆ There are so many existing zero-coupon bond issues on the market to choose from that investors may ladder their maturities to provide regular cash flows.

◆ There are different types of zero-coupon bonds with special features which make them attractive investment vehicles for investors with specific needs.

◆ Zero-coupon bonds are excellent vehicles for IRAs, Keogh accounts and pension plans due to their tax-deferred growth and predictable amounts at maturity.

Disadvantages of Zero-Coupon Bonds

◆ The tax consequences of paying taxes annually on accrued (phantom) interest which is not received until maturity creates a negative cash flow.

◆ Zero-coupon bond prices are extremely volatile: when market rates of interest rise, zero-coupon bond prices may plunge significantly, resulting in large capital losses should the investor be forced to sell.

◆ When interest rates do go up, investors in zero-coupon bonds are not able to benefit because they are locked into a lower rate, and there is no coupon interest to reinvest.

◆ Many zero-coupon bonds have call provisions which allow the issuers to redeem them before maturity.

◆ If a zero-coupon bond issuer defaults, investors have more to lose than on conventional bonds, because with the latter, they would have received some interest which could have been reinvested.

◆ Commissions and/or markups tend to be higher (percentage wise) on zero-coupon bonds, making them less liquid than other fixed income securities.

◆ Certain zero-coupon bonds may not be as marketable as other conventional fixed income securities.

Caveats

When investing in zero-coupon bonds, outside of tax-deferred accounts such as IRAs, Keoghs and pension accounts, investors should be aware of the tax consequences. They can be quite complicated and it might necessitate the hiring of an accountant or tax professional to compute investors' tax liabilities. The Internal Revenue Service publishes two free guides which are quite helpful in determining the tax liability on zero-coupon bonds. These are IRS Publication 550 on "Investment Income and Expense," and IRS Publication 1212, "List of Original Issue Discount Obligations."

When computing the tax consequences of a zero-coupon bond, you should know what the yield is and when the security was issued. The latter point is important because the computation for the phantom interest will be different for zero-coupon bonds issued before December 31, 1984, than for those issued after that date.

If your tax situation is relatively uncomplicated and you do not think that you could cope figuring the tax liability yourself as a result of investing in zero-coupon bonds, and that you would have to hire a tax accountant, you would be better off investing in other fixed income investments.

Conclusion

Zero-coupon bonds are excellent investment vehicles for tax deferred accounts in that they provide a lump sum of money at a future date. When used for investment purposes outside of tax-deferred accounts, investors face the disadvantage of negative cash flows due to the taxation of phantom interest. For some investors, this is not a serious disadvantage and the other features of zero-coupon bonds are more important. Because of their volatility, zero-coupon bonds can provide aggressive rates of growth when interest rates decline. Those investors who do not successfully guess the direction of interest rates should be prepared to hold onto their bonds to maturity.

If investors plan to buy and sell zero-coupon bonds without holding them to maturity, they may be better off buying zero-coupon mutual funds. This will avoid the high transaction costs which can eat into profits and reduce yields.

To determine whether zero-coupon bonds should be purchased over Treasury bonds, you should compare the yields on similar maturities. If the difference is not significant, you may be better off with Treasury bonds, which have no default risk and are much more liquid and marketable.

A good strategy for investing in zero-coupon bonds is to buy good quality bonds with different maturities which will average the interest rate spread and hold them to maturity.

References

Bary, Andrew. "Trading Points." *Barron's*, March 15, 1993, page 57.

Fabozzi, Frank J. and T. Dessa Fabozzi. "Survey of Bonds and Mortgage-Backed Securities," in *Portfolio and Investment Management*. Edited by Frank J. Fabozzi. Chicago: Probus Publishing Co., 1989.

Mitchell, Constance. "Are LYONS becoming a Dying Breed?" *Wall Street Journal*, March 8, 1993, page C1.

Chapter 11
Fixed Income Mutual Funds

Key Concepts

◆ How mutual funds work

◆ The different types of bond funds

◆ How performance affects the choice of a mutual fund

◆ The significance of the prospectus

◆ The tax consequences of buying and selling shares

◆ The risks of mutual funds

◆ How to buy and sell mutual funds

◆ The advantages of mutual funds

◆ The disadvantages of mutual funds

◆ Caveats

◆ Whether to invest in individual bonds or mutual funds

In some respects, mutual funds have come close to being the ideal investment for millions of investors. Many of these investors are able to move their money in and out of different types of mutual funds just as portfolio managers would when overseeing a large portfolio. Mutual funds have allowed investors who do not have the time, knowledge, or expertise of different financial instruments to invest their money in stock, bonds, and money market funds.

Since the early 1980s, the number of mutual funds has grown rapidly to the point where quotations of mutual fund prices now occupy more than two full pages in the *Wall Street Journal*. The fact that there are more mutual funds than companies listed on the New York Stock Exchange means that investors should be as careful in selecting mutual funds as they are in investing in individual stocks and bonds.

Moreover, the management companies of these mutual funds compete very aggressively for investor's dollars. This is evidenced by all the print advertising in newspapers and magazines as well as the use of television to ensure that the mutual funds are seen and heard.

This increase in the clutter of "infomercials" compounds the complexity of the investor's decision as to which mutual fund to choose. The decision becomes more difficult for investors who take the advertising messages literally without reading the fine print and stepping back to analyze the investment objectives of the fund.

According to the advertisements, there appear to be no loser funds, only funds that are "number one" in something, or funds that have had remarkable yields. If the fine print is read, many of the funds may have achieved that yield for one week, or one month period, or achieved number one status in a limited setting. In fact, being number one at one point does not mean that the fund is assured of a rosy future. For example, the number one position may have been achieved by an exceptional manager who has long since left the fund. Results as reported by Lipper Analytical Services, Inc. show that poor performing funds can at some stage or another rank as number one performers for a short period of time. According to the editor of *Morningstar Mutual Funds,* a Chicago newsletter, virtually any fund can achieve number one status in something at a point in time (Clements 1993).

A high yield that is quoted may present only half the picture. A fund could earn a high yield, but the total return may be negative because of a decline in the fund's share price.

The advertisements do not include the fees charged by their funds. If investors pick a fund that is number one in something once upon a time, and had a wonderful yield, they will assume that they have invested wisely. Well, the fund that they may have chosen could, in essence, be a poor performer. Fees charged by that fund could be higher than those charged by other mutual funds in the same category of investments. Needless to say, that fund may have chosen riskier investment assets which may make that fund's share price more volatile.

Many investors are so confused that they turn to one of the many newsletters on the market. The hype from some of advertisements of these advisory newsletters may overwhelm investors and make the choice of a newsletter even more complex than the choice of a mutual fund. Some newsletters go so far as to predict the returns for certain funds into the future (Savage 1993).

Of course, the aim is to get investors to subscribe to the newsletter, so the messages promoted by many of them use a combination of hyperbole and fear to move investors in that direction. Implying that investors will choose the wrong fund makes investors even more unsure about choosing a fund. For example, currently, mutual fund advisory letters are touting gold and strategic metal funds, which outperformed all other funds in the first quarter of 1993. Needless to say, gold funds had the worst returns for the two years prior to this quarter when most of the newsletters were touting other types of funds.

For investors who are so confused that they are in a state of paralysis as to how to invest their money, there are *wrap accounts* which are advertised to answer the concerns of investors who don't know how to manage their money. These are offered by all the major brokerage firms and for an all inclusive flat fee, they will manage your investments by diversifying into stocks, bonds and money market accounts. Sounds ideal!

Many investors have been jolted to reality by the fees charged for some of these wrap accounts. Some wrap accounts have high annual fees which are not all-inclusive. This means that it does not include the management of their cash accounts. An additional fee is charged to manage money market and cash accounts, which in today's economic environment of low interest rates means that investors are losing money on their cash funds. Not all investors like to be fully invested in stocks and bonds. This means that their money in cash accounts may be earning only 2.9 percent per annum. With a two percent annual management fee levied, investors will earn negative rates of return after paying taxes and adjusting for inflation.

Performance is another widely touted reason for investing in brokerage firm's wrap account. However, many of the brokerage firms do not include their fees when factoring in their performance. This can make quite a difference to the actual performance of the account when investors find that they will be earning ±2 to 3 percent less than the advertised rate.

The high cost and the equivocal performance of many wrap accounts should also make investors think twice before jumping into these without a careful analysis. Besides cost and performance, investors should also look at potential conflicts of interest in the management of the wrap accounts. For example, does the broker favor securities underwritten by the same brokerage firm when choosing investment securities? (Schultz 1993).

The author is in agreement that it is confusing for investors to choose a mutual fund especially when there are over 4,000 of them available on the market. Moreover, investors may be equally confused by all of the conflicting advice and predictions offered by many of the newsletters. Consequently, the author's advice is to go back to the basics of investments:

◆ understand how mutual funds work;

◆ understand the basics of the types of investments that the fund invests in; and

◆ evaluate the performance of the fund from the prospectus.

By following these steps, investors will be able to narrow their choices of the different types of funds and then they will be in a better position to make a decision as to the overall choice of fund.

How Do Mutual Funds Work?

All mutual funds work in similar ways. A mutual fund makes investments on behalf of the investors in that fund. The money from investors is pooled, which allows the fund to diversify their acquisition of different securities such as stocks for stock funds and bonds for bond funds. The type of investments chosen is determined by the *objectives* of the mutual fund. For example, if a bond fund's objectives are to provide tax-free income, the fund will invest in municipal bonds. The fund will buy different municipal bond issues to achieve a diversified portfolio which will also reduce the risks of loss due to default.

When these securities pay out their interest, fundholders get a proportionate share. Thus, an investor who invests $1,000 will get the same rate of return as another investor who invested $100,000 in the fund.

When the prices of the securities fluctuate up or down, the total value of the fund is affected. These fluctuations in price are due to many different factors, such as the intrinsic risk of the types of securities in the portfolio, economic, market, and political factors. The objectives of the fund are important because they will indicate the type and quality of the investments the fund will choose. From these objectives, investors are better able to assess the risks the fund is willing to take to improve income (return) and/or capital gains. See Table 11–1 for a classification of fixed income securities by investment objectives.

Investors invest their money in mutual funds by buying shares at the net asset value (NAV). The fund's net asset value price of the shares is the total assets minus the liabilities of the fund divided by the number of outstanding shares.

It is easy for a fund to determine the market value of their assets at the end of each trading day. For instance, if the fund is a balanced fund, which means that it is invested in both common stocks and bonds, the investment company would find out the closing prices of the stocks and bonds for the day and multiply them by the number of shares of stocks and the number of bonds that the fund owns. These are added up and any liabilities (for example, accrued fees) that the fund has is subtracted. The resulting total is then divided by the number of shares outstanding to give the net asset value price per share. A numerical example illustrates the process as follows:

Market Value of Stocks and Bonds	$5,000,000
Minus Total Liabilities	- 150,000
Net Worth	$4,850,000
Number of Shares Outstanding	750,000
Net Asset Value	$ 6.466 (4,850,000/750,000)

The net asset value may change every day due to the market fluctuation of the stock and bond prices. The net asset value is important for two reasons:

◆ this is the price that is used to determine the value of the investor's holding in the mutual fund (number of shares held multiplied by the net asset value price per share); and

◆ this is the price that new shares are purchased at or redeemed at when selling shares in the fund.

The net asset values of the different funds are quoted in the daily newspapers. Table 11-2 shows how mutual funds are listed in the newspapers. Some of the funds in two families of funds (Vanguard and Westcore) are shown for illustrative purposes.

In the Vanguard Group, the GNMA (Ginnie Mae) fund which invests in bonds (as opposed to the STAR fund which invests in stocks and bonds) has a net asset value of $10.53 per share. The investment objectives column indicates the types of investments a fund will invest in. A NL in the offer price column signifies that the fund is a no-load fund which means that investors can buy and sell shares at the net asset value of $10.53. The net asset value change column signifies the

Table 11–1 Types of Fixed Income Funds

Funds	Objectives
Corporate Bond Funds	Seek high levels of income. Invest in corporate bonds, Treasury bonds, and agency bonds.
High Yield Bond Funds	Seek higher yields by investing in less than investment grade bonds (junk bonds).
Municipal Bond Funds Long-Term Maturities	Seek income that is exempt from federal income taxes. Invest in bonds issued by state and local governments with long maturities.
Municipal Bond Funds Intermediate-Term Maturities	Seek income that is exempt from federal income taxes. Invest in bonds issued by state and local governments with intermediate-term maturities.
Municipal Bond Funds Short-Term Maturities	Invest in municipal securities with relatively short maturities. These are also known as tax exempt money market funds.
U.S. Government Income Funds	Invest in different types of government securities such as Treasury securities, agency securities and federally backed mortgage backed securities.
GNMA Funds	Invest in Government National Mortgage Association securities and other mortgage backed securities.
Global Income Funds	Invest in the bonds of companies and countries worldwide including those in the U.S.
Money Market Funds	Invest in money market securities with relatively short maturities.

Table 11–2 Mutual Fund Quotations

	Inv. Obj.	NAV	Offer Price	NAV Change
Vanguard Group:				
STAR	S&B	13.39	NL	+ 0.07
GNMA	BND	10.53	NL	+ 0.02
IG Corp	BND	9.20	NL	+ 0.02
Westcore:				
GNMA	BND	16.45	17.23	+ 0.02
ST Govt	BST	15.87	16.19	. . .

Source: *Wall Street Journal*

change in price from the previous day's closing price. The Vanguard GNMA fund closed $0.02 up from the previous day's closing price.

The two fund examples in the Westcore Group are load funds since they charge a commission to buy and sell their shares. This is evidenced by the offer price which is different from the net asset value price. To buy shares in Westcore's Short-Term Government Fund, investors would buy at the offer price of $16.19 per share and would sell their shares at the net asset value price ($15.87). The difference ($0.32 per share) between the offer price ($16.19) and the net asset value price ($15.87) represents the load or commission that investors will pay to buy or sell shares in this fund.

Investors may earn money from their mutual funds in three ways:

◆ when interest and/or dividends earned on the fund's investments are passed through to shareholders;

◆ when the fund's management sells investment securities at a profit, the capital gains are passed through to shareholders. If these securities are sold at a loss, the capital loss is offset against the gains of the fund and the net gain or loss is passed through to the shareholders;

◆ when the net asset value per share increases, the value of the shareholder's investment increases.

Investors in funds have the option of having their interest and capital gain payments paid out to them in check form or having them reinvested in the fund. The reinvested funds will be used to purchase additional shares in the fund.

Mutual funds can be open-end or closed-end. With open-end funds the investment company of the fund can issue an unlimited number of shares.

Investors may buy more shares from the mutual fund company or they may sell their shares back to the mutual fund company, which means that the number of shares will increase or decrease respectively. Closed-end funds issue a fixed number of shares, and when all are sold they do not issue more. In other words, they have a fixed capital structure. Closed-end funds are discussed in Chapter 12.

Mutual funds pay no taxes on income derived from their investments. Under the Internal Revenue Code, mutual funds serve as conduits through which the income from the investments is passed to shareholders in the form of interest or dividends and capital gains or losses. Individual investors pay taxes on their income.

Shareholders receive monthly and annual statements showing the interest, dividends, capital gains and losses, and other relevant data that should be retained for tax purposes. In fact, not only is the interest income important for tax purposes, but when investing in different fixed income mutual funds, investors should also keep track of the net asset value prices of the shares purchased and sold. This information will help in the computation of gains and losses when shares are redeemed.

The Different Types of Bond Funds

There are many different types of bond funds and their differences may be significant. The overriding differences between the types of bond funds are that they invest in different sectors of the bond markets. Municipal bond funds are very different from zero-coupon bond funds. Similarly, short term government funds differ from both municipal bond funds and zero-coupon bond funds. The types of securities that funds invest in will determine the risks of the fund, namely the reaction to changes in interest rates, credit quality and the risk of default, length of time to maturity, and the yield of the fund.

Money market funds are the only funds that maintain constant share prices. These are mostly $1 a share and the management company will keep the net asset value at $1 per share. Any expenses or short-term losses from the sale of securities will be deducted from the revenues generated from the investments to keep the share price constant. This is more easily accomplished for funds which invest in money market securities, which are short term, where there is not that much volatility in the prices of the investment assets.

All the other types of bond funds have share prices which fluctuate up and down depending on the value of the assets (investments) of the funds. Certain types of securities fluctuate more in price than other securities. For instance, Ginnie Mae securities will be much more volatile to changes in interest rates than similar maturity Treasury notes and bonds. In order to gauge the extent of the volatility in the mutual fund's price, investors should understand how the different bond securities will react to changes in interest rates.

A conservative investor should be aware that investing in a bond fund composed of junk bonds (high yield bond fund) can fluctuate as much as 50 percent in net asset value price. During the junk bond sell-off, some fund's prices declined by as much as 50 percent. Similarly, in the past there have been occasional sell offs in GNMA bond funds (1981 and 1982) and briefly in the municipal bond market in 1987. Currently, investors in adjustable rate mortgage funds have seen declines in net asset value prices even though interest rates have been declining. This is because homeowners have been refinancing their mortgages. These mortgages are paid back to their holders at 100 percent of their face value, but many funds may have paid a premium for these securities. These losses translate into lower net asset value prices.

Thus, understanding how individual types of bonds react to changes in interest rates will play more or less into how the fund prices will react to these changes. Generally, the higher the risk of the securities, the greater the potential return and the greater the potential loss on the down-side.

Bear in mind that as of this writing interest rates are at a six-year low, which means that bond prices as well as bond mutual fund share prices are at a six-year high. If market rates of interest decline further, the average price of bond funds will appreciate. However, if market rates of interest go up, there could be a sell off in bonds, which means that bond funds of all types will see a decline in price.

To lessen the potential price volatility, investors can invest in shorter maturity bond funds which tend to fluctuate less than longer term maturity funds. Money market funds which have constant share prices have an average maturity of 90 days. This is why money market funds are considered to be safe investments. Short-term funds have maturities of three years or less, which means that there is less volatility in net asset value prices due to changes in interest rates than longer maturity funds. Remember, less risk does not mean no risk. During several months in 1992, two-top rated short-term bond funds chalked up declines in their net asset values. Long-term maturity funds have average maturities in the range of 20 years which will see the greatest fluctuations in price as interest rates change. Fund managers are quick to take advantage of changing rates of interest by either increasing or decreasing the maturities of their investments. For instance, when interest rates are on their way down, fund managers will purchase bond issues with longer maturities which, of course, will increase the yield and the fund's total return.

The credit quality of the investments will have an influence on the price volatility as well as the yield. The lower the ratings of the individual bond issues in the fund, the higher the fluctuations in price and the greater the yields. Because of the many issues held in a bond fund, credit risk does not affect bond funds in the same way as it does when buying individual bond issues. For instance, most individual bond issues account for less than two percent of the total value of the typical large bond fund, which means that a default by the issuer would not have a significant impact on the net asset value price. The exception is the high risk bond fund. This type of fund invests in below investment grade bond issues, namely junk bonds where credit risk and the risk of default may be of greater concern. Investors in these funds are compensated with higher yields for bearing these risks which translate into greater net asset value price volatility.

With market rates of interest currently at a six-year low, many bond fund managers have been looking for exotic types of bond investments to boost their funds' yields. Collateralized mortgage obligations (CMOs) have been scooped up by not only the mortgage funds but also by funds investing in government and corporate bonds (Jereski 1993). Some bond funds hold as much as 15 percent of their assets in CMOs. CMOs have the potential of boosting returns for funds, but because of the complexities of this type of investment, it is difficult to price them on a daily basis.

Inverse floaters, which were described in the chapter on municipal bonds, have mainly been acquired by municipal bond funds to boost their yields. These, too, are difficult to price because of their volatility. In fact, Merrill Lynch, which prices most of the mortgage-backed securities in the market, will not price the volatile instruments (Jereski 1993). How does this affect the shareholder?

At best most shareholders are unaware of the fund's pricing problems and the fact that many funds use the approximate market values to compute their net asset value prices. This means that investors could be buying and selling shares in their bond funds at inexact prices.

By understanding the characteristics of the investments in the fund, shareholders will be better able to guage the extent of the fluctuations in the net asset value of the fund, but if investors/shareholders don't know what the fund is investing in, it becomes harder to anticipate the changes to net asset value prices. Investors don't know what the funds are invested in, if it is not clearly spelled out in the prospectus of the fund. The securities that the funds invest in are listed in the prospectus information, but the type and characteristics of the bonds are not fully disclosed. Hence, an investor might see the number of the bond in a mortgage pool with the coupon rate, but might not see information such as if it is a floating rate bond or a fixed rate bond, the weighted average life of the bond, or which tranche it is in if it is a CMO.

Pricing errors may occur much more frequently in the future because of the following factors:

◆ more complex derivative securities are being held by bond mutual funds;

◆ many bond issues are difficult to price. These are thinly traded issues and junk bonds which are not priced on a daily basis.

Even an error of a few cents in the pricing of the fund's share price can be costly. A few cents multiplied by several million shares outstanding can add up to a significant sum. In November 1992, T. Rowe Price made a mistake in the pricing of their International Bond fund and the investment company asked some shareholders to pay them back due to the three cent a share error (Eaton, 1993).

There is not much that the investor in bond mutual funds can do about this other than to be aware of the potential glitches that could occur in the pricing of their fund's bond investments.

How Does Performance Affect the Choice of Mutual Fund?

The overall performance of a fund pertains to the following:

◆ Yield

◆ Total return

◆ Expenses

As mentioned in the beginning of the chapter, most funds can boast attaining the number one position in some area of performance at some point in time throughout their existence. Similarly, good past performance may not be indicative of good future performance. Some funds that have performed well in the past have had poor performance thereafter. In fact, there are some funds that did well in the past that are no longer in existence today.

It is little wonder that with several thousand mutual funds on the market vying for investor's savings that many of the messages in their advertisements would lead you to believe that they have attained

2 + 2 = 5 performance. Even if funds do well during good times, investors should also examine how these funds have performed during the down markets. Several business magazines track the overall performance records (during up and down markets) of many of the mutual funds and this would be a better yardstick than the advertising messages of the individual mutual funds. *Forbes* magazine publishes annual performance ratings of mutual funds, and from this (or from other publications) investors can see how well bond funds performed in up markets as well as how the funds protected their capital during periods of declining bond prices.

New funds do not have track records and, therefore, investors may not have a yardstick on performance during a period of declining prices. This is especially so for funds that are created during bull markets.

Some organizations such as Morningstar rate a mutual fund's performance relative to other funds with the same investment objectives, but this too can be misleading for investors trying to choose a fund. First, the funds may not be comparable even though they have similar objectives; one fund may have riskier assets than another fund, and hence, a comparison would not be appropriate. Second, past performance may not be a reliable indicator of future performance.

In choosing a fund, investors are best off looking at what the fund invests in (as best as can be determined), and trying to determine the volatility in terms of up and down markets.

Yield is one aspect of performance. Yield is defined as the interest/dividends that are paid to shareholders as a percentage of the net asset value price. Money market funds quote yields over a seven-day period. This is an average dividend yield over seven days which can be annualized. Long-term bond funds also quote an annualized average yield but it is generally over 30 days.

Since 1988, the SEC has ruled that funds with average maturities longer than those of money market mutual funds quote the SEC standardized yield. The *SEC standardized yield* includes the interest or dividends accrued by the fund over 30 days as well as an adjustment to the prices of the bonds for the amount of the amortization of any discount or premium which was paid for the bond assets. The SEC standardized yield makes the comparison of different mutual funds more meaningful. Prior to this standardized rule, comparing the yield of one fund to the yield of another fund was an exercise in futility, if one of them used a formula which inflated its yield (Thau 1992).

The SEC standardized yield should be used for comparison purposes and not as a means to predict future yields. This yield is a measure of the fund's dividend distribution over a 30 day period, and is only one aspect of the fund's *total return*. Mutual funds pass on any gains or losses to shareholders, which can increase or decrease the fund's total return.

Another factor which affects total return is the fluctuation in net asset value. When the share price increases by six percent, this will effectively increase the total return by an additional six percent. Similarly, when the net asset value price of the fund declines, this will decrease the total return. This explains why funds can have a negative return. This happened when the European currencies went into turmoil towards the latter part of 1992 and affected short-term global bond mutual funds. These funds had high yields, but they were diminished by the steep declines in their net asset value prices.

The interest on reinvested dividends is another factor which may be in the total return. When the monthly interest or dividend paid out by the fund is reinvested to buy more shares, the yield earned on these reinvested shares will boost the overall return on the invested capital.

Therefore, when comparing the total returns quoted by the different funds, you need to make sure that you are comparing the same type of total return. As you can see, total return can include the following three components:

◆ dividends and capital gains or losses

◆ changes in net asset value

◆ dividends (interest) on reinvested dividends.

When total returns are quoted by funds, you should ask whether all of these are included in the computation. In other words, it would be a *cumulative total return* for the period. However, there are examples of funds that choose not to advertise a total cumulative return. Some high yield junk bond funds have at times chosen not to emphasize total returns, as they were negative due to the deep declines in junk bond prices. Instead they touted their high yields. Thus, basing your choice of fund on yield alone can be misleading as yields may be easier to manipulate. Investors should, therefore, look at the yield and the total return of the fund to get a more balanced picture.

Expenses are a key factor in differentiating the performance of the different bond funds. By painstakingly looking for funds with the highest yields, investors are only looking at half the picture. A fund with a high yield may also be the one that charges higher expenses which would put that fund behind some of the lower cost funds which have smaller yields. Fees will reduce the total return earned by the funds.

The mutual fund industry has been criticized for the proliferation of fees and charges. Granted, these are all disclosed by the mutual funds, but besides the conspicuous charges, investors need to know where to look to find the less obvious fees.

Load Funds versus No-Load Funds

Some mutual funds are no-load funds where the investor pays no commission or fee to buy or sell the shares of the fund. Investing $10,000 in a no-load fund will have every cent of the $10,000 going to buy shares in the fund. These no-load funds are easily identified in the newspapers by looking for "NL" under the offer price column in the mutual fund quotes.

A load fund charges a sales commission for buying shares in the fund. These fees can be quite substantial ranging to as much as 8.5 percent of the purchase price of the shares. The amount of the sales (load) charge per share can be determined by deducting the net asset value price from the offer price. Some funds give quantity discounts on their loads to investors who buy large blocks of shares. For example, the sales load might be five percent for amounts under $100,000, 4.25 percent for investing between $100,000 to $200,000, and 3.5 percent for amounts in excess of $200,000. You have to check when buying load funds whether they charge a load on reinvested dividends as well.

Some funds also charge a "back-load" or exit fee when you sell the shares in the fund. This could be a straight percentage or the percentage charged could decline the longer the shares are held in the fund.

The ultimate effect of load charges is to reduce the total return. The impact of the load charge is felt more greatly if the fund is held for a short period of time. For instance, if a fund has a yield of six percent and there is a four percent load to buy into the fund, the total return to the investor for the year is sharply reduced. If there is a back-end load to exit the fund, this could be even more expensive to the investor; if the share price has increased, it will be the load percentage of a larger amount.

Why then would so many investors invest in load funds when these commissions "eat away" so much of their returns? The author can only speculate on possible answers:

◆ investors may not want to decide which funds to invest in, and so they leave the decisions to their brokers and financial planners;

◆ brokers and financial planners earn their living from selling investments from which they are paid commissions. These include load funds.

◆ no-load funds do not pay commissions to brokers and financial planners.

Do Load Funds Outperform No-Load Funds?

There is no evidence to support the opinions expressed by many brokers and financial planners that load funds outperform no-load funds. According to CDA/Weisenberger, there was no difference between the performance of the average no-load funds and load funds over a five-year period (Clements 1993). In fact, when adjusting for sales commissions, investors would have been better off with no-load funds.

12 (b)-1 fees are less obvious than loads. These are charged by many funds to recover expenses for marketing and distribution. These fees are assessed annually and can be quite steep when added together with load fees. Many no-load funds tout the absence of sales commissions but tack on 12 (b)-1 fees which is like a hidden load. A one percent 12 (b)-1 fee may not sound as if it is very much, but this is $100 less per annum in your pocket on a $10,000 mutual fund investment.

In addition to the above mentioned charges, funds have *management fees* which are paid to managers who administer the fund's portfolio of investments. These can range from .5 percent to two percent of assets. High management fees will also take its toll on the investor's total return.

Thus, all fees bear watching as they reduce yields and total returns. Critics of the mutual fund industry have brought a sense of awareness of the proliferation of all these charges. However, investors should not be deceived by funds who claim to be what they are not. By lowering front-end loads or eliminating them altogether doesn't mean that a fund can't add it in somewhere else.

Funds have to disclose their fees, which means that investors can find them in the fund's prospectus. Management fees, 12 (b)-1 fees, redemption or back-end loads, and any other fees charged will be disclosed somewhere in the fund's prospectus. The financial newspapers also list the types of charges of the different funds in their periodic mutual fund performance reviews.

Some guidelines that you may want to follow to help you choose a fund:

◆ examine the performance records of the funds that you are interested in;

◆ compare their total expenses and fees;

◆ choose the fund which you feel will be the best choice in terms of performance. If there is no difference in the performance of your choice of funds, then go with the fund that has the lowest expenses.

What Is the Significance of the Prospectus?

Besides information which can be obtained about the different funds from business magazines, newspapers, and advisory services, essential information is provided by the mutual fund's prospectus. Currently, funds are required to send a prospectus to a potential investor before accepting investment funds. However, this may change as the SEC has a new proposal which it is testing. The proposal will allow mutual funds to eliminate sending a prospectus as long as the key points of the prospectus are included in their advertisements. The information in the advertisements would be legally binding in that if there are any facts which are not true investors can sue. However, there is a vast grey area of puffery which has the potential for causing tremendous confusion among investors. Imagine the "clever" letters advertisers of mutual funds could dream up to send as direct mail to potential investors:

Dear Potential Investor:

The markets are going to tumble in addition to . . .

No need for you to bear these hardships. Invest in XYZ Fund and reap the rewards . . .

Sincerely,

E.Z. Prey
Chairman, XYZ Fund

Although a prospectus is written in a manner which may vie with other literature as one of the best cures for insomnia, it still provides investors with information about the fund that they may not be able to get anywhere else.

You should look for the following in the prospectus.

Objectives

The objectives and policies of the fund will be somewhere near the front of the prospectus. The objectives describe the types of securities that the fund invests in, as well as the risk factors associated with the securities. For instance, if the prospectus states that the fund will buy securities which are less than investment grade, the investor should not be surprised to find that most of the bonds are junk bonds.

The investment policies will outline the latitude of the fund manager to invest in other types of securities. These may be the trading of futures contracts and the writing of options to hedge their bets on the direction of interest rates, and or to invest in derivative securities to boost the yield of the fund. Many so called conservative funds which supposedly hold government securities "only" have used derivative securities to boost their returns (Thau 1992). The greater the latitude in investing in these other types of securities, the greater the risks if events backfire.

Selected Per Share Data and Ratios

This selected per share data and ratios table in the prospectus summarizes the fund's performance over the time period shown. Table 11-3 gives an example of such a table. Although these may vary from fund to fund, essentially the format will be similar.

The investment activities section shows the amount of investment income earned on the securities held by the fund and these generally are passed on to the mutual fund shareholders. For instance, in 1993, all of the net investment income of $0.37 was distributed to the shareholders (line 4) but in 1992 only $0.30 of the $0.31 of net income was paid out to shareholders. In this year, the $0.01, which was not distributed to shareholders, increased the net asset value (line 7) in the capital changes section. (The capital loss and distribution of gains was reduced by this $0.01 which was not distributed).

Capital gains and losses will also affect the net asset value. Funds distribute their realized capital gains (line 6) but the unrealized capital gains (losses) will also increase (decrease) the net asset value.

Table 11–3   Selected Per Share Data and Ratios

	1993	1992	1991
Net Asset Value (NAV) Beginning of the Year	$10.02	$11.01	$10.73
Investment Activities			
line 1 Income	.40	.35	.55
line 2 Expenses	(.03)	(.04)	(.05)
line 3 Net Investment Income	.37	.31	.50
line 4 Distribution of Dividends	(.37)	(.30)	(.47)
Capital Changes			
line 5 Net Realized and Unrealized Gains (Losses) on Investments	$1.00	(.75)	1.50
line 6 Distributions of Realized Gains	(.70)	(.25)	1.25
line 7 Net Increase (Decrease) to NAV	.30	(.99)	.28
NAV Beginning of Year	10.02	11.01	10.73
NAV at End of Year	10.32	10.02	11.01
Ratio of Operating Expenses to Average Net Assets	.45%	.46%	.84%
Portfolio Turnover Rate	121%	135%	150%
Shares Outstanding (000)	10,600	8,451	6,339

The changes in the net asset value from year to year will give you some idea of the volatility in share price. For instance, for the year 1992, the net asset value decreased by $1.01 which is a 9.17 percent decrease. How comfortable would you feel in the short term if you invested $10,000 to have it decline to $9,082.65 (this is a 9.17 percent decline)?

Investors can calculate an average total return by taking into account these three sources of return (dividends distributed, capital gains distributed and the changes in share price) by using the following formula:

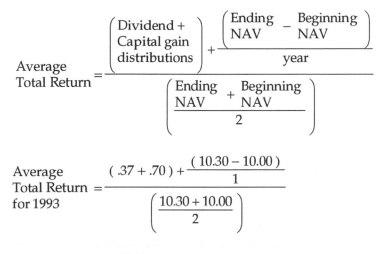

$$\text{Average Total Return} = \frac{\left(\begin{array}{c}\text{Dividend +}\\ \text{Capital gain}\\ \text{distributions}\end{array}\right) + \dfrac{\left(\dfrac{\text{Ending}}{\text{NAV}} - \dfrac{\text{Beginning}}{\text{NAV}}\right)}{\text{year}}}{\left(\dfrac{\dfrac{\text{Ending}}{\text{NAV}} + \dfrac{\text{Beginning}}{\text{NAV}}}{2}\right)}$$

$$\text{Average Total Return for 1993} = \frac{(.37 + .70) + \dfrac{(10.30 - 10.00)}{1}}{\left(\dfrac{10.30 + 10.00}{2}\right)}$$

$$= 13.50\%$$

Having calculated this simple yield of 13.5 percent indicates that an investor in this fund would have received double digit returns, resulting mainly from realized gains and increases in the NAV share price. The more volatile the net asset value of the fund, the greater the likelihood of unstable returns. Thus, when considering whether to invest in a particular fund don't go by the advertised yield alone, look at the total return.

The ratio of operating expenses to average net assets is fairly low in this hypothetical fund (close to 1/2 of 1 percent).

The portfolio turnover rate indicates how actively the assets in the fund are turned over. Bond funds tend to have high turnover rates and 150 percent would not be uncommon. A turnover rate of 100 percent indicates that all the investments in a portfolio would change once a year (Thau 1992).

Annual Expenses

Although annual expenses are shown in the Selected Per Share Data and Ratios section, mutual funds will have a separate table with a breakdown of their expenses in the prospectus. This would typically show the different load charges, redemption fees, shareholder accounting costs, 12 (b)-1 fees, distribution costs, and other expenses.

By examining the prospectus of the funds that you are interested in, you will be able to make a more informed choice than merely going by the advertised messages of the funds.

What Are the Tax Consequences
of Buying and Selling Shares in Mutual Funds?

Tax reporting on mutual funds can be complicated. Even if you buy and hold shares in a mutual fund there are tax consequences. Dividends which are paid to investors on a monthly basis may be automatically reinvested in that fund to buy more shares. At the end of the year, the mutual fund will send a Form 1099 to each mutual fundholder showing the amount of dividends and capital gains received for the year. Individual shareholders will pay taxes on these dividends and capital gains. Therefore, these dividends and capital gains need to be added into the cost basis when the investor sells the shares in the fund.

For example, suppose that an investor who had invested $10,000 in a fund two years ago and has received a total of $2,000 in dividends and capital gains in the fund to date, wishes to sell all the shares in the fund, and $14,000 is received. Thus, the investor's cost basis is $12,000 (not $10,000) and the gain on the sale of the shares is $2,000 ($14,000 - $12,000).

When investors sell only a part of their total fund, the procedure is different and may be tricky. This is further complicated when investors actively buy and sell shares as if it were a checking account. In fact, many mutual funds encourage investors to operate their funds like a checking account by providing check writing services. However, every time that an investor writes a check against a bond fund, there is a capital gain or loss tax consequence. This does not include money market funds which have a stable share price of $1. This action either causes a nightmare for the investor around tax time or will produce extra revenue for the investor's accountant in terms of the additional time spent.

The most important thing in an actively traded bond mutual fund (or any mutual fund for that matter) is to keep good records. For each fund, keep a separate folder and store all the monthly statements showing purchases and sales of shares, dividends and capital gain distributions.

By keeping records of all transactions, investors will be able to determine the cost basis of shares sold. This can be done using either an average cost or a FIFO basis. FIFO is first in, first out, which means that the cost of the first shares purchased in the fund will be used first as the shares sold. Table 11–4 illustrates the FIFO method of calculat-

Table 11–4 Calculation of Gains/Losses
on the Sale of Shares

Summary of GNMA Bond Fund

Date	Transaction	Dollar Amount	Share Price	# of Shares	Total # of shares
06/14	Invest	$10,000	$10.00	1,000	1,000
11/26	Invest	4,500	9.00	500	1,500
11/30	Redeem (sell)	12,000	10.00	1,200	300
12/31	Income Dividends	1,000	10.00	100	400

To Calculate Gain/Loss on a FIFO Basis

Sold 1,200 shares at $10.00 per share   Sale Price $12,000

Cost Basis

06/14 1,000 shares at $10.00	$10,000	
11/30 200 shares at $9.00	1,800	
Total Cost		$11,800
Gain		200

GNMA Bond Fund After Sale

Date	Transaction	Dollar Amount	Share Price	# of Shares	Total #
11/26	Invested	$2,700	$ 9.00	300	300
12/31	Income Dividends	1,000	10.00	100	400

ing capital gains or losses on the partial sale of shares in a mutual fund. The example shows that the earliest shares purchased are the first to be used in the sale of shares. After all, the shares of the invested funds are sold, the basis of the dividends and capital gains shares will be used to determine any gains or losses.

Several funds provide the gains and losses on an average cost basis when investors sell shares in these funds. The average cost basis can get quite complex with additional sales and purchases of shares. Hence, some bond funds don't allow their shareholders to write checks against their accounts.

To minimize any tax hassles, investors are better off not writing checks from their bond funds for their short term cash needs. This only creates gains or losses where the investor would have been better off investing the money needed for short-term purposes in a money market fund, which alleviates these tax problems.

Whether you trade actively or not, the solution to tax computations is to keep good records. If you can't determine the cost basis of your shares, an accountant will be able to do, so provided you keep good records. If you don't have all the records of your purchases and sales, you may not be able to prove your cost basis to the IRS (Internal Revenue Service) if disputed.

What Are the Risks of Mutual Funds?

The major risk with bond mutual funds is the *risk of loss of funds invested* through a decline in net asset value. The longer the maturity of the fund, the greater the possible decline in net asset value. This is because of interest rate risk. When interest rates rise, bond prices (and net asset values of bond funds) decline. Similarly, when interest rates go down, bond prices (and the net asset values of bond funds) appreciate.

Credit risk will affect those funds that invest in below investment grade bonds such as junk bonds. When there is nervousness about defaults in junk bonds, a major sell off in the junk bond market is provoked, which in the past has resulted in steep declines in junk bond prices and the net asset values of bond funds. However, as explained earlier in the chapter, credit risk may not be as significant for bond funds as it is for individual bonds. This is because funds are large and diversified with many different issues. Generally, the loss from the default of one or two issues would have a small overall impact on a fund.

As a result of some bank failures and the shaky financial status of some savings and loan associations, some investors are naturally concerned about the *risk of insolvency* of mutual funds. There is always the risk that a mutual fund could go under, but the chances of this happening are small. The key distinction between banks and mutual funds is the way that mutual funds are set up, which reduces the risks of failure and loss due to fraud. Typically mutual funds are corporations owned by shareholders. A separate management company is contracted by the shareholders to run the fund's daily operations. The management company oversees the investments of the fund, but they do not have possession of these assets (investments). The assets (investments) are held by a custodian such as a bank. Thus, if the management company gets into financial trouble, they cannot get access to the assets of the fund.

Another safeguard is that the shareholder's accounts are maintained by a transfer agent. The transfer agent keeps track of the purchases and redemptions of the shareholders. In addition, management companies carry fidelity bonds, which are a form of insurance to protect the investments of the fund against malfeasance or fraud perpetrated by the employees.

Besides these safeguards, there are two other factors which differentiate mutual funds from corporations such as banks and savings and loan associations:

◆ mutual funds must be able to redeem shares on demand which means that a portion of the investment assets must be liquid; and

◆ mutual funds must be able to price their investments at the end of each day known as marking to market.

Hence, mutual funds cannot hide their financial difficulties as easily as banks and savings and loans.

In addition to these checks and balances, mutual funds are regulated by the SEC. Thus, it is unlikely that investors in mutual funds will have to worry about losing money due to the financial collapse of a mutual fund or through fraud. However, investors should be aware that they can lose money through purchasing a fund whose investments perform poorly in the markets.

How to Buy and Sell Mutual Funds

Buying and selling shares in bond mutual funds can be accomplished in several ways, depending on whether the fund is a load or no-load fund.

Investors can buy into no-load mutual funds by dealing directly with the mutual fund. Most if not all funds have 800 telephone numbers. Mutual funds will send a prospectus along with an application form to open an account to first time investors. Once investors have opened accounts with the fund, they can purchase additional shares by sending a check along with a preprinted account stub detached from the account statement. As mentioned earlier, there are no sales commissions with no-load funds and so these are not sold by brokers. Shares in no-load funds are bought and sold at their net asset values.

Load funds are sold through brokers and salespeople who charge commissions every time new shares are bought. Some funds also charge a redemption fee which is a back-end fee or reverse load for selling shares. If the percentage loads are the same (for front or back-end), it may be preferable to go for a reverse load rather than a front load because all the money is invested immediately with the back-end load (Faerber 1992).

Financial planners, brokers and sales people may try to convince you to buy load funds because of claims of better performance than no-load funds. There is no evidence to support this premise. In fact, according to a study by Morningstar, a Chicago firm that tracks mutual funds, no-load bond funds consistently outperformed load funds over three-, five- and 10-year periods through March 31, 1993 (McGough 1993). However, there may be some truth to the claim that no-load bond funds are much more volatile than load funds during expanding and contracting markets.

Banks and discount brokerage firms have also entered the mutual fund arena and they too sell mutual funds. This, of course, complicates the choice of mutual funds, but investors who feel confident enough to choose their own funds are better off with no-load funds. The difference saved may be minimal over a short period of time, but this difference can grow substantially over a 10-year period due to the compounding of interest (time value of money).

A good source of information on mutual funds is a reference book by Wiesenberger called "Investment Companies" available in most libraries. In it, you can review the long run performance of the funds that you are interested in.

What Are the Advantages of Mutual Funds?

◆ Mutual funds offer small investors the opportunity to own a fraction of a diversified portfolio. For instance, investing $2,500 in a bond fund gives the investor a share of an excellent cross section of bonds. Investors would need to invest at least $50,000 in individual bonds to have a diversified portfolio.

◆ Mutual funds provide administrative and custodial duties: record-keeping of all transactions, monthly statements, information for tax purposes, as well as the safekeeping of all securities.

◆ Mutual funds are professionally managed. Many investors do not have the time or the expertise to manage their bond portfolios.

◆ Mutual fund companies redeem shares on demand. In the case of no-load funds, they are redeemed at net asset values.

◆ Investors have the option of being able to reinvest dividends and capital gains automatically for more shares in the fund or have them paid out on a monthly basis.

◆ Investors in a family of funds can switch from one fund to another as market conditions change. For example, when interest rates are going up, investors can switch money from their bond funds to money market funds.

◆ Levels of risk, return, and stability of income and principal vary-with the type of fund chosen. Most families of mutual funds offer a range of different types of bond funds with various characteristics.

What Are the Disadvantages of Mutual Bond Funds?

◆ Professional management does not guarantee superior performance. Many funds underperform the market over long periods of time.

◆ When load charges and fees are included, total returns may be significantly less than if investors bought individual bonds and held them to maturity.

◆ Investors have no choice over the investment securities that portfolio managers make.

◆ Investors have no control over the distribution of hidden capital gains, which can upset very careful tax planning. Since investment companies do not pay taxes, income and capital gains are passed through to the shareholders.

Caveats

♦ Choose a mutual fund family which has a wide range of different funds allowing you greater flexibility to transfer from one fund type to another.

♦ Avoid funds which have high sales charges, redemption fees and high management and expense ratios.

♦ Keep all the records of income and capital gains distributions, as well as the dates, amounts and share prices of all purchases and redemptions of shares. This can alleviate a potential nightmare at tax time.

Should You Invest in Bond Mutual Funds or in Individual Bonds?

Bond mutual funds have been very popular among investors. As of March 1993, a record $622 billion was invested in bond mutual funds according to the Investment Company Institute (Herman 1993). This amount was more than for either stock mutual funds or money market funds.

As stated earlier, the advantages of bond mutual funds are: professional management; diversification; being able to invest small amounts of money; and ease of buying and selling. For many investors, these advantages outweigh the disadvantages of mutual funds. Mutual funds may be the most practical way for investors to buy many bond types. These would be bonds which sell in high denominations such as certain mortgage-backed bonds, certain agency bonds and some municipal issues. Another factor in favor of mutual funds is the complexity of certain types of bonds. The complexities of mortgage-backed bonds, zero-coupon bonds, convertible issues, and derivative securities may exclude most investors from buying them as individual bonds. Mutual funds, therefore, allow investors to own many different complex types of bonds.

It certainly makes sense to invest in junk bond mutual funds rather than individual junk bonds. The diversification achieved by mutual funds minimizes the impact from any unexpected defaults. Professional managers of these funds have quicker access to information about the different issues as well as greater expertise than the average investor.

However, there is a strong argument for buying individual bonds over mutual funds in certain cases. Rates of return on individual bonds are often greater than those earned from mutual funds. This is true even for no-load funds, because besides sales commissions, there are other fees (12 (b)-1, operating fees) which eat into the returns of mutual funds. By investing in individual bonds, investors avoid these fees.

The second powerful argument for individual bonds is that if they are bought and held until maturity, interest rate risk is avoided. Changes in interest rates affect the price of both individual bonds and bond mutual funds. However, if investors have a set time for which they will not need their money, they can invest in individual bonds with corresponding maturities (to their needs) and not worry what happens to interest rates. This does not apply to bond mutual funds. If interest rates go up, there will be a decline in the net asset value of share prices of bond funds.

Bonds such as Treasury securities are easy to buy and by owning these individual Treasury securities, investors can eliminate many of the fees which mutual funds charge, thereby increasing their returns. Moreover, when these are bought directly from the Federal Reserve Banks or branches, investors do not pay any commissions. Buying and holding Treasury securities makes more sense than investing in Treasury bond funds. However, if investors do not plan on holding the bonds through maturity, funds may be a better alternative.

Buying U.S. Treasury notes requires a minimum amount of $5,000. Investors with less than $5,000 are precluded from buying Treasury notes. For example, if an investor has only $4,980 to invest, individual Treasury notes are out of the question until that investor has $5,000. Similarly, if an investor has $5,950, only $5,000 could be used to buy individual Treasury notes, whereas investors could invest all of their proceeds in a U.S. government bond mutual fund. Once investors have opened a fund account, they can invest in increments of as little as $100 in many funds.

Thus, bond mutual funds offer investors a convenient way to invest small amounts as well as large amounts of money. Investors could, of course, buy individual U.S. Treasury notes for the minimum amounts and invest any marginal dollars in existing bond mutual funds.

Investing in bond mutual funds is good for investors who do not have enough money to diversify their investments, and who also do not have the time, expertise or inclination to select and manage individual bonds. In addition, there are a wide range of different bond funds which offer investors the opportunity to invest in the types of bond securities which would be difficult to buy on an individual basis.

References

Clements, Jonathan. "The 25 Facts Every Fund Investor Should Know." *Wall Street Journal,* March 5, 1993, page C1.

Eaton, Leslie. "Price Fixing. Costly Mistakes in Valuing Shares." *Barron's,* April 19, 1993, page 35.

Faerber, Esmé. *Managing Your Investments, Savings, and Credit.* Chicago: Probus Publishing Co., 1992.

Herman, Tom. "Bond vs Bond Mutual Funds: Which Are Better for You?" *Wall Street Journal,* April 30, 1993, page C1.

Jereski, Laura. "What Price CMOs? Funds Have No Idea." *Wall Street Journal,* April 12, 1993, page C1.

McGough, Robert. "Banks vs Brokers: Who's Got the Best Funds?" *Wall Street Journal,* May 7, 1993, page C1.

Savage, Stephen. "Refrigerator Rules. ABCs for Today's Complex Fund Climate." *Barron's,* February 15, 1993, page 43.

Schultz, Ellen. "How to Unwrap a Wrap Account." *Wall Street Journal,* February 5, 1993, page C1.

Thau, Annette. *The Bond Book.* Chicago: Probus Publishing Co., 1992.

Chapter 12

Closed-End Funds

Key Concepts

◆ Unit investment trusts

◆ The risks of closed-end funds and unit investment trusts

◆ How to buy and sell closed-end funds and unit investment trusts

◆ Their advantages

◆ Their disadvantages

◆ Caveats

◆ Whether they are a suitable investment vehicle

Closed-end funds bear similarities to open-end mutual funds, but there are some significant differences. As pointed out in the previous chapter, open-end mutual funds issue an unlimited number of shares. When investors buy more shares in an open-end fund, more money is available to the fund manager to buy more investment assets.

Closed-end funds have a fixed number of shares outstanding, and after these are sold, the fund does not issue any new shares. Shares of closed-end funds are traded on the stock exchanges or on the over-the-counter market. Most closed-end funds are traded on the New York Stock Exchange with some on the American Stock Exchange and a few on the over-the-counter market.

Since there is a fixed number of shares in a closed-end fund, investors who want to invest in an existing fund (as opposed to a new fund) have to buy shares from shareholders who are willing to sell their shares on the market. Thus, the price of the shares of the closed-end bond fund will fluctuate up and down depending on not only the supply and demand for the shares, but also on other factors such as the return of the fund, average maturity of the assets of the fund, net asset value and other fundamental factors of the fund.

Like open-end mutual funds, the net asset value is important in the valuation of the share price. However, unlike open-end funds, share prices of closed-end funds can sell above or below their net asset values. For example, when interest rates decline there may be heavy demand for closed-end funds which could push up their share prices above their net asset values. Hence, these funds would trade at a premium. Similarly, when interest rates go up, shares of closed-end bond funds could trade at significant discounts to their net asset values. For example, a closed-end bond fund could have a net asset value of $9 per share and be selling at $7.50 per share (trading at a $1.50 discount per share). At times, the discounts to net asset values of closed-end funds can be as much as 20-30 percent.

The type of assets held in the fund and their maturities will also affect the share price. The longer the maturity, the greater the volatility in share price.

Like open-end funds there are many different closed-end funds. There are stock funds, bond funds, international funds, and specialized funds. Among the bond funds there are corporate bond funds, municipal bond funds, government bond funds, international bond funds, and balanced funds. Balanced funds invest in both stocks and bonds.

Depending on the investment objectives of the closed-end fund, the professional managers (of the funds) will invest in different financial assets to make up a diversified portfolio. Even though closed-end funds do not issue new shares to expand their capital structure, their portfolio assets can and do change. Existing bond issues may be sold and new ones bought for the portfolio. Thus, when bond issues mature, the proceeds received are used to buy new issues. Closed-end funds, like open-end funds, never mature.

Net asset values for closed-end funds are calculated in much the same way as for open-end funds. The total assets minus any liabilities equals the net worth for the fund, which is divided by the fixed number of shares to give the net asset value per share.

Occasionally, closed-end funds become open-end mutual funds and the net asset value becomes the price that the shares trade at through the mutual fund. That is, if it becomes a no-load fund. For a load fund, there will be an additional commission that will be added to the net asset value.

What Are Unit Investment Trusts?

In the closed-end bond fund market, unit investment trusts have become very popular. More than $6 billion has been invested in unit trusts over the past year (1992), and roughly $11 billion of unit trusts are managed by three firms (Blackrock Financial Management, Hyperion Capital Management and Piper Jaffrey) (Bary 1993). Brokerage firms such as Merrill Lynch and Bear Stearns, as well as Nuveen and Van Kampen and Merritt sponsor unit trusts.

Unit investment trusts have been seductively marketed as the investment which earns high current income as well as returning investors' entire investments when the trust assets mature. Theoretically, this is possible, but in practice this may not always be possible. By examining how unit trusts work, the difficulties of living up to these lofty promises will become apparent.

A unit investment trust, like a closed-end fund, will sell a fixed number of shares. For instance, assume that the trust sells one million shares at $10 per share for a total of $10 million. Sales commissions of $500,000 would be deducted leaving the unit trust (same for a closed-end bond fund) $9.5 million to invest in different bond issues. The trust (closed-end fund) will then remit the earnings on the investments after management fees to the shareholders. When the different investments mature, the trust will pay back the proceeds from the investments to the shareholders. (Closed-end funds differ in that when issues mature, the proceeds are reinvested in other issues). This is how unit investment trusts and closed-end funds work.

However, before looking at the factors that could make it difficult for the trust to live up to its promise of high income and the full return of principal it may be more useful to examine some of the differences between unit trusts and closed-end funds.

Generally, with unit investment trusts, the portfolio of investments stay the same once they have been bought. In other words, no new bonds are bought and no existing bonds are sold. Theoretically, as the bond issues approach maturity, so will the prices of the individual bonds rise towards their par prices. Again theoretically, management fees should be lower on unit investment trusts than closed-end funds because the portfolio remains unmanaged. In fact, there should be no management fees on a unit investment trust because the portfolio is unmanaged, but in most instances, this is not the case. With closed-end bond funds, the portfolio changes as issues are bought and sold.

Shares of unit investment trusts, like closed-end bond funds, trade on the secondary markets. However, in certain conditions, shares in unit investment trusts can be illiquid. This happens when interest rates are rising and new investors would not want to buy into a trust with bond investments that are locked into lower yields. Hence, existing unit trust shareholders may have difficulty selling their shares due to illiquidity.

What Are the Risks of Closed-End Bond Funds and Unit Investment Trusts?

Both closed-end bond funds and unit investment trusts are subject to *interest rate risk*. When market rates of interest increase prices of the bond issues held in both the portfolios of unit trusts and closed-end bond funds will go down. This, of course, means that the share prices will fall.

Moreover, if there is selling pressure on the shares, the decline in share prices will be even greater than the decline in the net asset values. The opposite is true as well; if interest rates fall, there will be appreciation in the assets and, of course, in the share price.

Interest rate risk has another effect on unit investment trusts. The yields of the fixed coupon bonds will theoretically remain the same despite changes in interest rates, because the assets in the portfolio remain the same; whereas with closed-end bond funds, when the assets mature or are sold, new issues with higher (or lower) coupons will be bought. Thus, yields on closed-end bond funds will fluctuate more than those on unit investment trusts. However, if unit investment trusts invest in mortgage securities and interest-only strips, a reduction in interest rates would cause a reduced return for shareholders. Interest-only strips fall in price when interest rates decline. This has happened to some of the Hyperion Trust funds which have had negative rates of return on some trusts and poor returns on others (Bary 1993a).

Many unit investment trusts have used leverage to increase their yields. Leverage is where the trusts use borrowed money to supplement amounts invested by shareholders to invest in portfolio assets. Currently, this has worked well for many trusts because of the yield curve, which is the relationship between long-term and short-term rates. Currently, short-term rates are lower than long-term interest rates. Therefore, trusts have been borrowing on a short-term basis (3.5 percent) and investing the funds in long-term issues (seven to eight percent). This strategy worked well for trusts during the 1992-1993 period because interest rates have been coming down and are at their lowest levels in 20 years as of this writing.

However, this is a risky strategy because if interest rates bottom out and begin to rise, not only will borrowing costs climb, but the increased costs will cut into the yields paid to shareholders. Moreover, prices of the different bond securities held in the portfolio will decline in price which, of course, translates into lower share prices. Thus, the use of leverage adds further risks when compounded with changes in interest rates.

There is the *risk that share prices of both closed-end funds and unit investment trusts can fall way below net asset values* due to excess selling pressure on the stock markets. Then, of course, there is always the danger of not being able to recoup the original price paid for the shares when selling.

Unit investment trust shareholders have the added risk that they may not get back the full amount of their original investments. This could be due to a number of factors. Bond issues may be called before maturity with the call price being less than the face value. Other factors are the composition of the trust's assets, commissions and high management fees charged to the trust, the dividend yields, and as mentioned earlier, the use of leverage.

In many cases the managers of unit investment trusts and closed-end bond funds charge generous annual fees as well as up-front commissions for the original sale of the shares. These funds will not only have to earn spectacular returns so that the managers of these funds (trusts) can collect their fees without eroding yields significantly, but they will also have to rake up some capital gains to be able to recoup the sales commissions in order to return to the shareholders their entire investments at maturity. This explains why many investment trusts use leverage and resort to derivative securities to try and boost their returns.

When interest rates fall, there is the risk that bond issues will be called. This means that shareholders of unit trusts will get their money back, which is reinvested at lower rates of interest. This reduces overall returns.

The types of investments that the fund or trust holds will have a marked effect on the net asset value and the volatility of the share price. Unfortunately, for the original shareholders of closed-end bond funds and unit investment trusts, there is no way of knowing the composition of the portfolio investments when they originally subscribe to the shares of the fund/trust. The original shareholders will invest their money to buy the shares and only then will the managers of the fund/trust buy the investment assets. Thus, shareholders may not be able to anticipate the *levels of risk of the assets* until the portfolio has been constituted. The composition may include low quality bonds in addition to complex derivative securities for the purpose of boosting the yields of the portfolio. This strategy could backfire, low quality securities could deteriorate and interest rates could face unanticipated changes in direction, thus sending prices of these funds/trusts into a steep decline. Thus, investors trying to exit the fund/trust would experience losses through the decline in the share price.

What you see is not always what you get with advertised yields. Certain funds will include capital gains as well as returns of principal from mortgage backed securities to boost their yield figures. The true yield on a closed-end fund is only the net investment income per share (after management fees) divided by the price per share. This is the current yield. For closed-end funds where there is no maturity, a yield to maturity calculation is not meaningful. The total return for closed-end funds depends on the yield of the investments and the fluctuations in share price.

With unit investment trusts the selling feature is often a high yield. In a low interest rate climate many trusts will disregard the risks of high yielding lower quality securities for their portfolios. This happened to many unit investment trusts that loaded up on Washington Public Power Securities before they defaulted, resulting in losses which fell to the shareholders (Thau 1992).

In summary, investors in unit investment trusts should look beyond the advertised yield and scrutinize the make-up of the portfolio of investments. In reality, shareholders of unit investment trusts have no protection against both the deterioration of the quality of the investments in the portfolio or interest rate risk (Thau 1992). Similarly, if there is an exodus of shareholders from unit investment trusts and closed-end funds, shareholders may find it difficult to sell their shares without taking large losses.

How to Buy and Sell Closed-End Funds and Unit Investment Trusts

When closed-end funds and unit investment trusts are newly issued, the shares are underwritten by brokerage firms and sold by brokers. Brokerage fees can be as high as 8 percent, which means that the investor's investment is immediately reduced by 8 percent. For instance, if a fund or trust sells one million shares at $10 per share for $10 million, it will have only $9.2 million to invest after deducting $800,000 (eight percent) for brokerage commissions. This means that after shareholders have paid $10 per share to invest in the new fund or trust, the shares will drop in value and trade at a discount. This is known as a quick erosion in capital and is a well documented phenomenon for closed-end funds and unit investment trusts. This will not be a topic of conversation brought up by brokers who stand to earn high commissions from the sale of these shares. Many brokers assert that closed-end funds are sold commission free. This is a play on words because it may be commission free, but in its place is a hefty underwriting charge which is absorbed by the shareholders. Investors would do better to wait until the funds or trusts are listed on the stock exchanges than to buy them at issue only to see the shares drop in price.

Another reason not to buy closed-end funds or unit investment trusts at issue is that the portfolio of assets has not been constituted so investors do not know what they are getting and they most certainly won't know what the yields will be. Unit investment trust sponsors do not like to see the shares of their trusts fall to discounts, and so they often advertise above market yields to keep the shares from trading at discounts to their net asset values.

The advice from an expert, Thomas Herzfeld, who follows closed-end funds and unit investment trusts is to pay attention to the price of the funds that you are interested in, and the time to buy is when the discount is three percent wider than the normal discount for the fund (Thau 1992).

Common sense suggests that besides the attractiveness of buying into a fund when its shares are selling below their net asset values there are other factors to consider:

◆ the yield is important particularly if investors are buying into the fund in order to get the income. Examine the yield, total return and expense ratios before investing;

◆ the frequency that dividends are paid—semi-annually, quarterly, or monthly;

◆ the composition of the assets and the credit quality of the assets;

◆ the average length of time to maturity of the portfolio investments.

Information on closed-end funds can be found in Thomas J. Herzfeld Advisors annual "Encyclopedia of Closed-End Funds," Value Line Investment Survey, Standard & Poor's Record Sheets, Moody's Finance Manuals, Wiesenberger's "Investment Companies" (in most public libraries).

Share prices of the listed closed-end funds and unit investment trusts can be found in the stock exchange sections of the daily newspapers. For example, the following is a quote of the Hyperion Trust 97 listed on the New York Stock Exchange from the *New York Times* May 8, 1993:

365 day						Sales				
Hi	**Low**	**Stock**	**Div**	**%**	**P/E**	**100s**	**High**	**Low**	**Last**	**Chg**
10⅛	9½	Hy Tst 97	.70	7.7	–	6008	9¾	9⅛	9⅛	-⅝

Reading from left to right:

◆ the first two columns indicate the year's high of $10 1/8 per share- and the low of $9 1/2 per share;

◆ the name of the stock is the Hyperion Unit Trust with a maturity in 1997;

◆ the dividend is $0.70 per share;

◆ the yield percentage is 7.7 percent which is the dividend divided by the last price of the day (.70/9.125);

◆ the sales volume indicates the number of shares traded that day which was 600,800 shares;

◆ the high, low and last indicate that the high price on the day quoted was $9.75, the low price for that day's trading was $9.125 and the last price was the closing price of $9.125.

◆ the change column indicates that the share price closed down 5/8th of a point from the previous day's close.

Barron's, the weekly financial newspaper, publishes a comprehensive list of closed-end funds including unit investment trusts. For example, the information provided on Hyperion Trust 1997 from *Barron's* closed-end bond funds for the week ending May 17, 1993, provides different information than is offered in the daily financial newspapers:

Fund Name	Stock Exchange	NAV	Market Price	Prem/ Discount	52 Week Market Return
Hyperion 1997 Tm	N	9.01	9¾	+8.2	N/A

◆ Hyperion 1997 Term Trust trades on the New York Stock Exchange;

◆ the net asset value as of the week's close was $9.01;

◆ the closing market price for the week was $9.75;

◆ the "+" indicates that the market price was trading at a premium of 8.2% over its net asset value $\frac{(9.75 - 9.01)}{9.01} = 8.2\%$

A "-" indicates that the fund/trust is trading at a discount to its net asset value;

◆ the 52-week return for Hyperion 1997 Term Trust is not applicable because the Trust has not been on the market for a full year (began on October 23,1992).

By combining the information in the daily newspapers with that provided by *Barron's,* investors can better follow the closed-end funds that they are interested in buying or selling. Shares listed on the exchanges are sold through brokers.

Before buying closed-end funds or trusts, ask your broker or call the fund sponsor for the annual or quarterly report.

What Are the Advantages of Closed-End Funds and Unit Investment Trusts?

◆ Investors can buy into closed-end funds and trusts trading at discounts to their net asset values which may offer the potential for capital gains and increased yields. The downside of this strategy could lead to capital losses if the discount to the net asset value widens.

◆ The shares of the larger actively traded closed-end funds and trusts can easily be bought and sold on the stock exchanges. The less actively traded funds will not be as liquid. For income seeking investors, most unit investment trusts pay dividends on a monthly basis.

◆ Unit investment trusts have maturities when investors will have all (or most) of their capital returned to them.

What Are the Disadvantages of Closed-End Funds and Unit Investment Trusts?

◆ Both closed-end funds and unit investment trusts are subject to interest rate risk. Unit investment trusts have no protection against a rise in interest rates, because their portfolio of investments is fixed.

◆ There is the risk that the prices of shares of funds and trusts can move independently to the value of the securities that are held in the fund's/trust's portfolios. More investors exiting the fund/trust than buying the fund/trust will have the effect of driving the price down despite the fact that the assets in the fund are doing well. This often represents a buying opportunity when the fund's (trust's) shares trade at a deep discount to its net asset value.

◆ Brokerage commissions along with management fees can be high which eat into the yields of closed-end funds and unit investment trusts.

◆ Some of the shares of the smaller less actively traded funds and trusts may be illiquid.

◆ Buying into funds and trusts when they are first offered to shareholders means that these shareholders are investing into an unknown portfolio of assets. This is of particular significance for unit investment trusts in that investors cannot gauge the level of risk in the composition of the assets and whether the trust will use leverage to try and increase yields.

◆ Unit investment trusts offer no protection against the credit deterioration of their assets since their portfolios are fixed.

Caveats

◆ Investors should avoid investing in closed-end bond funds and unit investment trusts when they are first offered to the public because a percentage of their initial funds will go toward paying underwriting fees and selling commissions. For example, if investors pay $10 per share and $0.80 goes toward these expenses, net asset values will fall to $9.20 directly after issuance.

◆ Compare the long-term performance of closed-end funds and unit investment trusts before investing. Some have not performed well and investors may want to avoid those with poor long-term track records.

◆ Examine the fees charged before buying into closed-end funds and unit investment trusts. Fees can be high.

Are Closed-End Funds and Unit Investment Trusts Suitable for Me?

Under certain conditions, closed-end funds and unit investment trusts have provided investors with profitable returns in the past. Currently, bargains in these types of investments are becoming harder to find. According to Lipper Analytical Services, closed-end bond funds are trading at an average premium of 2.5 percent to their net asset values (Clements 1993). This means that investors would be paying on average $1.025 for every $1 of assets to invest in closed-end funds (not taking into account brokerage fees to buy the shares).

It is far more advantageous for investors to wait until they can buy into closed-end funds and unit investment trusts when they are trading at discounts to their net asset values. In fact, many investment advisors recommend buying closed-end funds and unit investment trusts when they are trading at large discounts by historical standards to their net asset values and selling them when they have small discounts or premiums.

You should also look out for closed-end funds which are to be converted to open-end funds. If the shares of these funds are trading at discounts to their net asset values, they will rise to their net asset value price at the date of conversion. This also represents a buying opportunity.

Unit investment trusts need to be examined carefully before buying because of their inherent characteristics. They have maturity dates, therefore investors will have their principal returned to them at a specified time. Whether they get all of their principal back is questionable. If interest rates continue to go down and the unit investment trust benefits from the use of leverage, shareholders should get close, if not all of their original principal back. However, if interest rates rise and borrowing costs climb, the return of their entire principal may be jeopardized.

With both closed-end funds and unit investment trusts, share prices will fluctuate due to supply and demand for the shares on the stock market. Thus, if investors cannot find closed-end funds or unit investment trusts that are trading at discounts and they do not want the added risks of further fluctuations in price over net asset values, they should consider open-end mutual funds.

References

Bary, Andrew. "Whom Do You Trust?" *Barron's*, February 8, 1993, pages M8-M9.

Bary, Andrew. "Father Knows Best? How Lew Ranieri's Bond Funds Fared So Poorly." *Barron's*, May 17, 1993a, pages 14-15.

Clements, Jonathan. "Bargains in Closed-End Funds are Tougher to Find these Days." *Wall Street Journal*, April 5, 1993, page C1.

Thau, Annette. *The Bond Book*. Chicago: Probus Publishing Co., 1992.

Chapter 13

Portfolio Management

Key Concepts

◆ Investor objectives

◆ Investor characteristics

◆ Asset allocation

◆ Selection of individual investments

◆ Portfolio management

Managing a portfolio can mean different things to different people. On one extreme, it means buying the most conservative investments and holding them through maturity or indefinitely. On the other extreme, there are those investors who are busy changing their investments on a regular basis as if they were disposable diapers.

Managing a portfolio has some analogies to managing your health. Eating healthy foods, exercising regularly, and eating an apple a day works well for people who are in good health. However, for a person who has a major illness or something chronically wrong, the apple a day, exercise, and good health regimen alone won't rectify the overall problem.

Similarly, managing a portfolio of investments means assembling those investment securities which together will perform to achieve the investor's overall objectives. When this has been accomplished, the investor can sit back and eat an apple a day while monitoring the securities in the portfolio. However, in another scenario, if the investment assets are haphazardly chosen and the investor has not set objectives or goals for the portfolio, there is no way of telling how well or badly this portfolio is doing. It can be likened to a walk in space and you don't know where you are drifting to, which means that you will not have a clue where you will end up.

Thus, knowing what you want to accomplish from your investments allows you to manage your portfolio effectively. Buying and selling investments are relatively easy, but knowing what to buy and sell is more difficult. In essence, the choice of assets to hold is determined by the investor's objectives and personal characteristics.

Investor's Objectives

The investor's objectives will determine the purpose and time period for the investments. For instance, one investor may be saving for retirement in five years and another investor may be saving for retirement in 30 years. Although their objectives may be the same (saving for retirement), the time period and elements of risk tolerance are very different.

Thus, the first step in any plan is to determine long-range, medium-range and short-term objectives. For example, a young family with small children may have the following objectives:

Short-Term:

◆ buy a new car;

◆ save for a vacation.

Medium-Term:

◆ save for a downpayment on a house.

Long-Term:

◆ save for children's education;

◆ save for retirement.

Once objectives have been developed, it becomes easier to see what the investor can aim for from the portfolio. Before setting a strategy to achieve these objectives, investors should examine their personal circumstances, which will serve as a guide in the selection of the portfolio assets.

Characteristics of the Investor	
Marital Status:	single, married, widower
Family:	no children, young children, teenage children, empty nest
Age:	under 25, 25-39 years, 40-60 years, over 60
Education:	high school graduate, college degree, graduate degree

Income: stability and level, future growth prospects

Job/Profession: skills and expertise, ability to improve level of
                                     earnings

Net Worth/Size of Portfolio: level of income, assets and net worth will determine
                              the size of the portfolio

These variables will determine the types of investments and the level of risk that can be absorbed in the development and management of the portfolio. For example, a non-working widower who is dependent entirely on income generated from her investments will not be able to tolerate the high risks of investments in junk bonds, collateralized mortgage obligations, inverse floaters, or newly issued public offerings of common stocks. This portfolio of assets would need to generate income but not at the expense of capital preservation.

Likewise the sole breadwinner of a young family may be risk averse but the circumstances may allow for more emphasis on growth assets than purely preservation of capital. A prosperous litigation lawyer can withstand more risk in the hopes of expanding capital (net worth) without having to generate current income.

Thus, depending on the investor's characteristics, there will be a trade-off between assets generating current income versus assets seeking capital appreciation. If investors opt for capital appreciation assets, they may sacrifice on current income.

A portfolio of assets is created based on the investor's characteristics and steered by the investor's objectives.

Allocation of Assets

Asset allocation is a plan to invest in different types of securities so that the capital invested is protected against adverse factors in the market. This, in essence, is the opposite of putting all your eggs in one basket. Imagine an investor with an amount of $200,000 to invest who had invested it all in IBM stock bought at $100 per share a few years ago. The value of the portfolio currently would be cut in half to $100,000, as IBM is trading at $50 per share, as of this writing.

Developing a portfolio is generally based on the idea of holding a variety of investments rather than concentrating on a single investment. This is to reduce the risks of loss and even out the returns of the different investments.

The latter point can be illustrated with the following hypothetical example of a portfolio:

	Total Investment
Assume the investor buys:	
1,000 shares of XYZ Co. at $50 per share and	$ 50,000
100 convertible bonds of ABC Co. at $1,000 per bond	100,000
	$150,000
A year later the portfolio is valued as follows:	
1,000 shares of XYZ Co. at $70 per share and	$ 70,000
100 convertible bonds of ABC Co. at $800 per bond	80,000
	$150,000

The investor has spread the risks of loss by owning two different types of securities, as well as averaging the returns of the two types of investments. Certainly the investor would have done very much better had he invested totally in XYZ shares, but hindsight always produces the highest returns. The fact that we are not clairvoyant points to the benefits of diversifying across a broad segment of investments. In other words, diversification seeks a balance between the risk-return trade-off discussed in Chapter 2.

Classifying some of the different types of investments on a continuum of risk, we see that common stocks are considered to be the most risky (in terms of variability in share price) followed by long-term bonds, with the shorter maturities on the low-risk end. Bear in mind that there are many other types of investments which are riskier than common stocks, such as commodities and futures contracts. Similarly, there is a great variation of quality among common stocks. The common stock of the well established "blue chip" companies are considered to be less risky than the bonds of highly leveraged companies with suspect balance sheets.

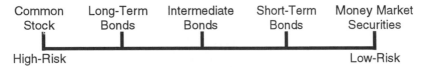

| Common | Long-Term | Intermediate | Short-Term | Money Market |
| Stock | Bonds | Bonds | Bonds | Securities |

High-Risk   Low-Risk

Common stocks are considered to be the most risky due to the volatility of stock prices. However, over long periods of time where the ups and downs of the stock market can be waited out, stocks have provided higher returns (see Chapter 2). Common stocks provide the growth in a portfolio and should be included among the investments.

The percentage allocated to common stocks will depend on the investor's objectives and personal characteristics. As mentioned earlier, a retired widower who is dependent on the income generated from the investments in the portfolio may not have any common stocks in the portfolio. However, if the portfolio generates more than a sufficient level of income for the widower's current needs, a small portion of the portfolio could be invested in common stocks to provide some growth in the portfolio for later years.

Bonds are sought by investors primarily for their ability to generate a steady stream of income. However, an often overlooked fact is that long-term bonds (15- to 30-year maturities) can also be quite risky. Although 30-year U.S. Treasury bonds are safe investments in that the U.S. government is not liable to default on the interest and principal payments, they can be quite volatile in price due to changes in interest rates. Corporate and other types of long-term bonds will be more volatile than Treasuries due to the increased risks of default.

Investors would have to weigh the advantages of taking on the greater risks of investing in other types of long-term bonds over Treasuries by examining their coupon yields. If the yields are significantly greater than those of long-term Treasuries, investors may want to contemplate purchasing these other types of long-term bonds.

However, total return includes transaction costs, which are very much less for Treasuries, particularly if these are bought directly through the Federal Reserve Bank or branches. If these bonds are held to maturity there will be no transaction costs. Besides coupon yield the second consideration is that interest on Treasury securities is exempt from state and local taxes.

Some of the volatility in price is reduced by shortening maturities to intermediate term bonds. Even though returns are reduced by shortening the length of time to maturity, intermediate-term bonds offer investors greater flexibility. For instance, if an investor's characteristics change, and that investor no longer is dependent on current income from investments, intermediate-term securities are generally much more liquid than longer term bonds and can be more easily changed to more growth oriented investments.

Low risk, low return securities such as certificates of deposit, Treasury bills and money market funds should account for the percentage of the investor's portfolio that will serve liquidity and emergency fund purposes. Many investors keep too large a percentage of their portfolio in these low-risk low return assets for various reasons.

Conservative investors who do not feel comfortable keeping only an amount equal to liquidity and emergency needs should increase the percentage. However, the returns from these low yielding investments often do not even keep pace with inflation without taking into account the effects of taxation on the interest.

There isn't a rigid formula for asset allocation. Rather, it is a good idea to think about the concept as a guideline when investing money. The percentage allocated to the different types of assets can always be changed depending on circumstances. As individual circumstances change, so will the investor's objectives. If the emphasis shifts, for example, to greater income generation and preservation of capital from capital growth, the percentage of the investments in the portfolio can be changed accordingly.

An example of asset allocation for a newlywed couple, who are both working professionals with no children might look like this:

> 70% Common stocks with emphasis on growth
>
> 15% Intermediate-term municipal bonds
>
> <u>15%</u> Money market securities
>
> 100%

However, when the wife decides to give up her career to stay home to bring up a new-born infant, the assets allocation may change to provide for greater income generation. The portfolio might be altered to look like this:

> 40% Long-term bonds
>
> 10% Intermediate term municipal bonds
>
> 30% Money market securities
>
> <u>20%</u> Common stocks with half invested in "blue chip" companies and the rest in growth stocks
>
> 100%

What may work for one couple may not work for another couple. Asset allocation is very dependent on the investment objectives and the personal and financial situation of each investor. Thus, the formula for asset allocation that works for one family may not be appropriate for another.

The most important aspect of investing is having an asset allocation plan which signifies the broad mix of assets to strive for. Once these broad categories are determined, the individual assets may be purchased.

Selection of Individual Investments

In order to match the individual's objectives with the specific investments, you need to identify the characteristics of the different investments and their risks. Funds for immediate needs and emergency purposes should be liquid—in investments that can be converted easily into cash without a loss in principal. These would be money market mutual funds, checking accounts, and savings accounts. These are readily convertible into cash. By increasing the time horizon from immediate needs to short term needs, investors can marginally increase their rates of return by investing in certificates of deposit, Treasury bills, and commercial paper. However, of these, only Treasury bills are marketable, which means that they can be sold on the secondary market before maturity.

These individual investments (savings accounts, certificates of deposit, money market mutual funds, Treasury bills, commercial paper) provide some income which is taxable, are liquid but not marketable (except for Treasury bills), and they do not give the possibilities of capital gains. Although investors will not lose any of their principal by investing in this group of investments, there is a risk that the returns from these investments will not keep up with inflation.

The financing of intermediate term objectives, which stretch several years into the future, such as the purchase of a car, house or appliance, and/or the funding of a child's education, in addition to emergency uses of funds that will crop up in the future require investments which are relatively safe. These investments would need to produce a greater rate of return than leaving the money in a savings account or in short-term money market securities. Short- to intermediate-term bonds offer increased rates of return over money market securities as well as the possibility of capital gains or losses if the investor needs the money before maturity. Although investors will get increased rates of return from intermediate-term securities, investors will find that they are not as liquid as short-term securities. Treasury notes and bonds have no credit risk or risk of default. This means that with Treasury notes and bonds there is no need to diversify, whereas with corporate bonds it is a good idea for investors to spread the risks of default (and call) by buying the bonds of different issuers. Similarly, it is a good idea to diversify when investing in municipal bonds and some of the smaller agency bonds.

Financing a child's education in five years requires an investment that is relatively safe. Most people would not gamble with the money earmarked for their children's education. Thus, the credit quality of the issuer is important. Similarly, if the yield differential between Treasuries and other types of intermediate bonds is not significant, it may be advantageous to stick with Treasury securities. This is not only because they are free of default risk, but their interest payments are tax-free at the state and local levels of taxation. However, if the yield differential of other types of bonds (agency bonds, corporate bonds and municipals) over Treasuries is large, investors should invest in these other bonds. Then again, it becomes important to choose a diversified portfolio rather than invest all the intermediate term funds in the securities of one issuer. Federal taxes and changes in the individual tax rates may steer the choice towards municipal bonds.

Long-term objectives, such as saving for retirement or an infant's college education in 18 years, require investments that offer long-term growth prospects as well as greater returns. The level of risk that can be withstood on these investments will depend on the individual investor's circumstances.

A more conservative long-term portfolio would consist of long term bonds, "blue chip" stocks and conservative growth stocks. The emphasis of this strategy is to invest in good quality bonds and the stocks of established companies which pay dividends and offer the prospects of steady growth over a long period of time. Securities offering capital growth are important even in conservative portfolios, providing some cover against any possible erosion in future purchasing power because of inflation.

A more speculative portfolio where the investor can absorb greater levels of risk and strive for greater growth and returns would include growth stocks, stocks of small emerging companies, convertible bonds, junk bonds, real estate, options, commodities, and futures. By including the last three types of investments, options, commodities, and futures, the author is not advocating that these should play a major role in a portfolio. For a speculative investor who understands the nuances of these investments, these securities should account for no more than five percent of the total portfolio. Gambling in a casino is not included as an investment option! The other assets mentioned offer the investor the opportunity for large gains, but the risks of loss are also greater. Foreign bonds and stocks should also be considered, but investors should do their homework first so that they understand the risks fully. International mutual funds may be more helpful to spread some of the risks, although there will always be currency risks when investing in off-shore investments.

Some investors may not feel comfortable buying individual bonds and stocks, and they should stick with mutual funds. Investors willing to make their own investment decisions on individual securities can eliminate the fees and expenses charged by mutual funds. However, they would need to make sure that the brokerage commissions charged are discounted and competitive. Many full service brokers will discount their commissions, if they know that the investors have done their homework and they will lose them to discount brokers if the commissions are not matched.

When considering the different types of securities to choose for a portfolio, investors should weigh the characteristics of the type of investment along with the risks to assist them in their overall choice. See Table 13–1 for a summary of the strategies to reduce the different types of risks.

Management of the Portfolio

Investors need to be continually aware that not only do their objectives and individual characteristics change over time, but that their investments need to be monitored due to changing financial conditions and markets. Companies change and their securities may no longer fulfill the criteria that they were purchased for. For example, IBM, which has currently posted its largest loss in its history is not the same company that it was 10 years ago. IBM's securities (stocks and bonds) which were once considered to be as solid as a rock, might not be perceived in that light today in certain portfolios. Not all investments in the portfolio will realize their projected returns and so investors managing their portfolios will need to sell these and replace them with other investments. This does not mean that all or most of the investments in the portfolio should be continuously turned over. Only those investments which are not likely to achieve the goals specified should be liquidated.

The management of bond portfolios does not generally require as much attention as stock portfolios. In fact, bonds are much more conducive to a passive management style since they pay a fixed stream of income and mature at a specified date. By selecting a con-

---

Table 13–1 Summary of Strategies to Manage Risk

Investment	Risk	Strategy
Common Stock	Market Risk	Invest for a Long Period of Time
	Financial Risk	Diversification Invest in Companies with Low Leverage
Bonds	Interest Rate Risk	Interest Rate Management Strategies
	When Market Rates Are Declining	Increase the Maturities of the Bond Issues
	When Market Rates Are Increasing	Shorter Maturities Ladder Maturities in the Portfolio
	Credit Risk	Invest in Higher Quality Issues (above Investment Grade) Shorten Maturities
	Purchasing Power Risk (When Inflation Increases)	Shorten Maturities Requires Active Portfolio Management

---

venient maturity date for the issue, the investor can wait until the issue matures to get back the principal. Not only does this strategy minimize transaction costs, but it also makes fluctuations in the value of the issue before maturity meaningless. However, if the investor needs the money for any reason before maturity, the current market value would be important.

Many investors follow a more active management style than the buy-hold strategy. Such a strategy involves replacing existing bonds in the portfolio with new bonds. This is referred to as *bond swapping*. This strategy may be used for tax purposes in order to reduce capital gains taxes. At the end of the tax year, if an investor has capital gains from other transactions, the investor can sell some bonds, whose prices have declined, for a loss to offset some or all of the capital gains. (If the investor has bonds in the portfolio which have not declined in price, this strategy cannot be used.) The proceeds from the sale of the bonds are used to buy similar type bonds (same maturity and quality). By swapping one set of bonds for another set of similar bonds, the investor has benefited by generating a tax loss which brings about tax savings.

Other reasons for swapping bonds could be to improve yields (a lower yielding bond swapped for a higher yielding bond) or to take advantage of price differentials between different types of bonds. For example, selling agency bonds and replacing them with higher yielding corporate bonds.

Anticipation of changes in interest rates could prompt investors to swap bonds with different maturities. If higher market rates of interest are anticipated, the investor would swap existing bonds for shorter maturities. Anticipation of lower rates of interest would lead to swapping bonds for longer maturities.

Management of Interest Rate Risk

Instead of trying to anticipate market rates of interest, investors could pursue a number of strategies which allow for changes in interest rates.

Using a *matching strategy,* an investor determines the holding period or time frame for the investments, and then selects a bond portfolio with a duration equal to the holding period. For instance, if the holding period is seven years, a bond portfolio with a duration equal to seven years is selected. Duration, which was discussed more fully in Chapter 2, is a measure of the average time it takes for the bondholder to receive the interest and principal.

The duration value is determined by three factors: the maturity of the bond, the market rates of interest, and the coupon rate. Duration has a positive correlation with maturity (the longer the maturity, the greater the duration) and a negative correlation with coupon rates and market rates of interest (the larger the coupon rate the lower the duration, and similarly duration moves in the opposite direction to interest rates). By matching the duration to the time period when the funds will be needed interest rate risk is minimized. If interest rates rise, the value of the bonds in the portfolio will go down but the interest payments received will be reinvested at higher rates of interest. Similarly, if interest rates decline, the bonds in the portfolio will increase in price, but the interest payments will be reinvested at lower interest rates. Through the use of duration, a portfolio can be protected against the changes in market rates of interest.

The *laddering strategy* is another method to cope with changes in market rates of interest. It is a passive strategy which consists of constructing a portfolio of bonds with different maturities over a time period. For example, a 10-year laddered portfolio would have 10 percent of the bond issues with a maturity of one year; another 10 percent of the bond issues with a maturity of two years, and so on. When the first year's bonds mature, the investor can reinvest the funds (if they are not needed by the investor) in issues with a 10-year maturity to maintain the original laddering structure.

The advantages of laddering are:

♦ funds become due on a yearly basis to provide for any short-term needs;

♦ short-term bonds generally earn more than leaving funds in money market securities;

♦ the impact on the valuations of the portfolio is reduced because of the fluctuations in interest rates;

The disadvantage of laddering is that if the investor anticipates a change in interest rates, the investor would have to sell most of the bond issues in the portfolio to react fully to the anticipated changes. For instance, in the 10-year laddering example, if interest rates go up, the investor would want to replace 9/10ths of the portfolio with higher coupon shorter maturity investments. The same would be true for lower anticipated interest rates. The investor would want to replace most of short-term maturities with longer term higher yielding coupon issues.

The *barbell or dumbbell strategy* is used to counter the major disadvantage of laddering (having to liquidate a large percentage of the portfolio to take advantage of anticipated changes in interest rates). A barbell strategy involves using only short-term and long-term bonds. By eliminating intermediate term bonds from the portfolio, the investor is better positioned to take advantage of anticipated changes in interest rates. If half the portfolio is invested in short-term bonds and lower rates are anticipated, the investor would sell the short-term bonds and reinvest in long-term bond issues. The opposite happens when higher market rates are anticipated, the long-term bonds are swapped for short-term bonds.

The advantages of the barbell strategy are:

◆ by eliminating intermediate-term bonds from the portfolio, investors will get increased liquidity from the short-term bonds and increased returns from holding long-term issues;

◆ only half the issues need to be swapped in the event of anticipated changes in interest rates;

◆ if market rates of interest are correctly anticipated, the impact of the changes will be reduced.

However, the major disadvantage is that if interest rates are incorrectly anticipated the investor could experience greater losses.

These strategies (matching, laddering, and barbell) are attempts to eliminate the effects of changes in interest rates on a portfolio. However, a key ingredient for the successful management of a bond portfolio is accurate forecasting of interest rates.

Conclusion

Portfolio management begins with clear objectives as to what is expected from the portfolio. With careful analysis of personal and financial characteristics, an asset allocation plan of the categories of investments for the portfolio is made. The next step is the choice of the individual investments and the extent of the diversification among these investments. Finally the management of the portfolio will be guided by the investment objectives. Managing a successful portfolio is more than selecting good investments.

The different types of investment assets can be complex. Investors should invest in only those investments which they fully understand. If the investor does not follow or fully understand the nuances of investing in individual stocks or bonds, the investor should stick with mutual funds. Besides the investments mentioned in this book, there are many others which were not discussed. This does not mean that they are not important, or that they do not have a place in your portfolio.

Glossary

Accrued Interest. Interest that has been earned but not yet paid.

Adjustable Rate Mortgage. A mortgage with an interest rate that changes periodically to reflect the movement of a specified index of current interest rates.

Annual Report. A published report of a publicly traded company that contains audited financial statements, auditor's report, chairman's report, review of the company's operations, and future prospects.

Ask Price. The price at which a dealer is willing to sell a security.

Asset Allocation. Dividing investment funds among different types of investment assets.

Back-End Load. A fee charged by an open-end mutual fund to investors when they sell their shares back to the mutual fund.

Balance Sheet. A financial statement that indicates the wealth of a company at a point in time.

Bankers' Acceptance. A short-term debt instrument. The acceptance is a draft drawn on a bank for approval for future payments.

Barron's Confidence Index. A ratio of Barron's average of 10 high grade corporate bonds to the yield on the more speculative Dow Jones average of 40 bonds. It shows the yield spread between high grade bonds and more speculative bonds.

Basis Point. One basis point is equal to .01 percent. It is a measure of change on interest bearing securities.

Bid Price. The price at which a dealer is willing to purchase a security.

Bid-Ask Spread. The difference between the price that a dealer is willing to buy a security at (bid price) and the price that a dealer is willing to sell a security at (asked price).

Blue Chip Stock. The common stock of a very large established company.

Bond. The borrower of funds issues a security which stipulates the amount of the payments to the lender.

Bond Rating. A rating is given to the bond as to the likelihood that the issuer of the bond will default on the interest and principal payments.

Bond Swap. The selling of a given bond and the immediate replacement with another bond of similar characteristics to improve portfolio performance, yield, or to take advantage of tax losses.

Business Risk. Refers to the nature of the company: the uncertainty about the company's sales, profits, and rate of return.

Call Premium. The price above the principal that the issuer will pay bondholders for retiring their bonds when called.

Call Provision. A provision in the bond's indenture which allows the issuer to retire bonds before maturity.

Call Risk. The uncertainty associated with the call provision of a bond.

Certificate of Deposit. A time deposit issued by banks and savings and loan associations.

Closed-End Fund. An investment company that issues a fixed number of shares.

Collateral Trust Bond. A bond that is backed by other financial assets.

Collateralized Mortgage Obligations. A debt security based on a pool of mortgages which pay monthly interest and principal.

Commercial Paper. An unsecured IOU of large corporations.

Commodity-Backed Bonds. Bonds whose coupons or maturity values are indexed to a specific commodity such as gold, silver, or oil.

Conversion Price. The price per share that a convertible security can be exchanged for common stock.

Conversion Ratio. The number of common shares received for each convertible security at conversion.

Conversion Value. The value of the common stock represented by the convertible security (conversion ratio multiplied by the market price of the common stock).

Convertible Security. Convertible bonds and preferred stock which can be exchanged for a specified number of common shares of the issuing company at the option of the convertible holder.

Coupon Rate. The fixed rate of interest paid on a bond. The dollar amount of the interest payment is expressed as a percentage of the par value of the bond.

Credit Risk. The uncertainty associated with the financial condition of a company.

Currency Risk. The uncertainty that a particular currency may lose its value relative to another currency.

Current Yield. The dollar amount of the coupon payments divided by the market price of the bond.

Debenture. An unsecured bond.

Default Risk. The uncertainty that some or all of the investment will not be returned.

Derivative Security. A security whose value depends on the price of an underlying security or asset.

Diversification. Investing in different securities as opposed to concentrating on one security.

Duration. The weighted average number of years that the bondholder receives interest and principal payments.

Eurobond. An international bond denominated in a currency not native to the country in which they are issued.

Face Value/Par Value. The nominal value of a bond that is repaid to bondholders at maturity.

Financial Risk. The uncertainty associated with the way the company has financed its assets.

Fiscal Policy. The government's use of taxation, spending, and debt management to stimulate or inhibit economic goals.

Flower Bonds. A particular Treasury bond that can be redeemed at face value to settle federal estate taxes.

General Obligation Bond. A municipal bond backed by the full faith, credit, and taxing power of the issuer.

Global Fund. A mutual fund that invests in both U.S. and non-U.S. securities.

Graduated Payment Mortgage. A mortgage whose payments increase over the life of the loan.

Growth Fund. A mutual fund whose primary objective is capital appreciation.

Growth Stock. The common stock of a company that is growing faster than the norm.

High Yield Bond/Junk Bond. High risk, low rated speculative bonds.

Immunization. A bond portfolio management strategy using duration which allows an investor to be able to meet a stream of cash outflows despite changes in interest rates.

Income Bond. Debenture bond on which interest payments are made only if funds are earned.

Income Statement. A financial statement that shows earnings and profits over a period of time.

Indenture. A legal document which spells out the provisions of a bond issue.

Index Fund. A mutual fund that seeks to match the portfolio composition of a particular index.

Inflation. The increase in the prices of goods and services in an economy.

Initial Public Offering (IPO). The initial offering of shares to the public.

Interest Rate Risk. The uncertainty of returns on investments due to changes in market rates of interest.

International Fund. A mutual fund that invests in non-U.S. securities.

Inverse Floater. A derivative security which reflects the changes in price of the underlying bonds sold with them.

Investment Companies. Companies that sell shares in diversified portfolios of investments to investors.

Investment Grade Bond. Bonds whose ratings are BBB and above (by Standard & Poor's).

Junk Bond. Speculative bond with ratings below investment grade.

Keogh Plan. A retirement pension plan that can be used to shelter self-employment income.

Ladder. A technique used to construct a portfolio with different maturities over a time period.

Liquidity. The ability to be able to convert an investment into cash with a minimum capital loss.

Listed Security. A security that is traded on an organized security exchange.

Load Charge. A sales commission or fee charged by load mutual funds when investors buy or sell shares.

Load Fund. A mutual fund that charges a load fee.

Low-Load Fund. A mutual fund that charges a relatively low load when investors buy and sell shares in the fund.

Margin. The amount of cash an investor puts up to invest in a security with the balance borrowed from the brokerage firm.

Market Risk. Uncertainty over the movement of market prices of securities.

Marketability. To be able to sell an investment quickly.

Monetary Policy. The regulation of the supply of money and credit to affect the country's economic growth, inflation, unemployment and financial markets.

Money Market. The financial market where assets with maturities of one year or less are traded.

Money Market Funds. Mutual funds that invest in high quality money market securities.

Mortgage-Backed Security. A debt security backed by a pool of home mortgages.

Mortgage Bond. A bond that has specific assets pledged as collateral.

Municipal Bond. A debt security issued by state, county, city, and local governments to finance public needs.

Mutual Fund. An investment company that manages the funds for the shareholders who buy shares in the funds.

Net Asset Value. The total market value of the securities in a fund, less any liabilities, divided by the number of shares outstanding.

No-Load Fund. A mutual fund that does not charge a sales commission to buy shares in the fund.

Notes. Intermediate-term debt securities with maturities between one and 10 years.

Open-End Fund. A mutual fund that has no limit on the number of shares that it can issue.

Original Issue Discount Bond. A bond that is issued with a coupon that is below prevailing market yields and is sold at a discount.

Premium (Convertible Security). The difference between the market price and the conversion value on a convertible security.

Primary Market. The market for the sale for the first time of securities by the issuer to the public.

Prospectus. A condensed version of the registration statement filed with the SEC for a new issue designed to provide information to prospective investors.

Purchasing Power Risk. The uncertainty associated with inflation.

Put Feature. A provision that allows the investor to sell the security back to the issuer at a specified price.

Recession. A decline in the Gross National Product for two consecutive quarters.

Refunding. A provision in a bond indenture which allows the issuer to call the bonds with a higher coupon rate, and pay the holders with the proceeds from a newly issued lower coupon rate bond issue.

Registered Bond. A bond whose ownership is registered with the issuer.

Reinvestment Risk. The uncertainty related to the rate that interest payments received on a bond will be reinvested at.

Revenue Bond. A municipal bond that is backed solely by the revenues from a particular project, authority, or agency.

Secondary Market. The market in which already existing securities are bought and sold.

Serial Bond. A bond issue with portions maturing at different dates.

Series EE Bonds. A U.S. savings bond that pays a market-based interest rate which is a market average for five-year Treasury securities.

Series HH Bonds A U.S. savings bond that pays semi-annual interest.

Sinking Fund. A provision in a bond that allows an issuer to allocate funds to repay the principal or purchase the bonds on the market and retire them before maturity.

Subordinated Debenture. An unsecured bond whose claims are junior to other bonds of the issuer in the event of bankruptcy.

Substitution Swap. A bond swap where an investor exchanges one bond for another bond with a higher yield.

Syndicate. A group of investment bankers who share the underwriting and distribution responsibilities in an offering of securities to the public.

Tax-Exempt Bond. A security whose income is not taxable by the federal government.

Term Bond. A bond issue where all the bonds have the same maturity date.

Trade Deficit. An imbalance between a country's imports and exports. Imports exceed exports.

Treasury Bill. A short-term security issued by the U.S. Treasury.

Treasury Bond. A fixed income security issued by the U.S. Treasury with maturities over 10 years.

Treasury Note. A fixed income security issued by the U.S. Treasury with maturities ranging from one to 10 years.

Unit Investment Trust. A type of investment company that has a finite life and raises funds from investors to purchase a portfolio of investments.

Variable Rate Note. A debt security whose coupon rate fluctuates with a specified short-term rate.

Yankee Bond. Bond issued by a foreign company or government but sold in the U.S. and denominated in U.S. dollars.

Yield Curve. A curve showing interest rates at a particular point in time for securities with the same risk but different maturity dates.

Yield to Call. The return on a bond if it is held from a given purchase date to the call date.

Yield to Maturity. The annualized rate of return on a bond if it is held until the maturity date.

Zero-Coupon Bond. Bonds that are sold at a deep discount and pay no interest until maturity.

Index

About the Author

Esmé Faerber is an assistant professor of business and accounting at Rosemont College. She is also a consultant in accounting and finance. Professor Faerber is a licensed CPA in Pennsylvania. She is the author of *Managing Your Investments, Savings and Credit* (Probus, 1992).